**This Is Not Architecture**   Architecture is discussed, explained and identified almost entirely through its representations. Indeed, these representations are often treated as though they were architecture itself. Huge status is given to the imaginary project, the authentic set of photographs or the eminent critical account. This is a paradox. Architecture is fundamentally concerned with physical reality, yet we discuss and even define architecture (as opposed to building) through an elaborate construct of media representations: photography, journalism, criticism, exhibition, history, books, films, television and critical theory.

This book assembles architectural writers of different kinds — historians, journalists, theorists, computer-game designers, film-makers, architects and academics — to discuss how this process works and to comment on the culture and bias which each medium inevitably brings. Together, they build up a critical picture of the construct of partial representations on which our understanding of architecture is based.

Charles Jencks writes: 'The extra-heavy text five inches thick and weighing over five pounds replaced the coffee table book in the 1990s. Foster, Tschumi, Holl, MVRDV *et al.* followed Rem Koolhaas' *S,M,L,XL*. The figure of the old testament prophet reading the truth is Madelon Vriesendorp's Christmas card to her husband in 1995.' (See Chapter 13)

# This Is Not Architecture

Media constructions

Edited by Kester Rattenbury

London and New York

First published 2002
by Routledge
2 Park Square, Milton Park, Abingdon, Oxon, OX14 4RN

Simultaneously published in the USA and Canada
by Routledge
711 Third Avenue, New York, NY 10017

*Routledge is an imprint of the Taylor & Francis Group*

© 2002 Selection and editorial matter: Kester Rattenbury;
individual chapters: the contributors

The right of Kester Rattenbury to be identified as the Editor
of this work has been asserted by her in accordance
with the Copyright, Designs and Patents Act 1988

Typeset in Akzidenz Grotesk by
Bookcraft Ltd, Stroud, Gloucestershire

All rights reserved. No part of this book may be reprinted or reproduced or
utilised in any form or by any electronic, mechanical, or other means, now
known or hereafter invented, including photocopying and recording, or in
any information storage or retrieval system, without permission in writing
from the publishers.

*British Library Cataloguing in Publication Data*
A catalogue record for this book is available from the British Library

*Library of Congress Cataloging in Publication Data*
This is not architecture : media constructions / edited by Kester Rattenbury.
   p. cm.
    1. Mass media and architecture. I. Rattenbury, Kester.
NA2543.M37 T48 2001
704.9'44–dc21                         2001052025

ISBN 0–415–23406–9 (hbk)
ISBN 0–415–23180–9 (pbk)

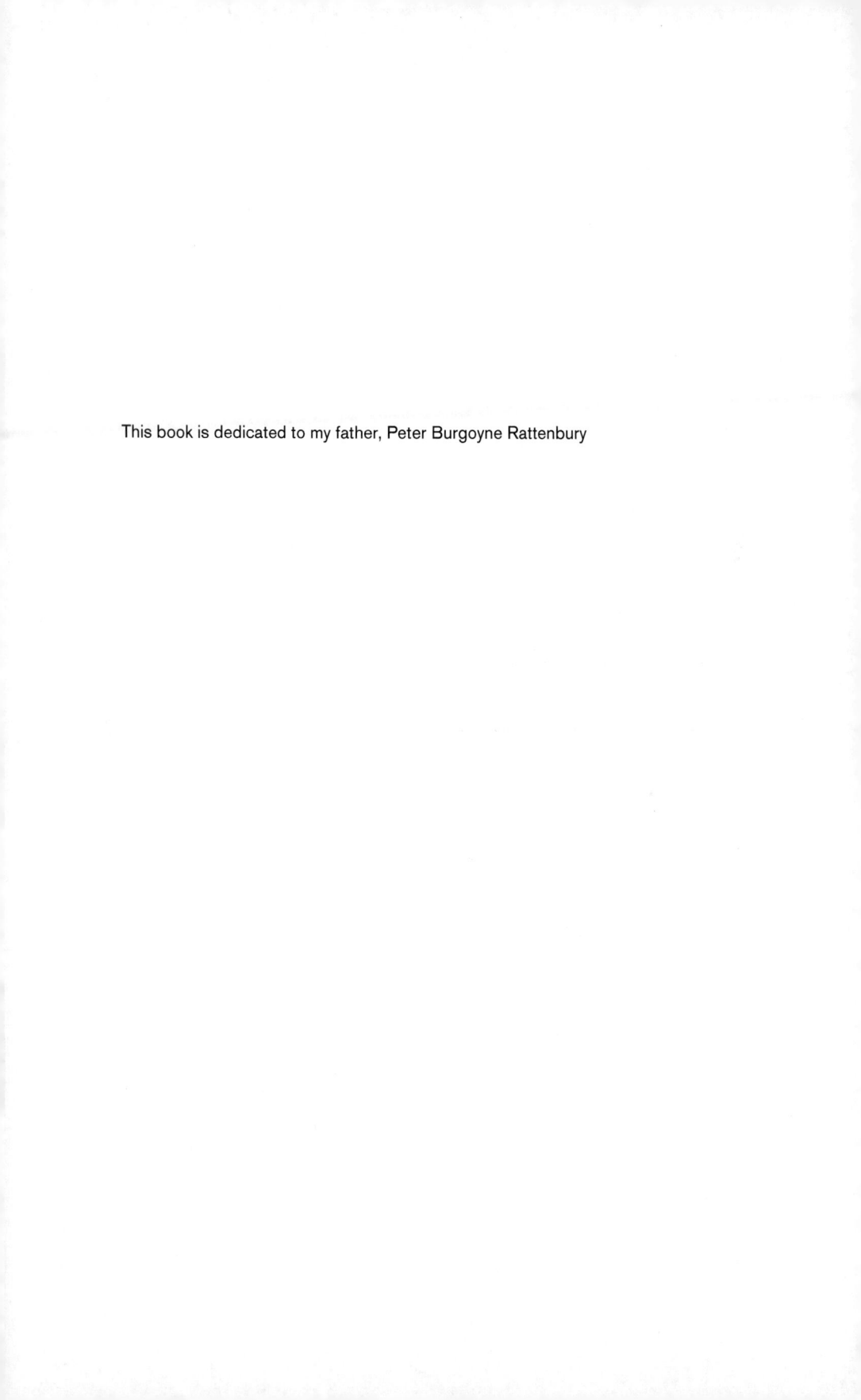

This book is dedicated to my father, Peter Burgoyne Rattenbury

**Contents**

| | |
|---|---|
| List of illustrations | ix |
| Notes on contributors | xii |
| Illustration credits | xvii |
| Acknowledgements | xix |
| Introduction | xxi |

**Part 1  A partial history of virtual reality** ... 1

**1** The revelation of order: perspective and architectural representation ... 3
*Alberto Pérez-Gómez*

**2** On the origins of architectural photography ... 26
*James S. Ackerman*

**3** Architectural cinematography ... 37
*Patrick Keiller*

**4** The revenge of place ... 45
*William J. Mitchell*

**Part 2  The shape of representation** ... 55

**5** Iconic pictures ... 57
*Kester Rattenbury with contributions from Catherine Cooke and Jonathan Hill*

**6** Think of it as a farm! Exhibitions, books, buildings ... 91
*An interview with Peter Smithson*

**7** Diagrams: interactive instruments in operation ... 99
*Ben van Berkel and Caroline Bos*

**8** The height of the kick: designing gameplay ... 110
*Philip Campbell*

| | | |
|---|---|---|
| **9** | Foto-graph, Foto-shop<br>David Greene | 121 |

| **Part 3** | **The reporting of architecture** | **125** |
|---|---|---|
| **10** | Framing icons: Two Girls, two audiences.<br>The photographing of Case Study House #22<br>Pierluigi Serraino | 127 |
| **11** | Naturally biased: architecture in the UK national press<br>Kester Rattenbury | 136 |
| **12** | The architectural book: image and accident<br>Alan Powers | 157 |
| **13** | Post-Modernism and the revenge of the book<br>Charles Jencks | 174 |
| **14** | Architectural publishing: an alphabetical guide<br>Paul Finch | 198 |

| **Part 4** | **The construction of theory** | **205** |
|---|---|---|
| **15** | Architectureproduction<br>Beatriz Colomina | 207 |
| **16** | From dematerialisation to depoliticisation in architecture<br>Clare Melhuish | 222 |
| **17** | *Wallpaper\** person: notes on the behaviour of a new species<br>Neil Leach | 231 |
| **18** | Everything counts in large amounts (the sound of geography collapsing)<br>FAT | 244 |

| Index | 253 |
|---|---|

# Illustrations

**Chapter 1**

| | |
|---|---|
| Gordon Matta-Clark, *Office Baroque* or *Walk Through Panoramic Arabesque* | 4 |
| J.-N.-L. Durand, 'mechanism of composition', the basic design tool in his *Précis* | 4 |
| Dürer, illustration of perspective device | 6 |
| Jean Martin, illustration of optical correction | 8 |
| Vignola, perspective machine | 8 |
| Vincenzo Scamozzi, Villa Bardellini shown as shadow tracer | 9 |
| Daniele Barbaro, plan, section and elevation of a temple | 11 |
| Barbaro and Andrea Palladio, elevation and plan of the Classical theatre | 12 |
| Juan Bautista Villalpando, *El Templo a Vista de Pajaro* | 13 |
| Andrea Pozzo, diagram explaining how to project a perspective drawing onto a vault | 14 |
| Pozzo, fresco in San Ignazio, Rome | 14 |
| Pozzo, drawing method: plan, elevation and perspective | 15 |
| A. Bosse, *Les Perspecteurs* | 16 |
| Ferdinando Galli da Bibiena, *scena per angolo* | 18 |
| J.-N.-L. Durand, plate from *Précis des Leçons d'Architecture* | 20 |
| Gaspard Monge, universal spatial matrix of descriptive geometry | 21 |
| A. Parsey, three-point perspective from *The Science of Vision* | 21 |
| Auguste Choisy, axonometric from *L'Art de Bâtir chez les Romains* | 22 |
| G.B. Piranesi, plate from the *Carceri* | 23 |
| John Hejduk, frontal axonometric of Bernstein House | 23 |

**Chapter 2**

| | |
|---|---|
| Augustus Charles Pugin, view of St Étienne, Caen | 27 |
| Henri Le Secq, church of the Madeleine, Paris, south façade | 29 |
| Hippolyte Bayard, church of the Madeleine, Paris, interior of façade portico | 30 |
| John Constable, *Salisbury Cathedral, View Across the Bishop's Grounds* | 31 |
| Roger Fenton, Ely Cathedral, view across the close | 31 |
| Anonymous French photographer, colonnade at Palmyrna | 32 |

## Chapter 3
    Patrick Keiller, Montalcino, Italy, 1983, from *The End*     39

## Chapter 4
    J.B. Handelsman, *'You can access me by saying simply "Agnes"'*     47

## Chapter 5
    Giovanni Battista Piranesi, *Ruins of a Sculpture Gallery at Hadrian's Villa, Tivoli* (actually the Large Baths)     60
    Archigram/Ron Herron, *Walking Cities*, coloured version in the desert     62
    Le Corbusier, photos of the Villa Savoye and the Villa at Garches     64
    Sir John Soane, aerial cutaway of the Bank of England     66
    James Stirling, worm's-eye of the Florey Building     68
    Zaha Hadid, The Peak     70
    Robert Venturi, *Recommendation for a Monument*     72
    Bernard Tschumi, Parc de la Villette     74, 75
    Andrea Palladio, final façade study for San Petronio, Bologna     76
    Vladimir Tatlin, *Monument to the Third International* (The Comintern)     78
    Fritz Lang, *Metropolis*     84
    Mies van der Rohe, photos of the original German Pavilion, Barcelona     86, 88

## Chapter 6
    Max Risselada, *Chronology*     92–3
    Nigel Henderson's basement in Bethnal Green     95

## Chapter 7
    UN Studio, from blob to box and back again     99
    UN Studio, station area, Arnhem – spatial flow     101
    UN Studio, IFCCA – Penn Station, New York     103
    UN Studio, IFCCA – Penn Station, New York     106
    UN Studio, Klein bottle     108

## Chapter 8
    Philip Campbell/Quantic Dream, Global Location Profile – 'Fahrenheit'     112
    Campbell/Quantic Dream, Environment Locators – 'Fahrenheit'     117

## Chapter 10
    Julius Shulman, photo of Pierre Koenig's Case Study House #22: no girls     128
    Shulman, photo of Pierre Koenig's Case Study House #22: 'Two Girls'     130

## Chapter 11
    The nation's number one architectural critic: Prince Charles     137
    Scandal, controversy and disaster? Tower blocks being blown up     143

| Illustrations

| Mies van der Rohe's original, never-to-be-built Mansion House scheme | 147 |
| The Stirling Wilford scheme for Number 1 Poultry | 149 |
| Carl Laubin, paintings of the Royal Opera House redevelopment | 152 |

**Chapter 12**

| Andrea Palladio, title page from *I Quattro Libri* | 158 |
| Johann Bernhard Fisher von Erlach, Dinocrates, Colossus of Mount Athos | 158 |
| Gateway to the Admiralty, Whitehall, from *Works in Architecture* by Robert and James Adam | 163 |
| C.N. Ledoux, aerial view of the city of Chaux | 165 |
| Ledoux, Besançon, 'Coup-d'oeil générale du théâtre' | 165 |
| J.B. Papworth, 'A Cottage Orné designed for an exposed or elevated situation' | 167 |
| Karl Freidrich Schinkel, perspective of the upper gallery of the Altes Museum | 167 |

**Chapter 13**

| Robert Venturi, *Complexity and Contradiction in Architecture* | 177 |
| Venturi and Denise Scott Brown, Medical Research Building, UCLA | 178 |
| James Stirling and Michael Wilford, Die Neuestaatsgalerie | 180 |
| Charles Jencks, *The Language of Post-Modern Architecture* | 181 |
| Robert Venturi, the Duck versus the Decorated Shed | 183 |
| Gae Aulenti and Act, Musée d'Orsay conversion | 185 |
| Charles Jencks, *The Language of Post-Modern Architecture* | 187 |
| Kisho Kurokawa, Museum of Contemporary Art, Hiroshima | 188 |
| Daniel Libeskind, Jewish Museum extension to the Berlin Museum | 190 |
| Charles Jencks, *The Architecture of the Jumping Universe* | 191 |
| Rem Koolhaas and Bruce Mau, *S,M,L,XL* | 192–3 |

**Chapter 14**

| Louis Hellman, cartoon | 199 |

**Chapter 15**

| Bernard Tschumi, 'Advertisements for Architecture', 1976 | 218–19 |

**Chapter 16**

| Le Corbusier, Dom-Ino – prototype of concrete building principle | 223 |
| Central Asian yurt | 224 |

**Chapter 18**

| FAT, Reality and myth in a world of consultants | 246 |

## Notes on contributors

**James S. Ackerman**
is Professor Emeritus of Fine Arts at Harvard University. His many books include *Palladio's Villas* (1967), *The Villa: Form and Ideology of Country Houses* (1990), *Distance Points: Studies in Theory and Renaissance Art and Architecture* (1991), which won the American Institute of Architects Award in History and Theory in 1992, and *Conventions of Architectural Drawing: Representation and Misrepresentation* (2000). He has lectured widely, holds many academic fellowships, awards and prizes, has written many essays and articles on the history of architecture, on critical and historical theory and on the interaction of art and science, and has worked on films on Renaissance Rome and Palladio's influence in America. In 1998 he was awarded the Paul Kristeller Lifetime Achievement Award of the Renaissance Society of America.

**Ben van Berkel and Caroline Bos**
have their architectural practice, UN Studio, in Amsterdam. UN Studio presents itself as a network of specialists in architecture, urban development and infrastructure. Besides the architectural works they lecture at several architectural schools around the world and participate with their theoretical writings in debates on architecture and new media.

**Philip Campbell**
is Creative Director at Electronic Arts, CA, one of the world's biggest computer games companies. Trained and qualified as an architect in the UK before moving to the USA, he has been using computers to solve creative problems for more than fifteen years in fields including architecture and theme park design and as game designer for the Tomb Raider franchise. He has just completed *James Bond: Agent Under Fire* for Sony Playstation 2, Nintendo Gamecube and Microsoft XBox.

**Beatriz Colomina**
is Professor of Architecture at Princeton University and Director of Graduate Studies (PhD programme). She has written extensively on questions of architecture

and the modern institutions of representation, particularly the printed media, photography, advertising, film and TV. Her books include *Privacy and Publicity: Modern Architecture as Mass Media* (1994), which was awarded the 1995 International Book Award by the American Institute of Architects and has been translated into many languages, *Sexuality and Space* (editor, 1992), which was awarded the 1993 International Book Award, and *Architectureproduction* (editor, 1988). She is a member of the editorial boards of *Assemblage*, *Daidalos* and *Grey Room*, the recipient of many grants and fellowships, including those given by the Chicago Institute for Architecture, SOM Foundation, Graham Foundation, Fondation Le Corbusier and the Center for Advanced Studies in the Visual Arts in Washington. She is currently working on a book on the post-war American house and the relationships between domesticity and war.

**Catherine Cooke**
is a lecturer in the Department of Design and Innovation in the Faculty of Technology of the Open University in the UK. She is known for her research and many publications on the Russian avant-garde.

**FAT**
is a company that makes architecture and fine art, and things in between. FAT exists somewhere outside the old distinctions of high and low culture: completely selling out while remaining hardcore avant-garde; at one moment showing at *Manifesta*, then re-styling petrol stations for multinational corporations. Sometimes FAT sells T-shirts like it thinks it's a band, sometimes it designs buildings, sometimes it writes obscure texts in publications such as this. FAT lives and works in London, and at the moment is run by Sam Jacob, Sean Griffiths and Charles Holland.

**Paul Finch**
is Publishing Director of the *Architects' Journal* and the *Architectural Review*. He entered architectural and property journalism in 1972, was editor of *Building Design* from 1983 to 1994, and then editor of the *AJ* until 1999. He is Deputy Chair of the UK government's Commission for Architecture and the Built Environment, and Chair of its Design Review Committee.

**David Greene**
had the usual provincial suburban upbringing, followed by Art School and then down the motorway to London to begin a nervous twitchy career swerving from office to fashion to freelance practical speculations for developers for Archigram, which he

founded with Peter Cook. Over time, a seemingly irresistible drift into teaching and imagining an ephemeral architecture for the third industrial age occurred. He has taught variously in Europe, Scandinavia and North America; work published and exhibited similarly. He is currently Professor of Architecture at the University of Westminster.

**Jonathan Hill**

is Senior Lecturer at the Bartlett School of Architecture, University College London, where he is Director of the MPhil/PhD architectural design programme. Jonathan has had solo exhibitions at a number of venues, including the Haus der Architektur in Graz, Matthew Gallery at the University of Edinburgh and Architektur-Galerie am Weissenhof in Stuttgart. He is the author of *The Illegal Architect* and editor of *Occupying Architecture: Between the Architect and the User* and *Architecture – The Subject is Matter*.

**Charles Jencks**

is known for his books questioning Modernist architecture and for defining its successors: Late-, Neo- and Post-Modern architecture. He has published more than thirty books, including *Modern Movements in Architecture* (1972), the massively popular *The Language of Post-Modern Architecture* (1977), *The Architecture of the Jumping Universe* (1995), *Ecstatic Architecture* (1999) and *Le Corbusier and the Colonial Revolution in Architecture* (2000). He lives in London, but lectures widely around the world, designs furniture, gardens and interiors and has appeared on many TV programmes. In 1992 he won the NARA Gold Medal for Architecture.

**Patrick Keiller**

is an architect and film-maker, best known for his features *London* (1994) and *Robinson in Space* (1997), the latter extended as a book in 1999. He recently completed *The Dilapidated Dwelling*, a feature-length documentary for UK television.

**Neil Leach**

teaches at the Architectural Association and the University of Bath, where he is Professor of Architectural Theory. He has also been Visiting Professor at Columbia University, New York. He is author *of The Anaesthetics of Architecture* (1999) and *Millennium Culture* (1999); editor *of Rethinking Architecture* (1997), *Architecture and Revolution* (1999) *and The Hieroglyphics of Space* (2001); and co-translator *of L B Alberti, On the Art of Building in Ten Books* (1988).

### Clare Melhuish

is an architectural critic and commentator engaged in research at the interface of architecture and anthropology. She is author of *Modern House 2* (2000) and editor of *Architecture and Anthropology*, an anthology of work by architects and anthropologists (1996). She has contributed to numerous publications and is currently a columnist for the *Architects' Journal* in London.

### William J. Mitchell

is Professor of Architecture and Media Arts and Sciences and Dean of the School of Architecture and Urban Planning at MIT. His recent books include *E-topia*, *City of Bits* and *The Reconfigured Eye*.

### Alberto Pérez-Gómez

was educated in Mexico and Great Britain and has taught in Europe and North America, at the Architectural Association in London and at universities in Mexico, Houston, Syracuse, Toronto and Ottawa. He is now the Saidye Rosner Bronfman Professor of the History of Architecture at McGill University, where he has also been in charge of the history and theory of architecture graduate programme since 1987. He has been the Director of the School of Architecture at Carleton University and of the *Institut de Recherche en Histoire de l'Architecture* in Montreal. Dr Pérez-Gómez is the author of *Polyphilo or The Dark Forest Revisited* (1992), an erotic narrative/theory of architecture based on a kindred text from late fifteenth-century Venice. His first book, *Architecture and the Crisis of Modern Science* (1983), won the Alice Davis Hitchcock Award for architectural history in 1984. His most recent book, co-authored with Louise Pelletier and entitled *Architectural Representation and the Perspective Hinge,* was published in 1997. Dr Pérez-Gómez is co-editor of CHORA: *Intervals in the Philosophy of Architecture.*

### Alan Powers

is a lecturer in the School of Architecture and Landscape at the University of Greenwich and author of books on architecture and related issues. His monograph *Serge Chermayeff, Designer, Architect, Teacher* was published in 2001 and forms part of a continuing programme of research related to architecture and its culture in Britain in the middle years of the twentieth century. He is one of the editors of the journal *Twentieth Century Architecture*, published by the Twentieth Century Society, London.

### Kester Rattenbury

is an architectural journalist and teacher. She trained as an architect and did a PhD on the coverage of architecture in the mass media (1990), before becoming a journalist and reviewer for *Building Design* magazine. She went on to work freelance, writing more than 600 lecture and exhibition reviews, building studies and interviews for UK magazines and newspapers. She taught design in the degree school at the University of Greenwich for eight years and currently teaches in the diploma school at the University of Westminster. She has contributed to many books, publications and exhibitions including *Architecture and Film*, the Cedric Price *Magnet* exhibition, *The House Book* and the BA tourist guide to the London Eye. She won Arts Council funding for *This Is Not Architecture* in 1998.

### Pierluigi Serraino

authored *Modernism Rediscovered* (2000). Serraino graduated from the School of Architecture of the University of Rome 'La Sapienza' in 1994. He earned his Master of Architecture at SCI-Arc in Los Angeles and an MA at UCLA. His projects and writings have been published internationally in *Hunch*, *Space & Society*, *Global Architecture*, *Parametro* and *Rassegna*, among others. Serraino lives and works in San Francisco. serraino@uclink4.berkeley.edu

## Illustration credits

The authors and the publishers would like to thank the following individuals and institutions for giving permission to reproduce illustrations. Every effort has been made to ensure that all material has been properly cleared; but if there have been any omissions I will endeavour to set them right in future editions.

British Architectural Library, RIBA, London  p. 60
Bunn, Stephanie  p. 224
Campbell, Philip and Quantic Dream 2000–2002  pp. 112, 117
Centre Canadien d'Architecture/Canadian Centre for Architecture, Montreal  pp. 29, 31 (right), 68
Cooke, Catherine  p. 78
Donat, John  p. 147
Dover Publications Inc p. 163
FAT  p. 246
Fondation Le Corbusier/ADAGP, Paris and DACS, London, 2001  pp. 64, 223
George Eastman House Collection, Rochester  p. 30
Gregg International Publishers  p. 167
Harenburg Kommunikation, Dortmund  p. 158 (bottom)
Hellman, Louis  p. 199
Henderson, Nigel  p. 95
Hoepli, Ulrich, Milan  p. 158 (top)
Jane Crawford Collection, New York  p. 4 (left)
Keiller, Patrick  p. 39
Mies van der Rohe Archive, Museum of Modern Art, New York  pp. 86, 88, cover
New Yorker Collection (1997) J.B. Handelsman from cartoonbank.com  p. 47
Office of Zaha Hadid  p. 70
Princeton Architectural Press  p. 165
Provost and Fellows of Worcester College, Oxford, and the Conway Library, Courtauld Institute of Art  p. 76
Risselada, Max  pp. 92–3
Ron Herron Archive  p. 62
Shulman, Julius  pp. 128, 130

Smithson, Peter  p. 95
Trustees of Sir John Soane's Museum, London  p. 66
Tschumi, Bernard  pp. 74, 75, 218, 219
UFA, Transit Films and the Murnau Stiftung  p. 84
UN Studio, Amsterdam and Cynthia Davidson, Anyone Corporation, New York  pp. 99, 101, 103, 106, 108
Venturi Scott Brown and Associates, *Learning from Las Vegas*, MIT Press  pp. 72, 178, 183
Venturi Scott Brown and Associates, *Complexity and Contradiction in Architecture*, Museum of Modern Art  p. 177
Victoria and Albert Museum  p. 31 (left)
Von Holtzbrinck Publishing Service p. 167 (bottom)
Young, Richard  p. 137

# Acknowledgements

This is a book that has developed as an idea over a number of years: first through my PhD research on bias in the reporting of architecture, then through years as an architectural journalist, both full-time in the news-based structure of UK trade magazines, then as a freelance writer, as a reviewer of hundreds of lectures on architecture by many eminent architects, writers and teachers, and finally as a teacher of architecture. Even so, the cumulative structure of the book and the argument it sketches out were adjusted, sometimes radically, by the specific nature of the content that was delivered and by the argument it built up.

I am deeply indebted to many people for their help and contributions. In particular, I would like to thank all the contributors and particularly those who, by signing up early, acted as bait for the others: James Ackerman, Charles Jencks and Patrick Keiller. Particular thanks go to Caroline Mallinder and Routledge for their unstinting support and to the Arts Council and Alicia Pivaro for funding and support of early research work. To Val Bacon, Mike Jenks and Roland Newman at what was then Oxford Polytechnic and to Peter Golding at the Centre for Mass Communications Research in Leicester for supporting the original PhD from which this interest originally arose. To everyone at the University of Greenwich and especially Corine Delage and to everyone at the University of Westminster and at *Building Design* for their practical and sympathetic support and advice.

Special thanks to all who individually provided advice, permission, information, time and help way beyond any call of duty: Catherine Cooke, Cynthia Davidson, Jeremy Dixon, Tim Dobbs, Paul Finch, Iona Foster, Sue Foster, Clare Gerrard, David Greene, Mark Hewitt, Jonathan Hill, Patrick Keiller, Robert Kennett, Sam Jacob, Charles Jencks, Anna Joynt, Sutherland Lyall, Clare Melhuish, Jeremy Melvin, Gail Novelle, Paul Oliver, Jay Rattenbury, Peter Smithson, Chris Watson, Steve Witherford, the Eames Office, the offices of Zaha Hadid and Bernard Tschumi, Venturi Scott Brown Associates, UN Studio and everyone who helped with the massive provision and clearing of pictures.

**Kester Rattenbury**

# Introduction

Of course, this is not architecture. This is a picture. This is a book. Yet it's almost impossible to conceive that a photo of the Barcelona Pavilion, on the front of an architectural book, is not architecture. As with Magritte's painting *This is not a Pipe*, it's hard to accept the construct – that what you're looking at is a representation and not the thing itself.

The assertion that this picture is not architecture doesn't ring entirely true. The photo of the Barcelona Pavilion is not just architecture, but one of the most famous examples of modern architecture in the world – and a print of one of the original photos of the original building too. Like Magritte's pipe, the representation is almost more definitive than the thing itself.

It's quite possibly a picture of a pipe that we learned to recognise first, before any physical object. If as children we learn to recognise and name things through looking at pictures in books, it's certainly the same for architects. Ninety-nine times out of a hundred, architecture students learn to identify and define architecture, and especially what is good or famous – or indeed, what is architecture in any form, as opposed to just the buildings they prefer – firstly by looking at representations. A photo, a drawing, a lecture, a magazine article or a book.

Architecture's relationship with its representations is peculiar, powerful and absolutely critical. Architecture is driven by belief in the nature of the real and the physical: the specific qualities of one thing – its material, form, arrangement, substance, detail – over another. It is absolutely rooted in the idea of 'the thing itself'. Yet it is discussed, illustrated, explained – even defined – almost entirely through its representations.

Indeed, architects (or at least people who write about or discuss architecture for the benefit of other architects) often fail to distinguish architecture from its representations. Unbuilt, imaginary, iconoclastic projects (Tatlin's Tower, Zaha Hadid's The Peak, most Italian Futurism, Piranesi, Archigram – you name it) have a roughly equivalent place in the architectural canon, as it is set out in books and magazines and lectures, as built iconoclastic projects – sometimes a greater one.

The culture of treating unbuilt, imaginary designs as architecture is essential to the design process as taught and used in the Western world. You design by means of representing a non-existent project. This is instilled in architectural students when imaginary projects are discussed in the studio as though they were real buildings, and it never leaves the culture. Unbuilt competitions and other proposals figure large in the CVs of most architects, young or old, famous or not, who seek the status of high architecture. Often, if you're unfamiliar with the projects, it's impossible to tell which, if any, actually exist in built form.

The promotion of the as-yet-fictional or always-to-be-fictional project is both the architect's tool and often, initially, their stock-in-trade. But built architecture itself is then recorded, discussed, designed and taught through a series of further representations: photographs, articles, books, critical accounts and, sometimes, retrospective drawings. These are often taken directly from the codes of the architect's first virtual representation, but they are also driven by their own representations. Indeed, it is often at this stage – when they get represented or published – that some projects rather than others get defined as architecture.

For 'architecture' is not just a broad, generic name we use to describe the built or inhabited world. It's a construction, a way of understanding certain parts of the built or inhabited world as being fundamentally different to other parts. It's to do with a constructed understanding of quality, class, interpretation, intention, meaning. And this seems to be not just conveyed but actually defined by this complex system of media representations, by an elaborate construct of drawings, photographs, newspaper articles, lectures, books, films, conferences and theoretical books whose subject matter is often (albeit inadvertently) the representations rather than the things themselves.

This is not architecture. Or at least, this is not the same as the substance of architecture itself as it is usually understood (though many people, as will be discussed, see architecture as a medium in itself). But even in the most physical understanding of architecture, the media that describe it shape what we understand it to be, and the way we design and build it. This constructed representation defines what we consider good, what we consider fashionable, what we consider popular. At a simple level, it is the terms through which architects select what to represent and to privilege – composing the façade, imagining the photo view, making the image for the client, commissioning the photographer. At several more complex levels, it affects how we interpret and value architecture. At the level of discussion, publication and reference, representation arguably surpasses the architecture itself.

There's a strong argument, probably even a historical one, that architecture – as distinct from building – is always that which is represented, and particularly that which is represented in the media aimed at architects. Architectural drawing evolved for description, not construction. Pevsner said Lincoln cathedral was architecture and a bicycle shed was a building. You could easily argue that, if he'd only put the bicycle shed in one of his books, it would have become architecture. And all forms of representation have their own bias, their own preferences, their own cultures, their own economic, cultural and personal drives. Representation will always be partial.

This book looks at how the many forms of representation, with their limitations and biases, feed directly into the architecture we make and discuss. Moreover, the book comes at a time when the information revolution, with its boom in new media, and the growth of critical theory are changing what we understand architecture to be – a time when publications on shopping centres and Disney (if not bicycle sheds) are now the highest of high-code architectural writing. If the selection of subject matter for architectural representations has shifted, this does not mean we are freer from the constructs of the media. It only means the constructions are more elaborate.

The aim of this book is to assemble the broadest practicable sample of what might more or less be called the representations of high architecture. The writers included here were specifically selected for their diversity: people whose views might be considered antithetical and who might therefore not usually appear in the same sort of publication. The book brings together publishers of trade magazines, such as Paul Finch, with influential critical theorists, like Beatriz Colomina; history professor James Ackerman with the experimental film essayist Patrick Keiller; chronicler of the information revolution William Mitchell with the provocative designers FAT; Charles Jencks with Peter Smithson; and so on. The range of styles of writing, terms of reference and subject matter is meant to be informative in itself.

The original structure planned for the book was overwhelmed both by the diversity and range of subject matter covered by the writers, by unexpected similarities and divergences in their arguments. What I found in the contributions was a description of a cumulative structure of partial representation. At ground level, I would argue, representation establishes the paradigms of high-code architecture and affects how architects see the world and which things get described as architecture. On top of this, photographs, journalism, exhibitions and books reinforce and promote a secondary layer of these paradigms, establishing a canon of famous architecture, while also bringing their own criteria and biases to bear. And on top of this is critical theory, with its own new infusion of specialised values, and often principally concerned with previous representations and arguments rather than the wide subject matter of buildings themselves. I have arranged the book to follow the structure of this argument as far as possible.

The book starts by taking a historical look at four of the key shifts in representation and media that have affected architecture: perspective, photography, film and e-technology. Part 2 then takes some examples of the direct relationship between representation and design in different media and examines how the nature of the representation affects our interpretation of the architectural subjects. Architectural publishing itself – whether books, magazines and journals or architectural coverage in the mainstream media – is of course complicit in the definition of architecture, and is the next stage in this cumulative construction of meaning. The authors in Part 3 describe the various influences that shape these publications. Finally, architectural theory appears as the pinnacle of this construction of mediation, referring to other critics and other representations as its main source of interest. The authors in the last chapters explore the effect of critical theory on architectural practice and publication and also how architecture itself – the buildings as much as the representations – can be considered a medium.

Architecture has its own communicative qualities, but whether we prefer to think of it as principally and essentially physical or principally and essentially communicative, our understanding of what exactly architecture is (as opposed to just plain old buildings) and what is good or interesting about it, seem to be the outcome of a cumulative structure of mediations. This structure has many influences and economic drives of its own – not least that it is in some part managed by architects and others who make a living through publishing, exhibiting, discussing or teaching architecture. Gradually, this book aims to uncover some of the forces and limits which shape our understanding of what architecture is and how we make it. The architecture, you could say, is in the medium.

**Kester Rattenbury**

Part 1
# A partial history of virtual reality

Virtual reality is an old story. Humans have been representing things throughout history. Indeed, it can be argued (as by Pier Luigi Cappucci at a lecture at London's Royal College of Art on 9 December 1997) that the prolific tendency to represent things is the human's main distinguishing characteristic.

It is often argued that the emergence of the architect as a recognised professional (as opposed to architecture itself, which is much older) was roughly simultaneous with – and profoundly linked to – the beginnings of perspective. Perspective evolved in the studios of the painters and sculptors of fourteenth-century Florence, overtaking the orthogonal drawings of the Gothic masons' workshops as the dominant architectural mode;[1] and it could be argued that perspective defined architecture as an authored art, rather than a collaborative craft. Since then, the definition of architecture – as an increasingly heavily represented culture before, after and instead of the fact – has been to some extent directed and framed by the tendencies of each medium in which it is shown. Those media used for generating it (such as architectural drawings of all kinds and various types of computer imaging) might have been more influential than those principally used for recording it (photography and film). But all have framed the way architects see the world and design their buildings.

All forms of media – speech, drawing, writing, perspective, photography, film, the various forms of computer information – have their own characteristics, biases and tendencies, as well as their own limitations. Matters outside their scope are implicitly and effectively downgraded – by sheer omission.

By bringing together the four writers in the book who deal directly with what might be called the four big shifts in architectural representation – perspective, photography, film and e-technology – Part 1 gives a kind of summarily assembled history of virtual reality. This is not necessarily the writers' main subject or their intention, and the contributions are of course offered first and foremost on their own account. But this grouping does allow a consideration of the specific possibilities and limitations of each medium – and what that medium allows us to describe and discuss.

All four writers describe modes of representation that are still current and dominant, and they introduce a field of arguments that connect through the book. In particular, there is the connection between the media's capacities and conventions and the ways in which we understand what is being represented. There is also the powerful idea that many of the conventions established in one medium are carried through without question into subsequent media (for example, perspective remains extremely dominant in composing photos, films and e-technology) – though of course these conventions are adjusted by the possibilities and limitations of the new medium. These arguments are inherent throughout the book, and it is useful to have them set out in the first instance.

It's particularly interesting that these four writers use very different types of language. By the final part of the book, which deals with theory, the arguments are often parallel, however diverse the style of writing. At this stage, and as an introduction, it's useful to see how varied (as well as how similar) architectural writing can be: what sorts of references are used and the audiences that are assumed – indeed, to what extent the scope of a particular type of writing itself shapes the nature of the argument being made.

**Note**

1    For this analysis I am indebted to James Ackerman's *The Reinvention of Architectural Drawing, 1250–1550*, given as the annual lecture at Sir John Soane's Museum in London 1998, and published by Sir John Soane's Museum.

Chapter 1
# The revelation of order
Perspective and architectural representation[1]
**Alberto Pérez-Gómez**

Tools of representation are never neutral. They underlie the conceptual elaboration of architectural projects and the whole process of the generation of form. Prompted by changing computer technologies, contemporary architects sometimes recognise the limitations of tools of ideation. Yet, plans, elevations and sections are ultimately expected to predict with accuracy an intended meaning as it may appear for an embodied subject in built work. Indeed, no alternatives for the generation of meaningful form are seriously considered outside the domain of modern epistemological perspectivism – i.e., the understanding of the project as a 'picture'.

The expectation that architectural drawings and models, the product of the architect's work, must prefigure a work in a different dimension sets architecture apart from other arts. Yet today, the process of creation in architecture often assumes that the design and representation of a building demand a perfectly coordinated 'set' of projections. These projections are meant to act as the repository of a complete idea of a building, a city or a technological object. Devices such as drawings, prints, models, photographs and computer graphics are perceived as a necessary surrogate or transcription of the built work, with dire consequences for the ultimate result of the process. For purposes of descriptive documentation, depiction, construction or any imparting of objective information, the architectural profession continues to identify such projective architectural artefacts as reductive. These reductive representations rely on syntactic connections between images, with each piece only a part of a dissected whole. Representations in professional practice are easily reduced to the status of efficient neutral instruments devoid of inherent value. The space 'between dimensions' is a fertile ground for discovery. But the search itself, the 'process-work' that might yield true discoveries, is deemed to have little or no significance.

This assumption concerning the status of architectural representation is an inheritance from the nineteenth century, particularly from the scientistic methodologies prescribed by Jean-Nicolas-Louis Durand in his *Précis des Leçons d'Architecture* (1802 and 1813).[2] Durand's legacy is the objectification of style and techniques, and the establishment of apparently irreconcilable alternatives: technological construction (functional) versus artistic architecture (formal), and the false dichotomy of necessary structure and contingent ornament. Though the formalisation of descriptive geometry in Durand's design method promoted a particularly simplistic objectification, the projective tool is a product of our technological world, grounded in the philosophical tradition of the Western world. It is one which we cannot simply reject – or simplistically pretend to leave behind.

A different use of projection, related to modern art and existential phenomenology, emerged from the same historical situation with the aim of transcending dehumanising technological values (often concealed in a world that we think we

Gordon Matta-Clark, *Office Baroque* or *Walk Through Panoramic Arabesque* (1977). The photograph, a literal section through the visual cone, destructures the reductive quality of section by presenting the actual 'sectioning' of an existing building and revealing its otherwise hidden interiority.

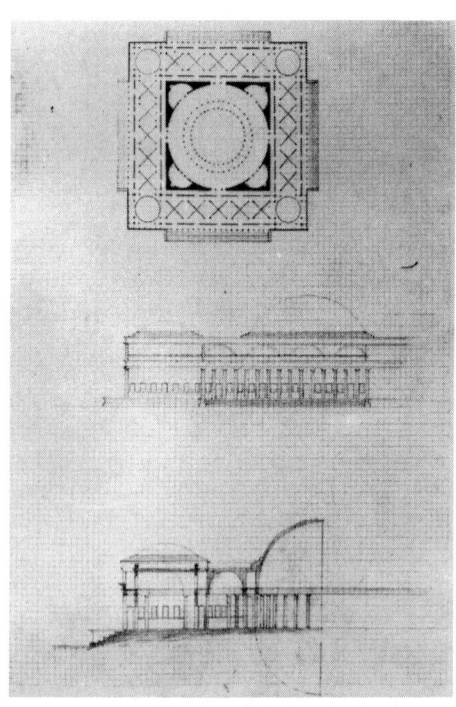

J.-N.-L. Durand's 'mechanism of composition' was the basic design tool in his *Précis*. The grid became an indispensable modular framework for architectural design in the student projects of the École Polytechnique and the École des Beaux Arts.

control) through the incorporation of a critical position. A careful consideration of this option, often a central issue in the artistic practices of the twentieth-century avant-garde, may help regenerate architecture's creative process, bringing about a truly relevant poetic practice in a Post-Modern world.

Today we recognise serious problems in our post-industrial cities and our scientistic way of conceiving and planning buildings. Even the most recent applications of computers to generate new (and structurally 'correct', i.e. 'natural') architectural forms assume an instrumental relationship between theory and practice in order to bypass the supposedly old-fashioned prejudice of 'culture', (i.e., the personal imagination), with its fictional and historical narratives. It is imperative that we do not take for granted certain scientific assumptions about architectural ideation, and that we redefine our tools in order to generate meaningful form.

Philosophers at the origins of our tradition perceived projection as the original site of ontological continuity between universal ideas and specific things. The labyrinth, that primordial image denoting architectural endeavour, is a projection linking time and place, representing architectural space: the hyphen between idea and experience, which is the place of language and culture, the Greek *chora*. Like music (realised only in time and often from a notation), architecture is itself a projection of architectural ideas, horizontal footprints and vertical effigies, disclosing a symbolic order in time, through rituals and programmes. Thus, contrary to Euclidean 'common sense', depth is not simply the objective 'third' dimension. Architecture concerns the making of a world that is not merely a comfortable or practical shelter, but that offers the inhabitant a formal order reflecting the depth of our human condition, analogous in vision to the interiority communicated by speech and poetry and to the immeasurable harmony conveyed by music.

There is an intimate relationship between architectural meaning and the *modus operandi* of the architect, between the richness of our cities as places of imagery and reverie, as structures of embodied knowledge for collective orientation, and the nature of architectural *techne*, the differing modes of architectural conception and implementation.[3] Since the Renaissance, the relationship between the intentions of architectural drawings and the built objects that they describe or depict has changed. Though subtle, these differences are none the less crucial.

When one examines the most important architectural treatises in their respective contexts, it becomes immediately evident that systematisation, which we take for granted in architectural drawing, was once less dominant in the process of development from the architectural idea to the actual built work. Prior to the Renaissance, architectural drawings were rare. In the Middle Ages architects did not conceive of the building as a whole, and the very notion of a scale was unknown. Gothic architecture, the most 'theoretical' of all medieval building practices, was none the less still a

One of Dürer's several illustrations of perspective devices, from his *Underwysung der Messung* (1538). A draughtsman uses a grid and an eyepiece to draw a nude figure with the correct proportions required by foreshortening.

question of construction, operating through well-established traditions and geometrical rules that could be directly applied on a site that was often encumbered by older buildings, which would eventually be demolished. Construction proceeded by rhetoric and geometry, raising the elevation from a footprint, while discussions concerning the unknown final figure of the building's face continued almost until the end. The master mason was responsible for participating in the act of construction, in the actualisation of the city of God on earth. Only the Architect of the Universe, however, was deemed responsible for the conclusion of the work at the end of time.

During the early Renaissance, the traditional understanding of architecture as a ritual act was not lost. Filarete, for instance, discussed in his treatise the four steps to be followed in architectural creation. He was careful to emphasise the autonomy among proportions, lines, models, and buildings, describing the connection between 'universes of ideation' in terms analogous to an alchemical transmutation, not to a mathematical transformation.[4] Unquestionably, however, it was during the fifteenth century that architecture came to be understood as a liberal art, and architectural ideas were thereby increasingly conceived as geometrical *lineamenti*, as bi-dimensional, orthogonal projections.

A gradual and complex transition from the classical (Graeco-Arabic) theory of vision to a new mathematical and geometrical rationalisation of the image was taking place. The medieval writings on perspective (such as those of Ibn Alhazen, Alkindi, Bacon, Peckham, Vitello and Grossatesta) had treated, principally, the physical and physiological phenomenon of vision. In the cultural context of the Middle Ages its application was specifically related to mathematics, the privileged vehicle for the clear understanding of theological truth. *Perspectiva naturalis*, seeking clear vision for humanity, was concerned not with representation but with an understanding of the modes of God's presence; Thomas Aquinas saw it as visual harmony and therefore associated it with music in the *quadrivium* of the liberal arts, not with drawing or any other graphic method. Humanity literally lived in the light of God, under God's benevolent gaze: the light of the golden heaven of the Byzantine frescoes and mosaics, or the sublime and vibrantly coloured space of the Gothic cathedrals.

The new understanding of the perspectival image in the Renaissance remained directly related to the Classical notion of optics as a science of the transmission of light rays. The pyramid of vision, the notion on which the Renaissance idea of the image as a window on the world was based, was inherited from the Euclidean visual cone. The eye was believed to project its visual rays onto the object, with perception occurring as a dynamic action of the beholder upon the world. Vitruvius (first century BC) had discussed the question of optical correction in architecture as a direct corollary of the Euclidean cone of vision, demonstrating an awareness (also present in some medieval building practice) of the dimensional distortions brought about by the position of an observer.

The issue, however (as is well known from the great examples of Classical architecture), was to avoid distorted perception. Architects were expected to correct certain visual aspects (by increasing the size of lettering placed on a high architrave, for example), in order to convey an experience of perfect adjustment or regularity to synaesthetic perception, always primarily tactile. Renaissance architectural theory and practice never questioned this aim.

Nor did certain fundamental assumptions about perception change during the Renaissance. When queried about the truth of parallel lines, anyone would have answered that obviously, in the world of action, those straight lines never meet. The hypothesis of a vanishing point at infinity was both unnecessary for the construction of perspective and ultimately inconceivable as the reality of perception in everyday life. Alberti's central point (*punto centrico*) of the perspective construction, for example, is often wrongly associated with such a 'vanishing' point. In fact, the point of convergence in the *construzione legittima* is determined and fixed by the point of sight as a 'counter-eye' on the 'window' or, in contemporary terms, the central point on the picture plane.[5] Even though fifteenth-century painters were experimenting with methods of linear perspective, the geometrisation of pictorial depth was not yet systematised and did not immediately transform either the quotidian experience of the world or the process of architectural creation. It was impossible for the Renaissance architect to conceive that the truth of the world could be reduced to its visual representation, a two-dimensional diaphanous section of the pyramid of vision.

**8** | Alberto Pérez-Gómez

Illustration of optical correction from Jean Martin's first French edition of Vitruvius's *Ten Books* (1547). The importance of optical correction is a pervasive discussion in treatises from Vitruvius to the eighteenth century, probably originating in Euclid's *Optics*. Optical correction compensates for the 'weakness' of sight so that buildings appear perfectly proportioned as we experience them synaesthetically, with all our senses.

Perspective machine, from Vignola, *Due Regole della Prospettiva Prattica* (1583). This curious machine shows two observers creating a perspective, seemingly in order to 'corroborate' the mathematical depth of the world, given that monocular vision was evidently inadequate. The perspective representation is emphatically 'artificial': it is created from instructions dictated by the observer who views the image. The drawing is made on a gridded page, suggesting that perspective could be used for operations that require precise measurement.

**9** | The revelation of order

During the sixteenth century, treatises on perspective tried to translate the primarily empirical understanding of perspective into a system, and they became increasingly distanced from treatises on optics. These new works, however, remained theoretical or mathematical elucidations and had almost no practical use in prescriptive representation.[6] In Vignola's *Due Regole della Prospettiva Prattica*, a 'second observer' was introduced and became the distance point that allowed for a mathematical regulation of the foreshortening. The distance point was projected on the picture plane, on the horizon line at a distance from the central point equal to the distance between the eye of the observer and the plane of the image. In other words, Vignola's method introduced a second observer at the same distance from the central point, looking perpendicularly at the beholder, thereby adding an element essential for the representation of stereoscopic vision. Before this, with the apex of the cone of vision as a simplified eye, *perspettiva artificialis* had been, strictly speaking, a (very imperfect) monocular construction.

Before Dürer, a plan was generally conceived as a composite 'footprint' of a building, and an elevation as a face. Vertical or horizontal sections were not commonly used before the sixteenth century, just as anatomy rarely involved the actual dissection of cadavers until the early modern era. It should not come as a surprise that perspective's emphasis on the truth of perception being a section through the cone of vision would be translated as a new emphasis on the importance of sections in architectural representation.

Sections became the legitimate embodiment of architectural ideas, precise as composite drawings could not be, and therefore more adequate to embody a Platonic conception of truth. Yet, the early use of sections betrays a fascination with the role of buildings as gnomons or shadow tracers. Vincenzo Scamozzi's design for a villa is a fascinating instance.[7] The coordination of the vertical and horizontal sections of the building reveal light and shadow as constitutive of the architecture's symbolic order, very much

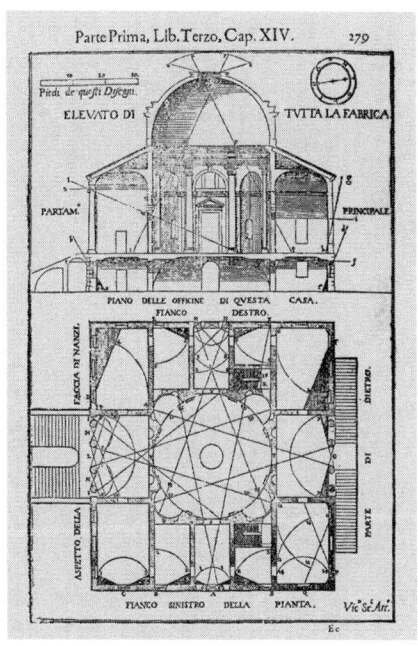

Vincenzo Scamozzi, Villa Bardellini shown as a shadow tracer, from his treatise *L'Idea dell'Architettura Universale* (1615)

in the spirit of Vitruvius, who had introduced gnomons as one of the three artefacts within the province of architecture, together with *machinae* and buildings.

The possibility of taking measure of time (and space), in the sense of poetic *mimesis*, was the original task of the architect, and this hadn't been forgotten in the Renaissance.[8] There was an overlapping of the notion of section as shadow or imprint, revealing the order of the 'day-ity', the presence of light, with that of section as a cut. The obsession to reveal clearly the insides of bodies, to magnify and dissect as a road to knowledge, is one that takes hold of European epistemology only after the mechanisation of physiology in the seventeenth century. Only then did light as divine emanation, as 'lighting' making the world of experience possible – indeed, as projection – become a passive medium, to the exclusion of shadows.

Today, many architects remain fascinated by the revelatory power of cutting, but it is clear that in science this operation has reached its limits. Further cutting in biology or particle smashing in physics does not reveal a greater interiority. More light without shadows is of no use. Objectified vision always leaves us on the outside, and the architect at the end of modernity must clearly understand this if the enframed vision is to be transcended. Understanding the nature of projections as ephemeral, dynamic, and endowed with shadows may generate an architecture that is once more experienced as a flowing musical composition, in time, its material surfaces presenting an ever-changing panorama to the viewer.

During the sixteenth century in Northern Italy, Daniele Barbaro, Palladio's friend and patron, emphasised that perspective was not an architectural idea in the Vitruvian sense. We may recall that in Vitruvius's *Ten Books* the Greek word *idea* refers to the three aspects of a mental image (perhaps akin to the Aristotelian *phantasm*) understood as the germ of a project. These *ideas* allowed the architect to imagine the disposition of a project's parts: *ichnographia* and *orthographia* would eventually be translated as plan and elevation but did not originally involve the systematic correspondence of descriptive geometry.[9] In his treatise on perspective, Barbaro offers a fascinating commentary on the Vitruvian passage. He believed that the translation of *sciographia* (the third Vitruvian idea) as perspective resulted from a misreading of *sciographia* as *scenographia* in the original text, whose application was important only in the building of stage sets. Thus he concludes that perspective, however important, was mainly recommended for painters and designers of stage sets.

It is worthwhile following Barbaro's commentary in some detail in order to understand its implications. The term sciagraphy (or sciography) derives etymologically from the Greek *skia* (shadow) and *graphou* (to describe). Scamozzi's villa comes immediately to mind. The etymology also speaks to the eventual relationship between the projection of shadows and linear perspective, an obligatory chapter in most seventeenth- and eighteenth-century treatises on the subject. In the architectural

**11** | The revelation of order

The plan, section and elevation of a temple appear together in one image from Barbaro's *Prattica della Perspettiva* (1569). This drawing, unique in Barbaro's treatise, is meant to show how *ichnographia*, *orthographia* and *sciographia* (section) belong to the same genre of drawings and constitute the 'ideas' to generate architecture. This composite drawing also includes the triangular *lineamenti*, the Platonic first figure of the cosmos, generating the dome.

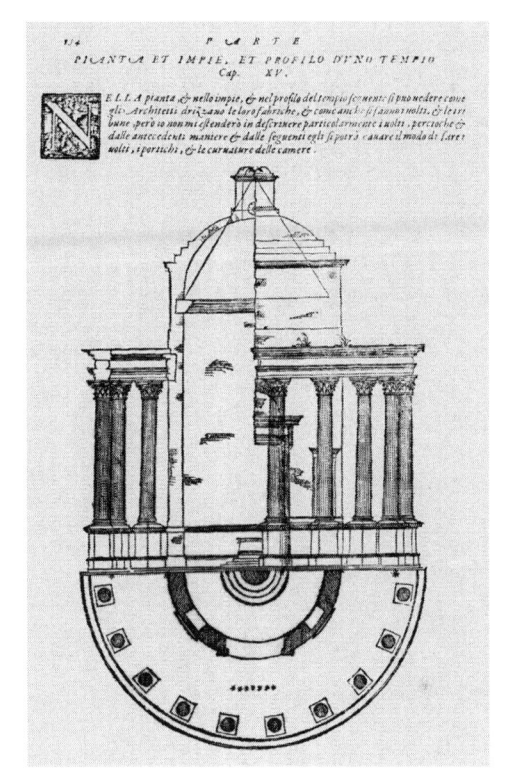

tradition, however, sciagraphy kept its meaning as a 'draught of a building, cut in its length and breath, to display the interior', in other words the profile, or section. This use of the term was still present in the nineteenth century.[10] Modern Latin dictionaries translate *scaenographia* (the actual term as it appears in the first existing Vitruvian manuscript) as the drawing of buildings in perspective, and generally assume that this word is synonymous to *sciagraphia*. The fact is that perspective was unknown in ancient Rome and even when Vitruvius speaks about the three types of stage sets appropriate to tragedy, comedy and satire (Book V, ch. 6), there is no mention of perspective in connection with Classical theatre. Vitruvius describes the fixed *scaena* as a royal palace façade with *periaktoi*, 'triangular pieces of machinery which revolve', placed beyond the doors, and whose three faces were decorated to correspond to each dramatic genre.[11]

Barbaro argues that *scaenographia*, which is 'related to the use of

12 | Alberto Pérez-Gómez

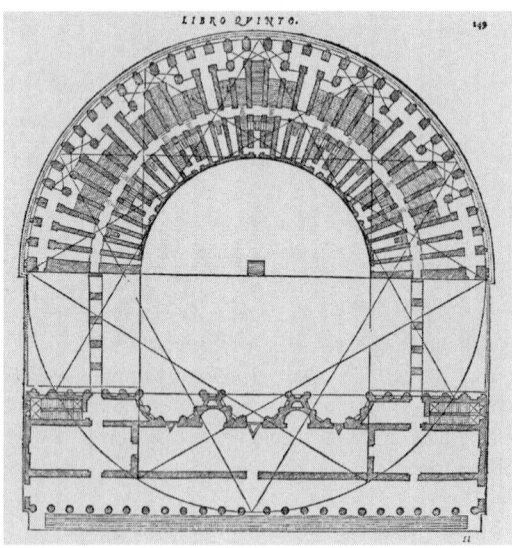

Elevation and plan of the Classical theatre, as interpreted by Barbaro and drawn by Palladio, from Barbaro's edition of Vitruvius's treatise (1567). The accompanying discussion includes the current debate about musical harmony, analogous to the mathematical order of the universe. The *periaktoi* are conceived as providing surfaces for perspectival painting, appropriate to the three genres of drama.

perspective', is the design of stages for the three dramatic genres. Appropriate types of building must be shown diminishing in size and receding to the horizon. He does not agree with 'those that wish to understand perspective (*perspettiva*) as one of the ideas that generate architectural design (*dispositione*)', ascribing to it the definition Vitruvius had given to *sciographia*. In his opinion it is plain that 'just as animals belong by nature to a certain species', the *idea* that belongs with plan (*ichnographia*) and elevation (*orthographia*) is the section (*profilo*), similar to the other two 'ideas' that constitute architectural order (*dispositione*). In Vitruvius's conception, the section 'allows for a greater knowledge of the quality and measurement of building, helps with the control of costs and the determination of the thickness of walls', etc. Barbaro, in fact, assumes that in antiquity 'perspective' was only applied to the painted representations on the side of the *periaktoi*.[12]

## Modernity and beyond

It was only during the seventeenth century that perspective became a generative *idea* in architecture, in the Vitruvian sense of the category. Both theology and science contributed to this shift. Within the Jesuit tradition, Juan Bautista Villalpando homologised perspective with plan and elevation in his exegetical work on Ezekiel's vision of the Temple of Jerusalem.[13] Emphasising the notion that the human architect must share the Divine Architect's capacity for visualising a future building, he insists that plans and elevations are similar to perspectives, as they are merely 'pictures' of a building-to-come.

The inception of the Cartesian modern world and the epistemological revolution brought about by modern science introduced, during the Baroque period, a conflict between symbolic and mechanistic views of the world.[14] A world of fixed essences and mathematical laws deployed in a homogeneous, geometrised space, much like the Platonic model of the heavens, was assumed by Galileo to be the truth of our experience of the physical world. As

Juan Bautista Villalpando, *El Templo a Vista de Pajaro* (from his *Ezechielem Explanationes*, 1604). The general view of the Temple of Jerusalem is presented as a 'parallel projection' kindred to God's own vision.

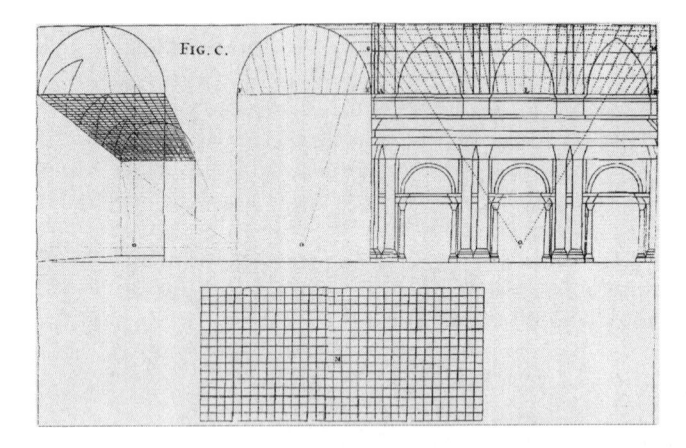

Diagram from Andrea Pozzo's treatise, explaining how to project a perspective drawing onto a vault according to the *quadratura* method

Andrea Pozzo, fresco in San Ignazio, Rome (1684–5). The vault above the nave is open to the sky through the devices of *quadratura*.

an example, Galileo believed, after postulating his law of inertia, that the essence of an object was not altered by motion. This notion, now an obvious 'truth' (as long as we keep making abstractions of contexts), was at odds with the traditional Aristotelian experience of the world in which perception, with its double horizon of mortal, embodied consciousness and a finite world of qualitative places, was accepted as the primary and legitimate access to reality. The new scientific conception eventually led to a scepticism regarding the physical presence of the external world. In the terms of Descartes, man became a subject (a thinking, rather than an embodied, self), confronting the world as *res extensa*, as an extension of his thinking ego. This dualistic conception of reality made it possible for perspective to become a model of human knowledge, a legitimate and scientific representation of the infinite world.

Baroque perspective in art and architecture, however, was a symbolic configuration, one that allowed reality to keep the qualities that it had always possessed in an Aristotelian world. During the seventeenth century the primacy of perception as the foundation of truth was hardly affected by the implications of this new science and philosophy. Perspective, now a legitimate architectural *idea*, became a privileged form of symbolisation. The architecture of the Jesuit churches by Andrea Pozzo, for example, can hardly be reduced to their section or elevation. Pozzo's frescoes are inextricably tied to the three-dimensionality of the architectural space, revealing transcendental truth in the human world. Rather than remaining in the two-dimensional field of representation, the perspective is projected from a precise point situated in lived space and fixed permanently on the pavement of the nave. The possibility of 'real order' for mortal existence appears only at the precise moment that a human presence occupies the station point of the 'illusionistic' *quadratura* fresco.

Even though the theory of perspective, as an offspring of the new science, was seen as a tool for controlling and dominating the physical reality of existence, the arts, gardening and architecture of the seventeenth century were still concerned with the revelation of a transcendentally ordered cosmos. Thus it can be argued that it was the geometrisation of the world that allowed access to a new transcendental truth.[15] Even though perspective became increasingly integrated with architecture, perspectival systematisation remained restricted to the creation of an illusion, qualitatively distinct from the constructed reality of the world. Perspective marked the moment of an epiphany, the revelation of meaning and the God-given geometric order of the world. For a brief time, illusion was the locus of ritual. The revelation of order occurred at the

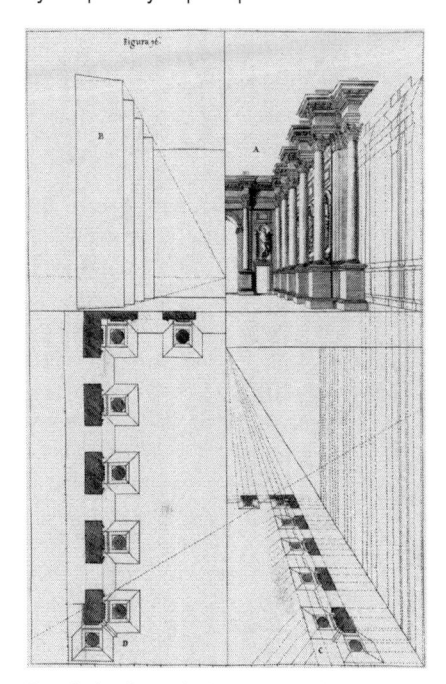

Pozzo's drawing method, demonstrated in his treatise (1700), was based on a correspondence between plan, elevation and perspective

precarious moment of coincidence between the vanishing point and the position of the observer.

While most seventeenth-century philosophers were still striving to formulate the appropriate articulation of the relation between the world of appearances and the 'absolute' truth of modern science, the work of Gérard Desargues appeared as an anomaly.[16] Desargues disregarded the transcendental dimension of geometry and the symbolic power of geometrical operations. He ignored the symbolic implications of infinity and thus transformed it into a 'material' reality. He sought to establish a general geometric science, one that might effectively become the basis for such diverse technical operations as perspective drawing, cutting of stone and wood for construction and the design of solar clocks.

Until Desargues, theories of perspective always associated the point of convergence of parallel lines with the apex of the cone of vision projected on the horizon line.[17] Desargues was apparently the first writer in the history of perspective to postulate a point at infinity.[18] He maintained that all lines in our ever changing, mortal and limited world actually converged at a real point, at an infinite distance, yet present at hand for human control and manipulation. Thus any system of parallel lines, or any specific geometrical figure, could be conceived as a variation of a single universal system of concurrent lines. Orthogonal projection as we understand it today was already for Desargues a simple case of perspective projection where the projective point was located at an infinite distance from the plane of projection.

Desargues's method allowed for the representation of complex volumes before construction, implementing an operation of deductive logic where vision, perception and experience were supposed to be practically irrelevant. Perspective became the basic (and

Les Perspecteurs, from A. Bosse, Manière universelle de M. Desargues (1648). This image poignantly conveys the belief in the power of perspective as a universal method to configure and construct the world – not merely to represent it. Moreover, every person inherently possesses this power.

paradigmatic) prescriptive science, a new kind of theory prophetic of the epistemological shift that would take place during the nineteenth century, and whose sole *raison d'être* was to control human action, the practice of applied sciences and our enframed technological world.[19] The scientific revolution had witnessed in Desargues's system the first attempt to endow representation with an objective autonomy. Nevertheless, the prevailing philosophical connotations of infinity, always associated with theological questions, as well as the resistance of traditionally minded painters, craftsmen and architects, made his system unacceptable to his contemporaries. Desargues's basic aims would eventually be fulfilled by Gaspard Monge's descriptive geometry near the end of the eighteenth century.

Despite European culture's reticence to demystify infinity, perspective soon ceased to be regarded as a preferred vehicle for transforming the world into a meaningful human order. Instead, it became a simple re-presentation of reality, a sort of empirical verification of the external world for human vision. Pozzo's treatise, *Rules and Examples of Perspective Proper for Painters and Architects* (Rome, 1693; English trans. London, 1700), occupies an interesting, perhaps paradoxical position as a work of transition. Starting from a plan and an elevation, his method of projection is a step-by-step set of instructions for perspective drawing that establishes the homology of projections and an absolutely fixed proportional relationship of orthogonal elements seen in perspective. Pozzo avoids the geometrical theory of perspective, and his theoretical discourse amounts to a collection of extremely simple rules and detailed examples of perspective constructions, perhaps the first truly applicable manual on perspective in the sense familiar to us. The consequential homology of 'lived' space and the geometric space of perspectival representation encouraged the architect to assume that the projection was capable of truly depicting a proposed architectural creation and, therefore, to 'design in perspective'. The qualitative spatiality of our existence was now identical to the objectified space of perspective, and architecture could be rendered as a picture.

In the eighteenth century artists, scientists and philosophers lost interest in the theory of perspective. Building practice, in fact, changed very little despite the potential of the new conceptual tools to transform architectural processes. The geometrisation of knowledge initiated with the inception of modern science in the seventeenth century was arrested by the focus on empirical theories spurred by Newton's work and by the identification of the inherent limitations of Euclidean geometry.[20]

In this context, architects seemed nevertheless ready to accept the notion that there was no conceptual distinction between a stage set constructed following the method *per angolo* of Ferdinando Galli da Bibiena, one where there was no longer a privileged point of view, and the permanent tectonic reality of their craft. Each and

Ferdinando Galli da Bibiena's *scena per angolo*, from his *Architettura Civile* (1711)

every individual spectator occupied an equivalent place in a world transformed into a two-point perspective. Reality was transformed into a universe of representation.

The Baroque illusion became a potential delusion in the Rococo church. Even the vanishing point of the frescoes became inaccessible to the spectator, the new aesthetic chasm now to be bridged by an act of faith, while the building appeared as a highly rhetorical, self-referential theatre, one where the traditional religious rituals were no longer unquestionable vehicles for existential orientation.[21] Humanity's participation in the symbolic (and divine) order of the world was starting to become a matter of self-conscious faith, rather than self-evident embodied knowledge, despite the pervasive (and unquestionably influential) Masonic affirmation of the coincidence between revealed and scientific truths.

Only after the nineteenth century and a systematisation of drawing methods could the process of translation between drawing and building become fully transparent and reduced to an equation. The key transformation in the history of architectural drawing was the inception of descriptive geometry as the paradigmatic discipline for the builder, whether architect or engineer. The École Polytechnique in Paris, founded after the French Revolution, trained the new professional class of eminent scientists and engineers of the nineteenth century. Descriptive geometry, the fundamental core subject, allowed for the first time a systematic reduction of three-dimensional objects to two dimensions, making the control and precision demanded by the industrial revolution possible. Perspective became an 'invisible hinge' among projections. It is no exaggeration to state that without this conceptual tool our technological world could not have come into existence.

With Durand's *Mécanisme de la composition* and its step-by-step instructions, came the codification of architectural history into types and styles, the use of the grid and axes, and transparent paper; and precise decimal measurements allowed for planning and cost estimates. Descriptive geometry became the 'assumption' behind all modern architectural endeavours, ranging from the often superficially artistic drawings of the École des Beaux Arts to the functional projects of the Bauhaus. The rendering of drawings in the Beaux Arts tradition does not change the essence of the architecture it represents, nor does it succeed in formulating an alternative to the architecture of the École Polytechnique. The Beaux Arts tradition does not retrieve myth through drawings, but rather only formalises appearances with a status of contingent 'ornament', in a similar way to 'Post-Modern Classical' styles. This is indeed at odds with the possibility of retrieving meaning through a phenomenological understanding of symbolisation.

In this context, it is easy to understand that true axonometry could only emerge as a preferred architectural tool after Durand, who was already suspicious of perspective and what he believed were deceiving painterly techniques. Conversely, 'new' theories of perspective became concerned with depicting 'retinal' images, such as curved or three-point perspectives. Despite similarities, it is in the early nineteenth century and not in the work of Pozzo that saw the inception of the tools taken for granted by twentieth-century architects.

Today the growing obsession with productivity and rationalisation has transformed the process of maturation from the idea to the built work into a systematic representation that leaves little place for the invisible to emerge from the process of translation. Computer graphics, with their seductive manipulation of viewpoints and illusions of three-dimensionality, are mostly a more sophisticated 'mechanism of composition'. The question concerning the application of computers to architecture is, of course, hotly debated and as yet unresolved. The instrument is not, simply, the equivalent of a pencil or a chisel that could easily allow one to transcend reduction. It is the culmination of the objectifying mentality

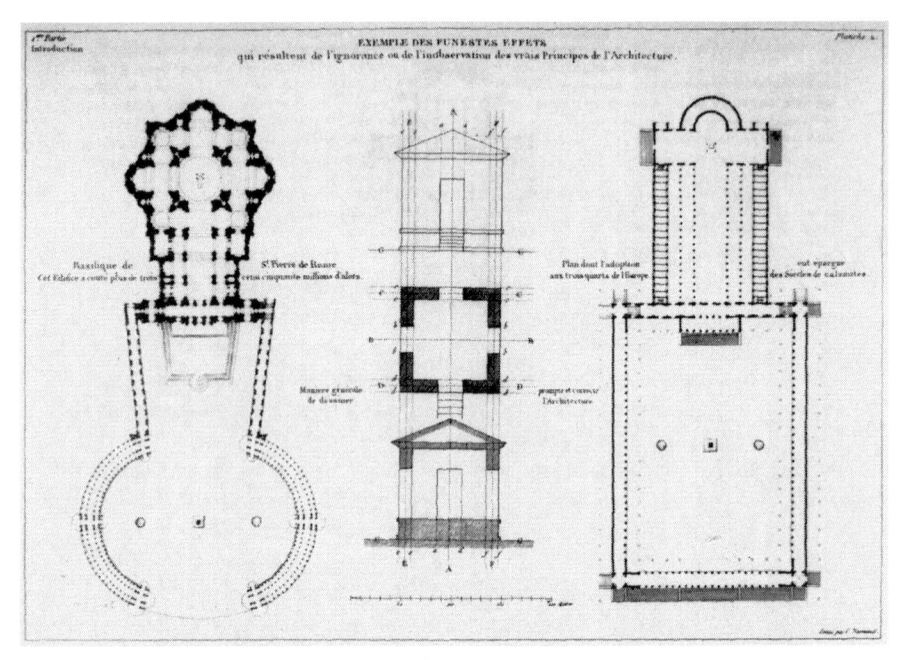

A plate from J.-N.-L. Durand, *Précis des Leçons d'Architecture* (1802). Durand's demonstration of the 'correct and effective way to design', illustrated in the centre of the plate, shows the precise coordination of plan, section and elevation, the 'set' that constitutes the 'objective idea' of a whole building. The comparison between the plans of the pre-Renaissance basilica of St Peter's in Rome and the modern sixteenth-century building purports to show the 'calamitous effects' evident in the modern example, resulting from the lack of observation of the 'true principles of architecture', ultimately epitomised by descriptive geometry.

of modernity and is, therefore, inherently perspectival, in precisely the sense that I have described in this article. Computer graphics tend to be just a much quicker and more facile tool that relies on mathematical projection, a basic tool of industrial production.

The tyranny of computer graphics is even more systematic than any other tool of representation in its rigorous establishment of a homogeneous space and its inability to combine different structures of reference. It is, of course, conceivable that the machine would transcend its binary logic and become a tool for a poetic disclosure in the realm of architecture. The issue – perhaps the hope – in our post-historical,

**21** | The revelation of order

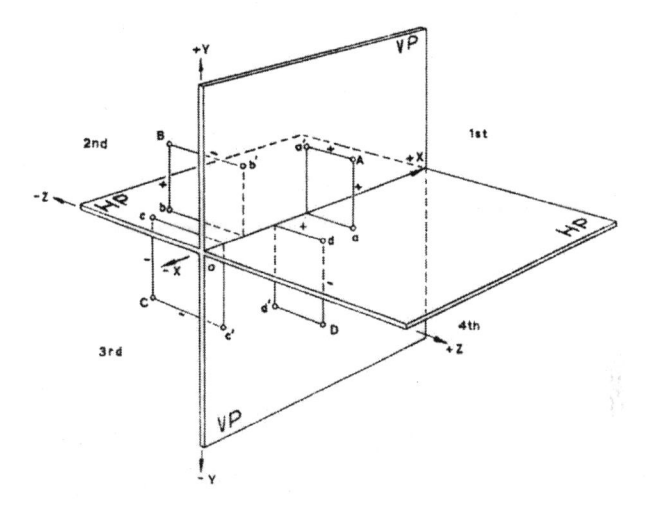

Gaspard Monge's universal spatial matrix of descriptive geometry (1790s), from R.G. Robertson, *Descriptive Geometry* (by courtesy of Sir Isaac Piton and Sons Ltd). While Desargues's system of reference retained a concrete initial position in relation to the volume being described, Monge's spatial matrix was construed as an a priori entity where all concrete phenomena could be objectively described by means of mathematical coordinates.

A three-point perspective, from A. Parsey, *The Science of Vision* (1840)

post-literate culture is to avoid delusion through electronic media and simulation, the pitfalls of further reductive, non-participatory representation. Conceivably, as a tool of representation, the computer may have the potential to head towards absolute fluidity or toward further fixation and reduction. The latter is the unfortunate result of the implementation of the technological will to power – control and domination. The fact is that the results of computer applications in architecture (whether merely graphic or, more recently, motivated by a desire to extrapolate 'complex natural orders' to practice), remain generally disappointing.

While descriptive geometry attempted a precise coincidence between the representation and the object, modern art remained fascinated by the enigmatic distance between the reality of the world and its projection. This fascination, with immediate roots in nineteenth-century photography and in optical apparatuses such as the stereoscope, was a response to the failure of the modern scientific mentality to acknowledge the unnameable dimension of representation, a poetic wholeness that can be recognised and yet is impossible to reduce to the discursive *logos* of science, while it no longer refers to an intersubjective cosmological picture. Artists since Piranesi and Ingres have explored that distance – the 'delay', or 'fourth dimension' in Marcel Duchamp's terms – between reality and the appearance of the world.

An axonometric representation from Auguste Choisy, *L'Art de Bâtir chez les Romains* (1873), demonstrating the 'determining' structural concept of a late Roman building

Defying reductionist assumptions without rejecting the modern power of abstraction, certain twentieth-century architects, including Le Corbusier, Alvar Aalto, Antoni Gaudí and John Hejduk, have used projections not as technical manipulations, but to discover something at once original and recognisable. These well-known architects have engaged the dark space 'between' dimensions in a work that privileges the process and is confident of the ability of the architect to 'discover', through embodied work, significant tactics for the production of a compassionate architecture. This

**23** | The revelation of order

G.B. Piranesi, plate from the *Carceri* (second state, 1760). The explosion of perspective into a temporal montage creates a poetic distance that invites participation while suggesting different modes of inhabitation than those expected in the Enlightenment world, where perspective has become the natural, eventually prosaic, depth of experience.

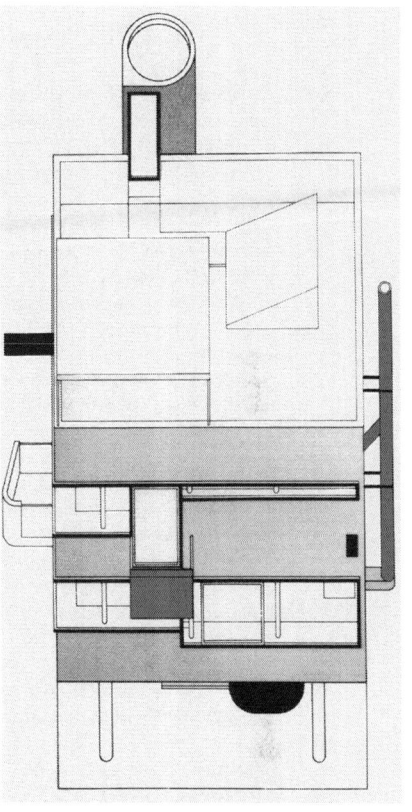

John Hejduk, frontal axonometric of Bernstein House (1968). Axonometry has the potential of opening up of a chasm in space, analogous to the unfamiliar gap between two familiar elements in a collage.

emerging 'architecture of resistance', a verb more often than a noun, celebrates dreams and the imagination without forgetting that it is made for the Other, and aims at revealing depth not as homologous to breadth and height (3D) but as a significant first dimension that remains mysterious and reminds us of our luminous opacity as mortals in a wondrous more-than-human world.

## Notes

1. For an extensive discussion of the issues presented in this article, see Alberto Pérez-Gómez and Louise Pelletier, *Architectural Representation and the Perspective Hinge* (Cambridge, MA: MIT Press, 1997). The historical research that underscores my present argument was the result of this major collaborative project.
2. J.-N.-L. Durand gave us the first architectural theory whose values were directly extrapolated from the aims of applied science and technology. Before Durand, never had the concern for meaning been subordinated to the pursuit of efficiency and economy in the products of design. For the purpose of this article it is particularly crucial to keep in mind the connection between this value system and its tools, i.e. Durand's *Mécanisme de la composition*, the first design methodology that was thoroughly dependent on the predictive quality of the projections of descriptive geometry.
3. See Alberto Pérez-Gómez, *Architecture and the Crisis of Modern Science* (Cambridge, MA: MIT Press, 1983), introduction and ch. 9, and 'Abstraction in Modern Architecture', *VIA* 9 (1988).
4. See Filarete's *Trattato* (reprint Milan: Il Polifilo, 1972), where he discusses in the form of a symposium the construction of the city of Sforzinda. There is also an English translation by John Spencer (New Haven and London: Yale University Press, 1965).
5. Leon Battista Alberti, *Della Pittura* (Florence, 1435).
6. The best examples of this mathematical treatment of perspective are to be found in Egnazio Danti's commentary on Jacopo Barozzi da Vignola's *Due Regole della Prospettiva Prattica* (Rome, 1583) and Guidobaldo del Monte's *Montis Perspectivae Libri Sex* (Pesaro, 1600).
7. Vincenzo Scamozzi, *L'Idea dell'Architettura Universale* (Venice, 1615), vol. 1, p. 138.
8. See A. Pérez-Gómez, 'The Myth of Dedalus', *AA Files* 10 (1985), and Indra K. McEwan, *Socrates' Ancestor* (Cambridge, MA: MIT Press, 1993).
9. Vitruvius, *The Ten Books on Architecture*, book I, ch. 2, trans. Morris Hicky Morgan (New York: Dover), pp. 13–14.
10. For example, in the *Encyclopaedia of Architecture* (London: Caxton, 1852).
11. In book I, ch. 2, Vitruvius describes this *scaenographia* as *frontis et laterum abscedentium adumbratio ad circinique centrum omnium linearum responsus*. Both Frank Granger (1931) and Morris Hicky Morgan (1914) in their translations of Vitruvius read this as perspective. Granger translates it as: 'Scenography (perspective) as in the shading of the front and the retreating sides, and the correspondence of all lines to the vanishing point [sic!] which is the centre of the circle.' Hicky Morgan's translation is also problematic: 'Perspective is the method of sketching a front with sides withdrawing into the background, the lines all meeting in the centre of a circle.' These modern translations fail to do justice to the original text, in which there is no allusion to a vanishing point or to linear perspective. Even if *scaenographia* means to 'draw buildings in perspective', the Latin origin of perspective, *perspicere*, is a verb that means simply 'to see clearly or carefully, to see through'.
12. Danielle Barbaro, *La Prattica della Perspettiva* (Venice, 1569), p. 130.
13. Juan Bautista Villalpando, *In Ezechielem Explanationes* (Rome, 1596, 1604). For this issue see Alberto Pérez-Gómez, 'Juan Bautista Villalpando's Divine Model in Architectural Theory', *CHORA* 3 (ed. by A. Pérez-Gómez and S. Parcell, 1997), p. 125–56.

14  See Alexander Koyré, *Metaphysics and Measurement* (London: Chapman & Hall, 1968) and Hans Blumenberg, *The Genesis of the Copernican World* (Cambridge, MA: MIT Press, 1987).

15  This is also revealed in the aims of philosophical systems throughout the seventeenth century. In his *Studies in a Geometry of Situation* (1679), for example, G.W. Leibniz proposed a science of extension that, unlike Cartesian analytic geometry, would be integral and not reducible to algebraic equations. But this project of a 'descriptive geometry' more universal than algebra could still magically describe the infinite qualitative variety of natural things. This transcendental geometry was part of Leibniz's lifelong dream to postulate a universal science, called by him at various times *lingua universalis*, *scientia universalis*, *calculus philosophicus* and *calculus universalis*. From all the disciplines of human knowledge, he tried to extrapolate the most simple constitutive elements in order to establish the rules of relation by which to organise the whole epistemological field into a 'calculus of concepts'.

16  For an extended analysis of the work of Desargues and a complete biography, see René Taton, *L'Oeuvre Mathématique de G. Desargues* (Paris: PUF, 1951). See also Pérez-Gómez, *Architecture and the Crisis of Modern Science*, ch. 5.

17  As I have already suggested, parallel lines did not converge in Euclidean space, where tactile considerations, derived from bodily spatiality, were still more important than purely visual information. See Maurice Merleau-Ponty, *Phenomenology of Perception*, part I, chs 1–3 (London and New York: Routledge, 1982).

18  Kepler had already introduced a point at infinity in a work on the conic sections, *Ad Vitellionem palalipomena quibus astronomiae pars optica traditur* (1604). He was interested in the laws of optics and generally in the nature and properties of light. Desargues was in fact the first to apply that notion to different theories on perspective and stereotomy. Such an accomplishment remains difficult to appreciate from a contemporary vantage point, which regards varieties of perspectival representation as the only true means of comprehending the external world.

19  Martin Heidegger emphasises that the enframed 'picture' implies a 'standing-together, system ... a unity that develops out of the projection of the objectivity of whatever is'. Although this objectivity is comprehensible only in relation to the Cartesian subjectivity, taking place in the mathematical space of analytic geometry, its absolute universality was only realised in the nineteenth century, particularly after the scientific refutation of Euclidean geometry. See 'The Age of the World Picture', in *The Question Concerning Technology and Other Essays* (New York, 1977), and below.

20  Thus, Diderot could state with assurance in his treatise *De l'interprétation de la nature* that 'before a hundred years there will be scarcely three geometricians left in Europe'. For more details about this aspect of eighteenth-century philosophy, see Yvon Belaval, 'La Crise de la Géométrisation de l'Univers dans la Philosophie des Lumières', *Revue Internationale de Philosophie* (Brussels, 1952).

21  Karsten Harries examines this problem in his excellent study *The Bavarian Rococo Church* (New Haven: Yale University Press, 1983).

Chapter 2
# On the origins of architectural photography
James S. Ackerman

The refinement of photographic processes during the 1830s culminated in the announcement to the public in 1839 of two quite different techniques – originating in France and England – for producing a permanent positive image. Both involved the use of a homemade camera box with a lens.[1] That of Louis-Jacques-Mandé Daguerre, which captured the object on a silver-plated metal ground (the daguerreotype), achieved a significantly greater precision of detail, but was limited to unique positive images. That of William Henry Fox Talbot, based on the production of a paper negative from which large numbers of positive prints could be made (which he called talbotypes, but soon renamed calotypes), was more effective in providing multiple copies and thus widespread access to visual information.[2]

In the early years of photography, when long exposures were required, architecture and landscape subjects were favoured partly because they did not move, but also because they satisfied a growing interest among the bourgeoisie in the world beyond everyday experience, manifested as well in an increase in travel – previously the prerogative of a privileged minority. Talbot capitalised on this feature of his work by publishing books of photographic prints (e.g. *Sun Pictures of Scotland*, 1845) that appealed to the current culture of Romanticism and to the proponents of the medieval revival: castles, ruined abbeys, ancient country houses, and the undisturbed moors and downs celebrated by Wordsworth and Sir Walter Scott, whose Scottish castle, Abbotsford, appears in three prints.

Talbot wrote in 1877,

> In the summer of 1835 I made in this way [i.e., with the use of small camerae obscurae and short focal-length lenses] a great number of representations of my house in the country, which is well suited to the purpose, from its ancient and remarkable architecture. And this building I believe to be the first that was ever yet known to have drawn its own picture.[3]

Like many early photographers, Talbot, a mathematician, physicist and chemist who kept in close contact with the scientific community, was unaware of – or unwilling to admit – the extent to which photographic images cannot simply be read as reflections of reality, but must depend on various elements of choice (of subject, position, framing, lighting, focus, etc.) and must reflect and address the ideology and taste of its time, though he must have appreciated the degree to which the techniques of photography themselves imposed certain expressive results (for example, the speed of exposure, the focal length of lenses, the graininess resulting from the use of paper negatives). The photograph of 1835 has not survived; probably it preceded the discovery of the essential fixing chemical. But existing photographs of Lacock Abbey are casual in their choice of viewpoint and not primarily intended as a record of an architectural subject.

Interest in Romantic and medieval subject matter had been nurtured by books and paintings since the early years of the nineteenth century. Large-scale, often multi-volume publications on medieval architecture with engraved illustrations and extensive historical and descriptive texts were widely available in England and France. Augustus Charles Pugin, father of the influential spokesman for the Gothic Revival, Augustus Welby N. Pugin, devoted his career to making drawings for the cutting of engraved plates in such publications (e.g., *The Architectural Antiquities of Normandy*, London, 1827–8). Illustrations of this type established conventions of architectural representation that were adopted, no doubt unconsciously, by photographers: the positions from which to shoot the façades and apsidal ends of churches, the interiors, the choice of details.

Augustus Charles Pugin, view of St Étienne, Caen (engraving), from *The Architectural Antiquities of Normandy* (London, 1827–8)

The engravings were inevitably more interpretative than early photographs: the engraving technique, requiring the incision of fine lines into metal plates, could not convey the nuanced effects of light and shade available to the photographer, and the style and 'hand' of the engraver exerted a greater influence on the way the object was interpreted than the disposition of the photographer – at least in the 'documentary' style of early photographic surveys. On the other hand, the camera had – and still has – limitations that did not affect the draughtsman: it could not, for example, capture the whole of a large-scale church façade with its towers, or an interior with its vaults, without distortion resulting from the nature of the lens, especially in sites cramped by surrounding buildings (the engraver could simply eliminate irrelevant obstructions at will); and it could not, before the invention of artificial illumination, capture ornamental and structural detail in poorly lit places, such as church interiors. In the end, both techniques were profoundly affected by convention and manner; they involve mis-representation as well as representation. The photograph prevailed over the engraving, however, because it could be produced and distributed more rapidly, and hence in greater quantity, more cheaply, and by practitioners less arduously trained.

It is impossible for these reasons to distinguish clearly a 'documentary' style of early architectural photographs from an interpretative one. Almost all photographers of the first half of the nineteenth century would have agreed with the statement by Fox Talbot to the effect that photographs make themselves – that is, that they are transparent records of what is in the world – and that this is what gives them their special status among images. The modern insistence on discussing and exhibiting as works of art those in which personal taste or style is found would, I believe, have struck the early practitioners as an attempt to deny them the uniqueness of their enterprise. In effect, from the early photographers' point of view, photographs are all documentary.

We could say that some were documentary by virtue of the nature of a public or private commission. Many photographers were engaged, particularly in France and England, to carry out programmes documenting national monuments. In 1851 the French government launched the *Missions Héliographiques*, assigning each of five specific regions to one of the pioneer photographers chosen by the Historic Monuments Commission (Edouard Baldus, Henri Le Secq, Hippolyte Bayard, O. Mestral and Gustave Le Gray). Baldus was also employed in the 1860s to provide a survey of structures serving the national railway system; his image of the shed of the station at Toulon is characteristic in its simplicity and clarity and in the photographer's capacity to see in industrial architecture a striking new category of building.

Because the purpose of the documentation programmes was to assemble archives of permanent relevance, the photographer was obliged to restrain as far as possible personal inclination and appeal to the taste of his time. This is implied by the statement issued in 1857 on the founding of the Architectural Photographic Association in England on the model of the French Société Héliographique, itself founded in 1851, for 'procuring and supplying to its members photographs of architectural works of all countries' with an eye to benefiting 'the architectural profession by obtaining absolutely correct representations of these works, and, to the public, by diffusing a knowledge of the best examples of architecture and thereby promoting an increased interest and love of the art'.[4]

The intention to produce 'objective' images also would have been true of many of the photographs of monuments and frequented sites made commercially for

Henri Le Secq, church of the Madeleine, Paris, south façade (1851–3)

mass distribution by entrepreneurs such as Louis-Desiré Blanquart-Evrard, who established in 1851–2 a printing and marketing establishment to produce books, albums and individual prints that could be ordered from a catalogue, which tended to repress idiosyncratic approaches in order to attract a variety of buyers.[5] Photographs were used also to document the building history of important structures. Baldus, for example, was employed to track the process of the new wing of the Louvre in Paris, and left thousands of prints, including a number of impressive panoramic images, in the archives; the same occurred in the construction of a major Second Empire enterprise, the Paris Opéra. Charles Marville was commissioned to record the huge demolition work carried out under Baron Haussmann's urban renewal scheme for the city of Paris.

The value of photography as a support for the restoration and conservation of historic monuments was also recognised by those charged with refurbishing medieval buildings. When Eugène Viollet-le-Duc was commissioned in 1847 to restore Notre-Dame in Paris, he ordered large numbers of daguerreotypes to document the existing state of the building, because of the exceptional capacity of the process to record fine detail; for his purposes, the fact that the images could not be reproduced in multiples was no drawback.

Of course, many photographs – knowingly or not – exploited the aesthetic potential of the medium and portrayed architecture expressively; in contrast to Henri Le Secq's record of the Church of the Madeleine in Paris (previous page), Bayard's image of the aisle behind the façade would not have recalled the impression of most visitors to the building; it is the record of a personal response, and its subject is as much the play of light and shadow as it is the church. This does not imply that Le Secq's image is a definitive record of the church; like the majority of architectural photographers of his time, Baldus has chosen an elevated viewpoint that would not have been available to the casual visitor, so as to avoid parallax (I do not believe, as has been suggested, that this typical decision was influenced by the orthogonal elevation standard in architectural draughting). The 'documentary' and the expressive photograph, however, were not necessarily the work of different photographers. Charles Nègre claimed that when visiting an architectural site he would take three kinds of photographs: for the architect, a general view 'with the aspect and precision of a geometric elevation'; for the sculptor, close-up views of the most interesting details; and for the painter, a picturesque view capturing the 'imposing effect' and 'poetic charm' of the monument.[6]

Hippolyte Bayard, church of the Madeleine, Paris, interior of façade portico

The long tradition of poetic landscape painting incorporating architectural elements, whose roots lay in the mid-seventeenth century in the work of artists such as Claude Lorrain, working in Italy, and Jacob van Ruisdael in Holland, had stimulated in the late eighteenth and early nineteenth century a taste for what theorists of architecture and landscape design called the 'Picturesque'. Early British photographers, from Talbot on, echoed the paintings of J.M.W. Turner and Constable, especially in

**31** | On the origins of architectural photography

John Constable, *Salisbury Cathedral, View Across the Bishop's Grounds* (1822–3)

Roger Fenton, Ely Cathedral, view across the close (late 1850s)

their approach to ecclesiastical monuments. When Roger Fenton chose, in photographing Ely Cathedral, to favour foliage over architecture, he must have had paintings like Constable's image of Salisbury Cathedral in mind. Between the extremes of documentation and expression fall photographs, such as those of August Salzmann, intended to convey the actuality of buildings by focusing on aspects such as massing, modulation of light and shadow, texture, relations to the surrounding physical context, and so on.

Photography was closely linked to the strengthening of European nationalism in the first half of the nineteenth century. The programmes launched to document particular aspects of each country's architecture underscored the nationalistic tendencies of the time. Subjects were chosen, perhaps subliminally, to reinforce a particular conception of the significance of certain periods of the past. In France and Britain, later medieval architecture was emphasised; British photographers did not show much interest in Anglo-Saxon buildings, although those would best have represented an indigenous achievement signifying architectural independence from France. This might be explained by the emphasis placed on late medieval sources by promoters of the Gothic Revival. Renaissance, Baroque and contemporary architecture attracted less attention in Britain and France, except for major public enterprises in the capital cities. In Italy, however, the Renaissance style, regarded as one of the major cultural achievements of the peninsula, accounted for a major proportion of the output. Italian photographers focused on urban architecture in major centres; few of the tourists who bought their prints ventured into the countryside looking for abbeys and villas.

Anonymous French photographer, colonnade at Palmyrna (late nineteenth century)

Photographic studies of non-European lands, like those of national monuments, were anticipated in printed publications of the early years of the century, from the time of Napoleon's conquest of Egypt.[7] The favoured sites were Egypt, with a focus on ancient monuments, and the Middle East, with an emphasis on places in the Holy Land known from the Bible. Greece (principally Athens) and Rome (principally the city) were represented by a lesser volume of prints, and Turkey, despite its treasure of Byzantine monuments, was barely noticed.[8] The photographers followed the trail of colonial conquest and the fashions of newly developed bourgeois travel, and saw their subjects, in the light of Orientalism,[9] as strange and exotic echoes of a far-distant past now in the control of decadent and indolent peoples (many photographs of native costumes and customs were produced alongside those of architecture). Where human beings appear in the photographs they almost invariably appear to be labourers, ne'er-do-wells or nomads, far removed from the self-presentation of enterprising Western Europeans.

One function of the architectural photograph particularly relevant to this volume is its use by the historian of architecture and by the architect as a resource in designing new buildings that employ references to historical styles. For the architectural designer, photographs can provide a rich resource and stimulus. The fact that photography became available at the height of the Gothic Revival and of the taste for the Picturesque made this especially evident. In contrast, architects working in the Classical Revival style (which continued to be practised alongside the Gothic Revival) found measured plans, sections and elevations in the tradition of Stuart and Revett's *The Antiquities of Athens* (1762) and Charles-Louis Clérisseau's *Antiquités de la France* (1778; on the Roman remains at Nîmes) more useful than photographs, because the strict rules of Classical composition and proportions could be conveyed more effectively in precisely measured architectural renderings.[10] Publications addressing the growing interest in the Gothic Revival and Picturesque architecture emphasised pictorial effects of massing, contrasts of light and shadow, texture and colour, and richness of ornament, all of which could be captured more effectively by the camera than by the draughtsman and engraver. But the potential of early architectural photography had already been suggested during the first three decades of the nineteenth century by new techniques of printing – the lithograph, the aquatint and the mezzotint – which were employed increasingly to convey these aspects of architecture and were the principal vehicles for the diffusion of the Picturesque: most of the villa and landscape publications used these techniques (e.g., J.B. Papworth, *Rural Residences*, 1813).

Photographs were a resource that not only expanded the designer's knowledge of familiar historical traditions but extended the scope of his knowledge to a wide spectrum of historical styles that were less accessible at first hand, especially those of the Egypt, Byzantium and the Middle East. In France, the influential Second Empire style promoted by the École des Beaux Arts employed a rich amalgam of ancient, Renaissance, Baroque and Rococo elements and ornamental motifs that made photographic archives a virtual necessity for practitioners.

In the second half of the nineteenth century architects increasingly became the patrons of photographers as it became evident that photographic portfolios could serve as a way of attracting clients. Henry Hobson Richardson must have sponsored or at least have encouraged photographic campaigns that surveyed his major buildings and that were published in *Monographs of American Architecture* (1886 on) and Mrs Schuyler van Rensselaer's *Henry Hobson Richardson and His Architecture* (1888).

Toward the end of the century innovative photographers (Frederick H. Evans, Edward Steichen, Alfred Stieglitz) turned away from a documentary approach and employed architectural subjects in the expression of a distinct personal style. Documentary photography became less experimental and varied. In the period of Modernist architecture, beginning in the second decade of the twentieth century, images of historical architecture were of less concern to the designer, but photographs of contemporary work, particularly those of the most eminent architects, powerfully affected the spread of the style.

Modern history of architecture had its origins in Western Europe at about the time when photographs of buildings became available to scholars.[11] Photographs did not create the discipline; but without them opportunities for the development of sophisticated research methods would not have been available to scholars, who had had access only to drawings and traditional prints. A method grounded on systems of classification could be developed without the capacity to make comparisons between buildings and groups of buildings. Photographs are fundamental to the practice of historical research and interpretation because they give scholars an almost infinitely expandable collection of visual records of buildings and details of buildings in their area of research.

With the development after the mid-nineteenth century of fine long-focus lenses and increasingly sensitive negatives permitting rapid exposure, many aspects of buildings could be revealed in photographs that were not accessible to the naked eye (whether due to their distance from the ground or the obscurity of detail in dark interiors). While there can be no effective substitute for experiencing buildings at first hand, our memory is incapable of storing all the visible aspects of any one work, much less the entire achievement of a particular body of work.

The beginnings of the modern discipline of architectural history – and the history of the other visual arts – can be traced back roughly to the period of early photography. Perhaps under the influence of the taxonomic method in science (in the botany of Linnaeus and others), scholars classified works of art according to style – the style of a historical period, a nation, an area, an individual designer. This required a method based on comparison – establishing a class of production through the determination of common traits among different objects. Comparative judgements with respect to style were also necessary to support a narrative of evolutionary change that already had been a feature of literary and art criticism in antiquity and the Renaissance. To this end, photographs became indispensable in ways that drawings and engravings could not: in consulting a graphic work, we have no way of determining how accurate a record it is; the photograph, on the other hand, though by no means a transparent reproduction, contains clues as to its degree of documentary reliability.

It is difficult to define precisely the motivations underlying the photographer's choice of architectural subject because we cannot be sure what portion of the work of the period has been preserved. Moreover, what we know of early photography through publication has emphasised the achievement of only a few countries – two of these, England and France, to a disproportionate degree. But, accepting these limitations, we can still see in the early history of architectural photography two basic principles: first, that modes of representation are not significantly altered when new techniques are discovered, but that they perpetuate pre-existing conventions; and second, that representation itself is not a reflection of some 'reality' in the world about us, but is a means of casting onto that world a concept – or unconscious sense – of what reality is.

## Notes

1. The following writings have been especially helpful to this essay: Michel Frizot (ed.), *A New History of Photography* (Cologne: Konemann, c. 1998); Peter Galassi, *Before Photography* (New York: New York Graphic Society, 1981); Joel Herschman and Cervin Robinson, *Architecture Transformed: A History of the Photography of Buildings From 1839 to the Present* (Cambridge, MA and New York: MIT Press, 1986); Edward Kaufman, 'Architecture and Travel in the Age of British Eclecticism', in *Photography and Its Image* (cat.), ed. E. Blau and E. Kaufman (Montreal: Canadian Centre of Architecture, 1989), pp. 58–85; Richard Pare, *Photography and Architecture 1839–1939* (Montreal: Canadian Centre of Architecture, 1982).
2. At about the same time Hippolyte Bayard in Paris produced direct positive prints in the camera that could be reproduced in multiples only by photographing them again. But because Bayard, who was an exceptional photographer, lacked the ability or interest to promote his invention effectively, he was given less credit than the others. In the course of the 1840s rapid improvements in paper 'film' techniques were developed, especially in France. See Jean-Claude Gautrand, *Hippolyte Bayard, Naissance de L'image Photographique* (Amiens, 1986).
3. H.F. Talbot, 'Early Researches in Photography', as quoted in Mike Weaver (ed.), *Henry Fox Talbot, Selected Texts and Bibliography*, p. 50, from Gaston Tissandier, *A History and Handbook of Photography* (London, 1878).
4. Information on the *Missions* and on Baldus is from the invaluable monograph by Malcolm Daniel and Barry Bergdoll, *The Photographs of Édouard Baldus* (New York and Montreal, 1995). See also Philippe Néagu, *La Mission Heliographique: Photographies de C. Nodier, Taylor, Voyages Pittoresques dans l'Ancienne France* (Paris, 1818), p. 3.
5. As quoted by Robert Sobieszic, *'This Edifice is Colossal': 19th Century Architectural Photography* (Rochester: George Eastman House, 1986), p. 3.
6. Isabelle Jammes, *Blanquart-Evrard et les Origines de l'Édition Photographique Française* (Geneva and Paris, 1981).
7. As quoted, from notebooks in the Archive Nationale, in Daniel and Bergdoll, *Baldus*, p. 32.
8. Reported in *La Déscription de l'Egypte, ou Receuil des Observations et des Recherches qui ont été faites en Egypte pendant l'Expédition de l'Armée Français* (Paris, 1809–22). Also see Carsten Niebuhr, *Reisebeschreibung nach Arabien und anderen umliegended Ländern* (Amsterdam, 1774–8); John Carne, *The Holy Land and Asia Minor* (London, 1836), etc.
9. An exception: John Frederick Lewis, *Lewis's Illustrations of Constantinople, Made During a Residence in That City in the Years 1835–6* (London, n.d.).

10   See W.J.T. Mitchell, 'Imperial Landscape', in *Landscape and Power*, ed. W.J.T. Mitchell (Chicago, 1994), and other studies in this volume; Linda Nochlin, 'The Imaginary Orient', *Art in America* (1983): pp. 119–31; Mary Louise Pratt, *Imperial Eyes: Travel Writing and Transculturation* (New York, 1992); Edmund Swinglehurst, *The Romantic Journey: The Story of Thomas Cook and Victorian Travel* (London, 1974).

11   I am indebted to Ralph Lieberman for many insights into the role of photography in the history of art, the dangers of historians' overdependence upon it and, in general, the limits of representation in architectural photography.

Chapter 3
# Architectural cinematography
Patrick Keiller

Since its invention, the cinema has offered glimpses of what Henri Lefebvre described, in another context, as 'the preconditions of another life'.[1] As the most extensive way of reconstructing experience of the world, it was also the most extensive way of getting out of it, and into another one. It's not surprising that so much of cinema was created by, and to some extent for, people with first-hand experience of emigration.

The new, virtual world of cinema was typically a world transformed – by eroticism, love, solidarity, crime, war or some similarly extraordinary experience. It differed from that offered by, say, the novel in that it was visible, and in that usually the spaces of the new world were made by photographing fragments of the old one. These fragments were very often specially created for the purpose, but in practice it seems to make very little difference whether the *décor* of a film is real or artificial, or even whether a film is fiction or documentary. The newness of the spaces of the cinema is a product, not of set-building, but of cinematography. It's the phenomenon of *photogénie*.

The earliest reference that I know of to something like this is made in Louis Aragon's essay *On Décor*, which was first published in September 1918 in Louis Delluc's *Le Film*. This was Aragon's first published writing, in which he wrote:

> To endow with a poetic value that which does not yet possess it, to wilfully restrict the field of vision so as to intensify expression: these are two properties that help make cinematic *décor* the adequate setting of modern beauty.[2]

The first part of this statement – 'to endow with a poetic value that which does not yet possess it' – anticipates Aragon's identification of the surrealist *frisson* in *Le Paysan de Paris*, the 'new kind of novel' based on descriptions of two of the several places in Paris that the Surrealists had adopted:

> I felt the great power that certain places, certain sights exercised over me ... The way I saw it, an object became transfigured: it took on neither the allegorical aspect nor the character of the symbol, it did not so much manifest an idea as constitute that very idea ... I acquired the habit of

constantly referring the whole matter to the judgement of a kind of *frisson* which guaranteed the soundness of this tricky operation.[3]

Later in the book Aragon identifies a similar sensation as that which accompanies the recognition of a poetic image, and it has always seemed to me that, as a sensibility, the surrealist *frisson* very much resembles the momentary insight, the instant of identification of an *image* that sometimes results in a successful photograph, or an image in a film. One wonders, even, if it was partly Aragon's experience of the cinema that led him to the surrealist subjectivity to actual everyday surroundings.

The second part of Aragon's statement – 'to wilfully restrict the field of vision so as to intensify expression' – effectively describes film space. Films are made of images with a field of view which is very narrow compared with experience of actual, three-dimensional space. The space of a film is assembled from fragments, their relationship inferred from cues in action, sound or narrative. Most film space is off screen – it's either remembered from preceding images, or heard, or merely the imaginary extension of the space on screen. Because it is reconstructed in this way, film space is always a fiction, even when the film is a documentary.

In his essay *Art of the Cinema*, Lev Kuleshov describes making a sequence in *Engineer Prite's Project* (1917–18):

> It was necessary for our leading characters, a father and his daughter, to walk across a meadow and look at a pole from which electric cables were strung. Due to technical circumstances, we were not able to shoot all this at the same location. We had to shoot the pole at one location and separately shoot the father and daughter in another place. We shot them looking upward, talking about the pole and walking on. We intercut the shot of the pole, taken elsewhere, into the walk across the meadow.
>
> This was the most ordinary, the most childlike thing – something which is done now at every step.
>
> It became apparent that through montage it was possible to create a new earthly terrain that did not exist anywhere …[4]

Before I ever thought of making a film, I had developed a habit of identifying examples of what might be described as 'found' architecture, and documenting them with colour slides. Many were industrial structures of various kinds, including some of the types photographed by Bernd and Hilla Becher, whose work I knew a little. I had also come across the Surrealists' adoption of particular sites in Paris – the Tour Saint-Jacques, the Porte Saint-Denis, the abattoirs of La Villette, the Parc des Buttes-Chaumont and so on – the last of which is one of Aragon's subjects in *Le Paysan de Paris*.

**39** | Architectural cinematography

What began as a search for individual buildings gradually widened to include all sorts of details of everyday surroundings – odd ruined shop fronts, roofscapes, scaffolding, the spaces of the London Underground and so on. The subjectivity involved was very like that described by Aragon, or the state of mind that Walter Benjamin describes in his essays about Marseilles. In the long run, the aim was to gradually refine the practice and to transform even the most familiar spaces of the city centre – Piccadilly Circus, say, or Regent Street – but it was difficult to progress beyond a certain point without some technique in making images. I recovered the idea, almost inadvertently, in making a film about London over ten years later,[5] by which time the process of defamiliarisation had become second nature.

By then I had made a number of short films, all of which were combinations of 16mm monochrome images of urban or rural landscapes and a fictional voice-over. To begin with, it had been difficult to see what one might make with sequences of architectural images, however intriguing, other than some kind of installation. To some extent, a sense of continuity could be achieved by making long takes with a moving camera (the first film was 20 minutes long, but contained only three shots) or by adopting the structure of a journey, but I had always thought that any film I might make would involve some kind of interior monologue. Ten years earlier, as an architecture student, I had seen Marker's *La Jetée*.

Patrick Keiller, Montalcino, Italy, 1983, from *The End*

The technique gradually evolved so that the films included more montage, with larger numbers of shorter shots. They were mostly made by undertaking journeys, but the pictures were rarely planned and were always subject to the unpredictability of natural light. The narration was always written after the footage had been shot and edited, so that the writing was determined by the picture, rather than the picture by the writing, and if one had put the pictures together in a different order, or had shot different pictures, some other equally plausible fiction might have been the result. It was very difficult to write coherent narration for an already edited sequence of brief, spontaneous images, but it seemed a suitably modern, or even postmodern, way to approach fiction. It also resembled the method of cinema newsreels. I found out later that other, more critically respected documentaries had been made in a similar way, without too many preconceptions. The combination of moving camera and interior monologue suggested some more-or-less comic attempt to represent consciousness, or perhaps artificial consciousness – the inner experience of an alienated and rather unreliable artificial *flâneur*. This was in homage both to *Frankenstein* and to the confessional voice-overs and subjective-camera sequences of *noir*.

The cinematography had also developed a distinct technique. Some of the best footage was shot directly after thunderstorms, or in windy weather at the coast. In this clear air, shadows were very sharp, detail was brightly illuminated, and the sky was darker, or at least not brighter than the ground. It was possible to produce footage of unusual sharpness and richness of detail that achieved an almost three-dimensional quality, despite the limitations of 16mm. This seemed to confirm the preference for monochrome and the old idea that the illusion of depth in photographs of architecture is often most convincing in fine grain, high contrast, deep focus, monochrome pictures.[6]

On the other hand, this preference for particular kinds of daylight made it increasingly difficult to produce pictures. The various stylistic traits – interior monologues, the compressed writing of the voice-overs, the reliance on atmospheric effects – also encouraged allusions to genre: Gothic fiction, or even Expressionism. The films were becoming stylised and increasingly difficult to make. The quasi-surrealism of the original project seemed to have been diminished in the attainment of technique.

The previous three films had been made by going away from London to more photogenic locations.[7] For various reasons, it looked as if the time had come to make a longer film, which suggested a more serious engagement with a subject. It also suggested a longer period of photography, which would be difficult if we had to go away. The political atmosphere of London seemed to be changing, and it would be a challenge to try to re-imagine familiar surroundings. I decided to risk making a film about where I lived.

In the early 1990s London did not seem a very promising camera subject, especially for someone obsessed with clear air. During the summer of 1989, when the film was conceived, the visibility along the river was often so poor that one could stand on a bridge and find it difficult to see the next one. On the other hand, in the absence of traditional London fog, perhaps the traffic fumes had possibilities. I wondered whether to make the film in colour, which might be more suited to the haze.

It had occurred to me that if the film was to be longer than its predecessors, it ought also to be wider. In any case, a feature-length film for theatrical distribution would conventionally offer the more extensive spectacle of 35mm cinematography, with the sharper resolution that I sought for making architectural images. It was not that much more expensive to shoot the film on 35mm stock. I was worried that it would be very difficult to make monochrome images of everyday surroundings in London – the film's documentary aspect implied less freedom to abandon a subject if it proved too difficult to get a decent shot out of it. Colour might not achieve the vertiginous three-dimensionality of monochrome pictures, but it would be much less dependent on the weather. I'd never liked the look of most 16mm colour – for some reason, I didn't think it would produce pictures that were sufficiently sharp or colour-saturated – but this aversion to 16mm colour did not seem to apply to 35mm. Colour also seemed more likely to produce pictures that were funny. Monochrome would have been too serious. For some time, I held on to the idea that some reels might be monochrome and some colour, like Warhol's *Chelsea Girls*, but in the end, after testing various filmstocks, we decided to shoot the film on a 35mm, fine grain, daylight colour stock that had recently been introduced by Eastman.

With colour, the camera became an instrument of criticism. A McDonald's, for instance, photographed in monochrome might merely have looked a bit bleak; in colour it got a laugh. The slightest sense of hyper-reality in the pictures seemed to be enough to unmask their subjects, especially if one stared at them a bit. I had already begun to use lenses with a longer focal length more often, with the result that the camera was hardly ever used without a tripod, and camera movement had become very infrequent. With colour, the camera hardly ever moved at all, the longer lenses were used even more, and the images were more often of details. This seemed to corroborate another idea one comes across in architectural photography, that colour suits images of detail.[8] It also recalled Aragon's formulation of *décor* – in re-imagining something as big as London, one tended to *restrict the field of vision*.

These characteristics – together with the adoption of rather stolid, often symmetrical compositions (easy to set up in a hurry) and the 4×3 screen ratio[9] – seemed to suit the spaces of London. There was an element of self-parody in the pictures, as if there was something inherently funny about their predictability. This quality was sometimes used to convey irony, affection and other meanings.

With the heavier 35mm equipment, and the frequent necessity to carry it some distance, each set-up was much more of a physical commitment than it had been before. This encouraged a tendency to linger, and make several shots, using different lenses and framing different details of the subject. Where there was a lot going on, it was possible to assemble action sequences, which created spaces that were more extensive than those of the earlier films. This was augmented by post-synchronised background sound which, laid over a group of shots, identified them as fragmentary views of the same location. None of this sound was ever recorded with the picture, and only rarely was it from the actual location. One of the sound effects in *London* had been recorded for *Blow-Up* over 25 years earlier. We chose this, without knowing what it was, because the level of background traffic roar was much lower than usual. One of the film's biggest fictions was that it reconstructed London as a quiet city, without the noise of traffic.

The film was organised as the record of a period of about ten months. The off-screen narrator described the work of a fictitious character who was researching what he described as the 'problem' of London, which seemed to be, in essence, that it wasn't Paris. There was a document, a plan, with a large reserve of ideas for subjects and itineraries, but the film effectively made itself up as the events of the year (1992) unfolded.[10] It was mostly photographed by a crew of two. We went out with the camera regularly on two days in every week, and shot some other material at night or at weekends. Apart from coverage of particular events, the photography was nearly always determined on the day, or at fairly short notice. Altogether there were about one hundred days of photography, and one hundred 400-foot rolls of film, about seven-and-a-half hours of material. We stopped when we thought we had enough material to make the film, which was about when we had expected. Most of the material in the film appears in the order it was shot. It was edited and written in more or less the same way as the earlier films, though there was more material and a lot of work post-synchronising sound – and for the first time I worked with an editor,[11] a collaboration that has survived this and subsequent projects.

Since *London*, I have made two more films of about the same length in more or less the same way,[12] though with tighter schedules and itineraries. In the latest film there is more camera movement. This film is not a satire but an investigation of some aspects of housing in the UK, a documentary made for television. It was shot in digital video and includes interviews with academics and other specialists.

At the moment, it looks as if the future of this architectural cinema depends on developing ways to assemble more extensive and ambitious fictional spaces. *London* and its sequel *Robinson in Space* set out to re-imagine actual spatial subjects. The latest film addresses the difficulty of making new spaces. The next project might explore the creation of a *new earthly terrain* like that of Kuleshov, a fictitious world made from fragments of the real one.

Film offers a kind of permanence to subjectivity. On a bad day, or in a bad light, even the architecture of Gaudí might lose its immediate appeal, but in a film one's transitory experience of some ordinary, everyday detail as breathtaking, euphoric or disturbing – a doorway, perhaps, or the angle between a fragment of brickwork and a pavement – can be registered on photographic emulsion and relived every time the material is viewed. On the other hand, when actual extra-ordinary architecture is depicted in films it's often easy to conclude that something is missing, as if the camera has nothing sufficiently revelatory to add, nothing to improve on a visit to the actual building.

At about the time I first began to think about making a film, I particularly admired the architecture of Hans Scharoun, on one hand, and *film noir*, on the other. Until recently it never occurred to me to look for a connection between them, other than perhaps Berlin. Scharoun's Philharmonie, for example, and (say) Fritz Lang's films of the 1940s and '50s – *The Big Heat*, *Human Desire* and so on – don't seem to have much in common until one remembers that both architect and film-maker share a background in the Expressionism of the 1920s. Quite what, if anything, this might mean isn't clear, though it's intriguing that Scharoun does seem to influence some present-day architects, who attempt connections with the spatiality of film. The architecture of Scharoun and Häring might just be seen as confirming the rationality of the apparently eccentric (though I doubt that they saw it that way), whereas *noir* reveals the irrationality of the normal, so perhaps the two are in some way complementary. Certainly, both extra-ordinary experience of everyday architecture (in film, especially *film noir*) and everyday experience of extra-ordinary architecture (Expressionism, Art Nouveau and so on) might be sought for similar reasons. The Surrealists, for instance, admired both Gaudí and *film noir*. For anyone in pursuit of, let's say, the *improvement* of everyday life, a medium that offers a heightened awareness of architecture – the medium of film – might be thought at least as compelling as an actually existing architecture of heightened awareness – an ecstatic architecture, whatever that might be.

## Notes

1. *The Production of Space*, trans. and ed. Donald Nicholson Smith (Oxford: Blackwell, 1991), pp. 189–90.
2. Reprinted in *The Shadow and its Shadow: Surrealist Writings on Cinema*, ed. Paul Hammond (London: British Film Institute, 1978), pp. 28–31.
3. Louis Aragon, *Paris Peasant*, trans. Simon Watson Taylor (Boston, MA: Exact Change, 1994), pp. 113, 115.

4   Reprinted in *Kuleshov on Film: Writings of Lev Kuleshov*, trans. and ed. Ronald Levaco (Berkeley: University of California Press, 1974), pp. 51–2.
5   *London* (85 minutes, 35mm colour, 1994), BFI Films, Connoisseur Academy Video.
6   See, for instance, the writings of the architectural photographer Eric De Maré.
7   These were *The End* (18 minutes, 1986), *Valtos* (11 minutes, 1987) and *The Clouds* (20 minutes, 1989), the first two independently produced with support from the Arts Council of Great Britain, the third made for the British Film Institute.
8   See, again, De Maré's writings.
9   Until the 1950s, cinema screens were 'Academy' ratio – 4×3 or 1.33:1 (the ratio of many of Turner's best known paintings, often 48×36 inches). With the advent of television, which used the same ratio, wider screen formats were introduced. These were initially achieved using anamorphic lenses which 'stretched' the entire 4×3 frame laterally. Gradually, however, all films were made to be projected at wider ratios, typically 1.75:1 or 1.85:1. Most films are now made with conventional lenses, with the frame masked to achieve the wider ratio. A large proportion of the frame is not used, and the image has to be magnified more in projection. To avoid this, and to enable the cinema, television and video versions of the film to be the same, the older Academy ratio was used. Also, as all the prints were made from the original camera negative, the picture was unusually sharp.
10  The film documents IRA bomb damage, the general election, the problems of the royal family, the ERM crisis and the parliamentary debates about the Maastricht Treaty, and two big demonstrations that followed the government's announcement of pit closures.
11  Larry Sider, also known for his work with Laura Mulvey and Peter Wollen and with the Brothers Quay.
12  *Robinson in Space* (82 minutes, 35mm colour, 1997), BBC Films, distributed by BFI Films and Connoisseur Academy Video, and *The Dilapidated Dwelling* (78 minutes, beta sx, 2000), an Illuminations production for Channel Four Television.

Chapter 4
# The revenge of place
William J. Mitchell

The special qualities of particular places are more important, not less so, in the digital electronic era. This will come as a surprise to acolytes of the now standard e-gospel – the narrative of an electronically shrunken planet, a weightless economy and an era of anything anywhere. Here is my counter-narrative; I offer three scenarios and an analysis.[1]

## Scenario 1: being vegetable

Sometimes the digital revolution makes me feel like I've been transported to VatVille.

Imagine a large collection of brains in vats. Let us equip each vat with an autonomous system for extracting necessary energy and nutrients from the surrounding environment – not so crazy, since that's exactly how trees work. And let us also provide fast Internet connections, IP addresses, and effective interfaces between the wet stuff and the silicon. That's VatVille.org (I ran Vatican.org through Network Solutions, but it's taken).

These brains have their limitations, but they can lead surprisingly interesting and productive lives. They can function efficiently as information workers (programmers, web page designers, stock traders or the like) plugged into the global digital economy. They don't have mattresses to put their earnings under, but they can accumulate them in online accounts, they can transfer them as they wish, and they can spend them through online transactions. They are far from powerless to affect the physical world; it's simple for them to order the transportation of physical materials and goods from place to place, and they can even operate a wide variety of online telerobotic devices – ranging from IP-enabled light switches to advanced weapons systems. They can inspect their surroundings through webcams, and they can download text, music and video files for their entertainment and cultural development. For social interaction they have online communities, chat rooms, instant messaging and even shared virtual worlds and online video games (such as Sony's 'Everquest') within which they can represent themselves by means of avatars. On the Internet, nobody knows you're a brain in a vat!

As far as I can tell, VatVille.org has little inherent geographic logic, and it can scatter itself across the surface of the globe in pretty arbitrary ways. It is hard to imagine a brain in a vat developing a preference for a particular location, since the sights, sounds and facilities of any location in the network are equally accessible from all locations in the network. It is not even clear (I will leave this one to the philosophers) that the brains in vats would have any conception of dwelling somewhere in particular. They park their core atoms at specific spots, it's true, but in another sense they exist everywhere at once.

If you look at VatVille.org from the outside, though, you can probably discern some rudimentary spatial patterns. Certain spots on the surface of the earth provide better access to energy and nutrients and are less subject to hazards and inconveniences than others, so you find vats more thickly clustered there. And, since it is cheaper to connect vats to nearby vats than to distant ones, you will find clusters around the locations of the earliest, pioneer vats, with high-speed backbones forming cluster-to-cluster connections. This clustering pattern is reinforced if the vats are not fully autonomous but depend on supplies of electricity, water and other needs via networks from central supply points. You can imagine developers selling gated vat farms.

I feel most like an inhabitant of VatVille.org when I'm alone in a hotel room, in a strange city, at night. My immediate surroundings provide few clues to where I am. The minibar, the little basket of toiletries and room service supply my basic needs. The television provides the same satellite channels pretty much anywhere. The telephone and (increasingly commonly) the high-speed network jack establish fast, two-way connections to the global digital telecommunications networks. My laptop computer creates the brain-to-bits interface. I can be all that a brain in a vat can be – picking up from where I left off in the last vat. And pretty soon I will move to a smaller but otherwise similar vat – an airline seat.

The now ubiquitous high-tech worker's cubicle is another good approximation of a brain vat. Fill your coffee cup, put on your Walkman, log in, and it doesn't much matter whether you're in Sunnyvale or Bangalore.

For me getting vatted is, at best, a tolerable temporary condition. (I don't want to live like a hydroponic tomato.) But proponents of teleserviced 'electronic cottages' seem to want to be brains in vats – 24/7/365. In this latest enactment of the anti-urban, agrarian-yearning subplot of the American dream, these nouveaux Thoreaus imagine themselves contentedly telecommuting from their Post-Modern cabins, far from the big city's problems, disturbances and people not like themselves. At the survivalist extreme, they are grimly prepared to keep the outside world at bay: brains in vats with guns.

### Scenario 2: being like a bee

At other times, the digital revolution seems to dump me in SwarmCity.

I first felt this when, one day, I was visiting Hadrian's Villa at Tivoli with a large group of friends and colleagues. We all had our tiny cell phones – switched on all the time, in the Italian manner. We scattered over the vast site in seemingly disorganised fashion, but we found ourselves continually summoning one another to points of interest and forming ad hoc clusters which quickly broke up and reconfigured, on the fly, as we pursued our individual but not unrelated interests and schedules. When someone informed us that there was a particularly fascinating discussion at some spot, we immediately converged on it. We took advantage of our rudimentary electronic intelligence system, and we swarmed.

Members of natural swarms, such as flocks of birds and schools of fish, depend upon direct observation of their terrain and of each other. The behaviour of the whole group emerges (by way of some satisfyingly elegant mathematics) from the numerous interactions among the behaviours of the constituent individuals.[2] It was the same with us in Tivoli, but our interconnections were electronically mediated.

A short while later I began to notice Japanese and Nordic kids similarly swarming through city streets. Their technology was slightly more advanced, it turned out. They were using their cell phones for wireless text messaging. As previous generations of rebellious teenagers had occupied their hands with cigarettes, these kids were into DoCoMo and Nokia. To watch them, you would think that the opposable thumb had evolved specifically for one-button control of handheld devices.

"You can access me by saying simply 'Agnes.' It is not necessary to add 'dot com.'"

The New Yorker Collection 1997 J.B. Handelsman from cartoonbank.com. All Rights Reserved.

Then, when the demonstrations against the WTO hit Seattle, I saw SwarmCity emerge full-blown. As the situation changed from moment to moment, the demonstrators used cell phones to coordinate instant gatherings at current sites of action. By now – several demonstrations later – the cops have figured out (at least for the moment) the best way to thwart this sort of strategy: you confiscate the phones.

Where brains in vats represent the endgame of sedenterisation, swarmers are electronically enhanced hunter-gatherers. They forage over their chosen terrains for currently available food, fuel, campsites, shelter, points of interest, the companionship of their friends, opportunities for confrontation, customers, victims, raves, or whatever.

They need mobility, either by being unencumbered on foot or through access to appropriate vehicles. And they become more formidable as their electronic intelligence repertoire grows – from simple voice and text communication to video, GPS positioning, navigation and tracking systems, mobile web access and geographically filtered delivery of information.

For really hardcore swarmers, cities don't need visible landmarks and edges to provide guidance, or the qualities of legibility and memorability that Kevin Lynch taught us to value in *The Image of the City*.³ They don't even need very much signage. Swarmers simply rely upon their electronics to deliver relevant information at the right moment, to guide them where they want to go and to tell them what they will find when they get there. In SwarmCity.org landmarks are physical places that (maybe temporarily) have lots of electronic pointers in their direction. And obscure backwaters are just places without pointers.

Lately, some of my hyper-ironic, thoroughly post-modernised Manhattan friends have been playing an extreme swarming game. For them, the landmarks are not the famous buildings that the tourists come to see. Instead, they are the inhabitants who – for the Warholian quarter-hour, at least – count as celebrities. When players spot these walking icons, they broadcast text messages: 'George Clooney at the produce rack in Balducci's!' For a few minutes, that's the place the electronic pointers pick out.

I think I got my swarmer spurs when I flew into DFW airport late one night, picked up a rental car with an electronic navigation system and let it guide me through the blandly undifferentiated landscape of suburban Dallas (completely unfamiliar terrain for me) to my destination. I would never have got there if the destination had not appeared on the guidance system's menu – in other words, if it had not been an electronically recognisable landmark. When I arrived, I had no mental map of where I had been. I might as well have been robomouse, blindly tracking signals from electronic cheese.

## Scenario 3: being vulnerable

And sometimes, the digital revolution makes me feel very vulnerable.

I wrote the first two of these scenarios before the horrifying destruction of the World Trade Center towers in New York. Then the events of 11 September 2001 suddenly brought the implications of VatVille and SwarmCity into vivid new relief. Space, power and violence don't fit together in the way they did before.

The World Trade Center towers were huge, specialised VatVilles – prominent, intense, immobile, spatially concentrated nodes in the global information economy. To the inhabitants, the twin towers seemed like cocoons, insulating them from the outside world to which they connected by increasingly diverse and sophisticated electronic means. Together with other large buildings in Manhattan's financial district, the towers operated as powerful command-and-control centres in the worldwide, electronically mediated financial system.[4] Their power and prominence made them inviting targets, and their spatial concentration made them tragically vulnerable ones.

Deliberate attack is not, of course, the only hazard to intensely focused concentrations of humanity and activity. Natural disasters, such as earthquakes, can be just as destructive. And as California has discovered, even economic and technological failures such as disruptions of power supply, though not as instantly life-threatening, can quickly destroy spatially concentrated enterprises. The lesson is that organisations that are distributed over many smaller, spatially distributed network nodes are more robust and defensible than those concentrated at a few large and prominent nodes. In the wake of 11 September, we are likely to see fewer trophy towers and more networked distributed systems.

By contrast, the terrorists who attacked the towers knew how to exploit SwarmCity. They were a mobile, dispersed network, relying on modern transportation and telecommunication capabilities for their effectiveness. Furthermore, to the frustration of the Pentagon's military strategists, they had no clearly identifiable, fixed locations or large concentration of lives and assets worth destroying. (Hence the urgent efforts to implicate governments that do have such concentrations and assets.) It was not like the old days of missile emplacements aimed at opposing capitals and mutually assured destruction.

And hijacking aircraft with pocket knives is far from the only way to turn SwarmCity against itself. Every competent terrorist now knows how to attach an explosive device to a mobile phone and remotely detonate it from anywhere in the world. And every competent teenage hacker knows how to execute the less violent but economically destructive strategies of hijacking computers and telecommunications systems by breaking into remote servers or by unleashing worms and viruses. As I was writing this, my technical staff put a new server online at MIT; within hours it had been broken into and temporarily hijacked by hackers from Romania.

The differences between VatVille and SwarmCity have important social, economic and cultural dimensions. And it is now evident that they have potentially deadly dimensions as well.

## Analysis

VatVille and SwarmCity are not, of course, particular places. They are general patterns that emerge when some of the familiar constraints on the locations of activities within the urban fabric are electronically loosened.

In general, we find particular activities at particular urban locations for some combination of three basic reasons. First, there are fixed attractions of the location – affordances that exist right there and are mostly unaffected by what happens elsewhere. In a dry region, for example, the fixed attraction may be a source of water; settlements are typically found at oases. Other fixed attractions include fertile agricultural land, mineral resources, favourable climate, scenic beauty and historical resonance.

Second, there are accessibility advantages – those that derive from convenient, efficient connections to related activities. Thus crossroads, ports and other nodes in transportation networks have traditionally offered economic benefits and have been favoured locations for settlements. Retail stores are located where there are plenty of customers, offices are located where workers can easily commute to them, and so on. These advantages are relative to conditions elsewhere in the network; if other activities relocate, if links in the network are broken or become clogged, or if new links are established, then the accessibility advantages of a particular location may rise or fall.

Third, there are stability advantages. A building to accommodate an activity represents an investment at a particular location, for example. If there are no prospective purchasers of the building, moving from that location means a loss of that investment. So there is advantage in staying put.

Essentially the same logic applies at the scale of buildings. By virtue of their sizes, shapes, orientations, views and so on, rooms have fixed attractions that suit them to accommodating particular activities. By virtue of their relationships to the circulation system, they also have accessibility advantages. And it takes time and effort to move furniture and equipment from one room to another, so there are advantages to keeping the uses of spaces stable – not moving things around too much, not creating excessive churn.

The distinctions among these types of advantages are clear enough to be useful for our purposes here, but they are not absolute. For example, it is worth noting, parenthetically, that accessibility advantages begin to look like fixed attractions when transportation networks and activity distributions are relatively stable over long periods. Similarly, apparently fixed attractions may disappear when resources run out, when technologies change, when overwhelming competition develops from unexpected quarters, and so on.

That's how architects and urban designers like to think about it. Economists prefer an equivalent framing of the issue in terms of costs, roughly as follows.[5] There are fixed costs of locating particular activities at particular locations; think of these as yearly rents. Then there are interactive costs; think of these as yearly transportation bills for commuting to work, for moving raw materials to a manufacturing location and finished goods from it, and the like. Finally, there are move costs; think of these as mover's bills and other relocation expenses resulting from transfer of an activity from one location to another. The total yearly cost of assigning some set of activities to a set of locations can be found by summing the fixed and interactive costs. If you allow movement of activities, you can also compute the total cost of a sequence of assignments; take the cost of each assignment over the time for which it exists, and add the move costs resulting from the transition between each assignment and the next.

The formulation of the economists clarifies the trade-offs. Often, for instance there is a trade-off between fixed and interactive costs – between highly accessible locations with correspondingly high rents and less accessible locations with lower rents but higher interaction costs. Similarly, an activity may be 'trapped' at an expensive or undesirable location because the move costs are too high. And the desirability of a potential move may be evaluated by calculating the time needed for it to pay off by means of more favourable fixed and interactive costs.

Let us now look at VatVille in these terms. It represents a condition under which you can get anything you want anywhere, and that's just as well, since it is very hard to move. More specifically, interactive costs are independent of distance, and move costs are high. Strategies for autonomously living off the land – collecting rainwater, growing your own food, employing photovoltaics and windmills for electricity generation, indifference to the outside world – are one way of getting to extreme VatVille. These simply reduce or eliminate the need to interact. Highly efficient networks connected to fixed delivery devices – such as high-bandwidth digital telecommunications systems connected to desktop computers – provide another way. These reduce the friction of distance. And digitally serviced office towers in central urban locations represent a mixed strategy: they get their traditional services from the local concentration of infrastructure and labour (much as a tall tree gets its nourishment from its local system of roots and leaves) while being linked globally, and are thus able to accumulate concentration and power, through electronics. You can drop out, you can plug in, or you can go for some combination of the two.

SwarmCity, it turns out, is the converse. This pattern emerges when local attractions and accessibility advantages matter a lot and may vary dynamically, when the availability of locations for assignment of activities fluctuates, and when the combination of good intelligence with very low move costs provides the opportunity to respond quickly as opportunities emerge. The produce rack at Balducci's is of great interest during the fleeting moment that the celebrity is there, an alert cell phone user provides the intelligence, and fleet-footed Manhattan pedestrians can swarm to the spot to gawk. Similarly, the search for a hotel room or a parking spot goes better if you have a continually updated electronic guide to current availability and price.

Think of SwarmCity as a dynamic pattern rather than a static one – a sequence, over time, of swift reassignments of activities to new locations. (You might imagine a computer's RAM, with its fixed array of locations and continually reassigned contents, as the most extreme version.) It is a pattern that effectively exploits distributed intelligence (the intelligence of the individual swarmers), that allows particularly efficient use of available real estate, and that encourages management of demand for both sites and channel capacity through dynamic variation of prices.

Electronically mediated swarming can take place at a variety of geographic scales and over a range of timescales. Pedestrians can swarm, over relatively local patches of terrain, when they have portable electronic devices such as cell phones and wireless PDAs. Drivers can swarm over metropolitan road networks when they have phones and electronic navigation systems. Office workers can swarm over temporarily assignable desks or cubicles when they have wirelessly networked laptop computers. GPS-equipped campers can swarm over national parks. Aircraft can swarm over airports when gates are dynamically assigned, by optimisation software, to respond to delays and unexpected events while minimising connection times for passengers and baggage. And electronically networked corporations can, increasingly, swarm their operations globally in response to varying local political conditions and labour markets.

**The revenge of place**

But what happens when ubiquitous digital networking, the miniaturisation and mobilisation of electronics, wireless technology and other factors combine to reduce interactive costs as well as move costs? The remaining component of the cost equation – the fixed cost of each particular place – becomes increasingly dominant. And the less the attractions of a place can be replicated or substituted for electronically, the more desirable and expensive it will be.

Take the beach, for example. There is a fixed quantity of it, you cannot reproduce it (except in very imperfect form), and you cannot move it. You have to be there to benefit from its advantages of climate, scenic beauty and recreational opportunity. And isolation need not diminish its value as it used to; you can telecommute from the beachfront, if you want. In a world where many distinctions among places are reduced, the particular value of the beach stands out even more vividly.

Or take listening to opera. You can inexpensively download MP3s of pretty much any performance you might want, anywhere you might care to listen to it. But there is only one La Scala. Opera fans will continue to seek the scarce tickets, and to pay the high prices, precisely because of its unique historical associations, cultural resonance and aura.

In an electronically mediated, networked world, places that have few unique local qualities, and decreased opportunity to take advantage of differences in accessibility, will compete (for citizens, tourists, visitors, customers, investments and so on) in a crowded and competitive market. Their value will inexorably be driven down.

Conversely, places that have unique, irreplicable, non-transferable advantages to offer will be the most highly desired real estate. They will be the nodes around which settlements form and swarms buzz. They will be the primary generators of new urban patterns. They will be the subjects of increasingly sophisticated, electronically executed search, pricing and allocation strategies.

And in all this, spatial diversification and dispersal matter. As the experience of many financial firms showed in the wake of 11 September, networked, dispersed organisations are far better able to continue effectively after the destruction of a node than more tightly concentrated ones – particularly if they can dynamically reassign functions to alternative sites. They are also less attractive and less vulnerable to violent physical attack, though network attack is another matter. They are less vulnerable to local peculiarities and restrictions; if you want to do stem cell research you had best not concentrate your facilities in the United States, and if you want to produce politically and sexually provocative multimedia you had best not concentrate them in Singapore. Much more positively, diversified distributed networks allow organisations to plug into unique local subcultures and to benefit from different types of cultural advantages. This is why major research and teaching institutions, such as MIT, are now distributing themselves globally through alliances and remote branches.

In other words, ubiquitous and efficient networks – particularly digital telecommunications networks – produce the commodification of accessibility. This reduces the capacity of places (both physical and online) to distinguish themselves simply by virtue of superior accessibility. To be competitive, they have to provide something that you cannot find anywhere else.

This is the revenge of place.

## Notes

1. This paper extends an exploration of the relationship between electronic technology and urban form that began with my *City of Bits: Space, Place, and the Infobahn* (Cambridge, MA: MIT Press, 1995) and continued with *E-topia: 'Urban life, Jim – but not as we know it'* (Cambridge, MA: MIT Press, 1999).
2. Mitchel Resnick, *Turtles, Termites, and Traffic Jams: Explorations in Massively Parallel Microworlds* (Cambridge, MA: MIT Press, 1997).
3. Kevin Lynch, *The Image of the City* (Cambridge, MA: MIT Press, 1960).
4. Saskia Sassen has brilliantly analysed this phenomenon in *The Global City*, new edn (Princeton, NJ: Princeton University Press, 2001). See also Saskia Sassen, 'Scale and Span in a Global Digital World', in Cynthia C. Davidson, *Anything* (Cambridge, MA: MIT Press, 2001), pp. 44–8.
5. Tjalling C. Koopmans and Martin Beckman, 'Assignment Problems and the Location of Economic Activities', *Econometrica* 25:1 (January 1957), pp. 53–76.

## Part 2
# The shape of representation

Each form of representation has its own specifics: its own criteria for selection, its own culture of tastes, its own production values, its own language, its own omissions.

Of course, these representations are profoundly different to the situations or buildings they purport to describe. All media, all representations are essentially, hugely and inevitably limited, partial and biased. Any medium, any form of representation selects certain elements, and it reproduces them depending on its own capabilities and biases. For example, the formal elevation – perfect in time, detail and completion, with all signs of occupancy, weather, age and time edited out. The photograph – carefully framed, composed and styled, and usually empty. The working drawing. The image for publication. The history book. The news item. Critical theory. And so on.

It's not always easy to see what these characteristics, limitations, biases and cultural codes are – or the way that they impact on architecture. It becomes impossible to dissociate the values of a medium from the architecture reproduced through it. Inevitably these values, criteria, limitations shape all kinds of architecture in various ways – from how it's imagined and designed, to how it's photographed and written about, to how it's used or interpreted and defined.

This part of the book aims to open up some examples of different types of architectural representation and to examine how this representation affects both the projects themselves and their interpretation. It also aims simply to focus attention on the characteristics of different media by bringing together several first-person accounts of producing architecture or producing architectural representations. With perspective, photography, film and e-technology already introduced, this part is more eclectic. It is, of course, in no way comprehensive, but it aims to sample some of the characteristics of the many diverse media that relate to architecture.

The first chapter, though, is not a first-person account. It's a picture essay: a small selection of architecture's many iconic images that are famous in their own right as pictures. It looks at them both as pictures and in terms of what such iconic pictures might tell us about our architectural beliefs.

Next is an interview with Peter Smithson who, with his wife Alison, made a hugely admired if often controversial career that included work in books and exhibitions as well as buildings. Smithson describes both the specific differences between these different sorts of work and the way in which they feed and support each other.

UN Studio architects Ben van Berkel and Caroline Bos are known for their work in diagrams, which they use as a form of process and analysis in the generation of a project. In their chapter, first printed in *ANY* magazine in the 1990s, they describe the relationship between the forms of the diagrams and their capacity to offer certain sorts of representational freedom.

Much has been written recently on the nature of architectural computer games and how this new, popular version of marketed space might affect our interpretation of real space. In his first-person account Philip Campbell, an architect turned game designer, exposes the design of game environments – and on a simpler level says something about how design responds to the ways people read perceived spaces.

Finally Archigram member David Greene, who has argued against the aestheticisation that the group's drawings seemed to bring, describes the curious facility of studio tutors and critics to mistake the architectural drawing for a building – and how much more likely this will become in the age of Photoshop.

The maverick nature of this part of the book, and the big jumps between the media and cultures described, is partly inevitable and partly intentional. Information about different media continues to be presented; but the grouping of these chapters is intended as a straightforward sample of some of the ideas, limitations and rules imposed by any kind of media, and how these affect what might be produced.

Chapter 5
**Iconic pictures**
**Kester Rattenbury with contributions from
Catherine Cooke and Jonathan Hill**

Architecture as taught, published and discussed by other architects relies on the recognition of a mass of famous pictures. Indeed, sometimes these can seem more iconically famous and even more satisfyingly 'architectural' than some of the buildings themselves.

Sometimes, of course, the image is all that exists of the architecture: the picture is effectively an architectural polemic for publication and debate with no intention of being built; or an unrealised proposal with all its idealism intact and unchanged by the realities of construction, context, use, abuse and time. Sometimes a view that was not principally 'architectural'– as presented in a film, say – offers such a strong architectural vision that it comes to be seen as almost as influential architecturally as architecture itself. Sometimes a photo or drawing – done either before or after construction – frames a specific architectural interpretation so successfully that it becomes the quintessential image: the 'real' or 'authentic' version of it, of which the occupied, adapted, economically handicapped, ageing or inaccessible building seems only a partly valid version. Sometimes, as the only record of a demolished building, it almost replaces the architecture in the idea of being 'real'. These pictures are indeed iconic in a way close to the religious sense: not merely a picture of architecture, but architecture itself. Such pictures are at the heart of our imaginary, image-based understanding of 'architecture' as a condition which applies not to the whole world but to certain, particular parts of it – even though, in many cases, they remain only pictures.

The idea of making a sample of some of these mythical architectural images and looking at them in their own right – outside the culture of the historical, critical or popular contexts in which they are usually seen, and with only short captions to accompany them – had two original purposes. The first was for fun, and as a kind of *Cole's Notes* of the pictures which you normally have to chase through architectural books of all sizes and shapes. The second purpose was to attempt to look at the pictures themselves, in their own right, stripped as far as possible from their native cultures, and to see how they work as images – what codes, constructions and ideas about architecture are loaded into them.

But when the pictures were put together, a third reason began to emerge. Set against each other (in a way at least partly determined by the technical constraints of colour printing in a book with a small print run), they form a nascent picture essay that describes a whole culture of architecture: what we consider valuable, interesting, essential, architectural.

In this, the collection of images is clearly not just a sample; it's a deliberate (if partly subconscious) editorial construction. The images were not selected in any scientific way or using any historical method. They are a deliberately loaded selection of 'high-code' architectural images as presented – almost exclusively – to architects. In particular, they are pictures that appeared or were referred to during my experience of the last ten years of London's 'architectural life' as an architectural journalist and teacher – not only in books or even exhibitions, which are naturally self-selecting in their subject and audience, but in lectures and student projects, which might be considered to be aimed at the heart of a more general architectural market.

This therefore is a fairly personal, London-based sample of high architectural images in the last ten years of the twentieth century. A sample from a different time or picked by a different person would presumably suggest a different interpretation or a different guise, and even this sample immediately suggests other pictures (those of Italian Futurism and the English Arts and Crafts movement come immediately to mind, each with their own, powerful pictorial culture, but which were possibly less fashionable during this period[1]). To extend this current sample further, though, starts to demand a system of categorisation which immediately starts to reassimilate them back into their various parent architectural publishing cultures – which is where they come from anyway.

Biased though it is, the sample is interesting. The pictures don't just represent their subject matter; they suggest a way of looking at the world. Of their kind they are extreme – grand, perfect, ruined, beautiful but sometimes uncomfortable or upsetting; and of their time they are profoundly iconoclastic – though the passage of time and frequent reproduction always tend to erode this effect. They are heroic: a world-view polemic offered in a single frame. They tell us not only how the world might be, but how we might see it.

The original intention in this chapter was to reduce text to a minimum, introducing the image itself in brief and relatively inexpert terms, but with references to key or interesting sources for more detailed and expert discussion. However, in sourcing the pictures I was inevitably involved in discussion with experts, and two of these people (Jonathan Hill and Catherine Cooke) kindly offered to write captions themselves. In both cases these captions ran over the length format. But the essays were so good and so apposite – and moreover stand as such a good introduction to the following chapters – that I have included them uncut as essays in their own right.

**GIOVANNI BATTISTA PIRANESI**

Ruins of a Sculpture Gallery at Hadrian's Villa, Tivoli
(actually the Large Baths)

> Piranesi's formidable output of over a thousand individual plates and their multiple impressions and revised states, constituted a revolution in communication unparalleled in their time. In a sense, this phenomenon characterised the contemporary European Enlightenment with its re-examination of the nature of the observed world, questioning of received ideas and dissemination of information to the widest audience possible

wrote John Wilton-Ely in *Giovanni Battista Piranesi, The Complete Etchings*.[2] If Piranesi's etchings look less than radical to any of us now, it is certainly due to the effects of time and familiarity. Piranesi's etchings and drawings constituted not just an information boom in themselves (and in their painterly techniques, with their focus on lighting, deterioration, human presence and fantasy), but a new way of representing the world, one in which, as Manfredo Tafuri writes in his seminal book, *The Sphere and the Labyrinth*, great architecture is forced to merge with the urban continuum.[3] Tafuri, indeed, argues for Piranesi as both Modernist and an early avant-gardist, overturning rational Enlightenment thought, using archaeology as 'the occasion for cryptic and allusive messages', and staging an attack on perspective as symbolic form.[4] Besides this, these *Vedute di Roma* plates were, of course, 'invitations to a voyage' – publicity material for the fashionable Grand Tour of Europe.[5]

Piranesi's influence is exponentially extensive – from Robert Adam, who accompanied him on visits to Hadrian's Villa, and John Soane, who heard him lecture in London, and whose buildings and drawings show his influence, to the great Romantic poet Samuel Taylor Coleridge, whose account of seeing his *Carceri* (described by Alberto Pérez-Gómez in Chapter 1) is given in Thomas de Quincey's *Confessions of an English Opium Eater* (1821). In more recent times Piranesi's influence has extended to Aldous Huxley, and to Sergey Eisenstein, who kept a copy of the *Carceri* on his wall and wrote in praise of Piranesi.

**ARCHIGRAM/RON HERRON**
Walking Cities (coloured version in the desert)

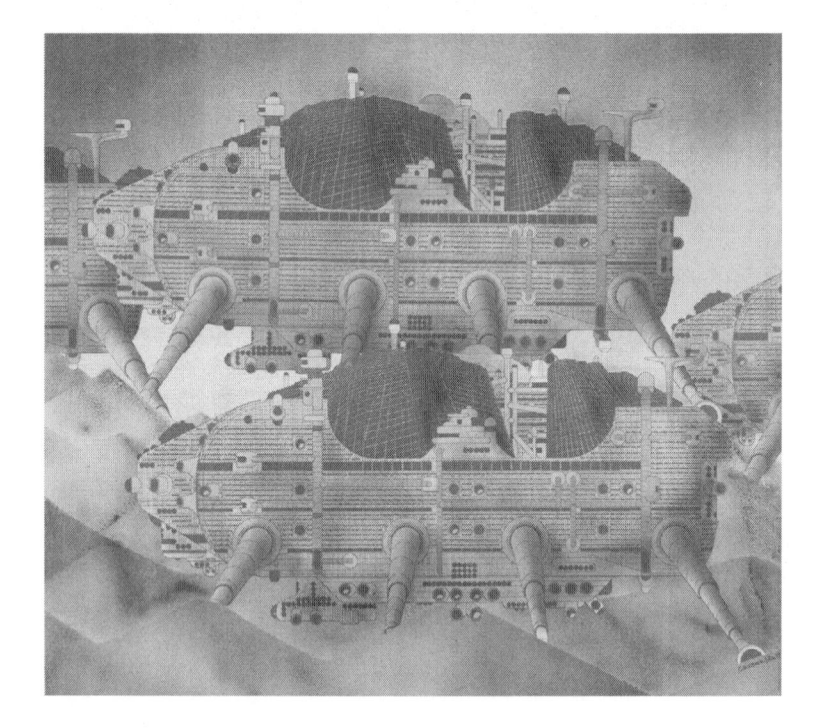

The fantastic images produced by the Archigram group are only part of a wider polemic, promoted through the Archigram magazine, projects and through other activities of members of the group, notably (and still) their role as the London schools' foremost teachers.

But it's still the drawings that crystallise the group's ideas for most people: spectacular imagery that at once refers to the conventions of the architectural drawing and overturns it. They propose projects that violently, graphically, funnily, upset the classical Bauhaus conception of dominant formal function. Archigram embraced aspects of the world excluded from the canon of high architecture: ephemera, electronics, technical innovations, advertising, vehicles, clothes, cars, lifestyles. The status of this drawing is thus a peculiar one, because the perfect artwork or precious drawing was in part antithetical to the group's aims and its cartoon, collage characteristics, once heretical, are now mainstream. Yet the drawing does still convey a challenge to the still dominant codes of a perfect, formal, established high architecture: its inherent Pop culture values remain visibly radical – though radically more acceptable and less uncomfortably avant-garde thirty years on.

# LE CORBUSIER
## Photos of the Villa Savoye and the Villa at Garches

During the 1990s Le Corbusier, 'probably the most written about architect this century',[6] came to seem again extraordinarily contemporary. His blatant use of fakery in published photos of his built work, his appropriation of advertising imagery, his staged filming of his buildings, the 'architectural promenade' that treated architecture as integral with event, and his use of gendered space (women and men rarely shared the same spaces[7]) seemed particularly potent, controversial or prescient.

In *Privacy and Publicity: Modern Architecture as Mass Media*, her seminal book exploring the different ways that Le Corbusier and Adolf Loos handled their representative media, Beatriz Colomina notes how Le Corbusier's photos direct the viewer's gaze out into the landscape (whereas Loos turns it inwards). She suggests that where, in Loos's photos, there is always the idea that someone is just about to enter the room, in Le Corbusier's photos someone has just left, leaving a door (or window) open, a loaf of bread or, as here, a big fish ('whatever one can make of it'), a hat, glasses, a lighter, cigarettes. 'We are following somebody, the traces of his existence presented to us in the form of a series of photographs of the interior.'[8] She notes the sense of voyeurism, of being out of bounds, our pursuit from room to room – and that the objects are always masculine, never a handbag or lipstick or item of female clothing ... 'where did the *gentleman* go?'[9]

Fondation Le Corbusier/ADAGP, Paris and DACS, London 2001

**SIR JOHN SOANE**
Aerial cutaway of the Bank of England
from the South-East

The fantastical pictures of the designs – real and imaginary – by Sir John Soane shown in Joseph Michael Gandy's watercolours are at least as well known as the buildings themselves. Soane was a famous proponent of the speculative paper project, but this painting represents a specific interpretation of a series of renovations and expansions to the Bank of England, which lasted forty-five years from 1788 to 1833. In his essay 'The Bank of England', Daniel Abramson says:

> The representation which comes closest to encapsulating Soane's achievement at the Bank of England is Joseph Michael Gandy's 1830 Royal Academy exhibition watercolour … As an allegory of the architect's ambitions, the aerial view depicts the Bank of England's building both poetically in ruins, like a Piranesi print, and professionally under construction, its walls, vaults and arches all freshly laid. The view illustrates the complex totality of Soane's greatest accomplishment and invests it with naturalistic authenticity. Gandy's view equates the Bank with the venerated ruins of antiquity, gifts London with urban grandeur and seizes representational control of Soane's architecture back from the commercial media. In effect, Gandy's view narrates Soane's lifelong struggle to construct for himself a modern professional identity, as both a poetic genius and a consummate professional.[10]

Abramson also refers to Joseph Schumpeter's argument that the picture is also a vision of capitalism itself: constantly both in ruins and being built.[11]

The Bank of England picture also came to have a particular potency when the bank was photographed by the eminent architectural photographer F.R. Yerbury during its demolition in 1925–6, in images oddly paralleling the painting.

Pen and watercolour drawing by Joseph Michael Gandy

**JAMES STIRLING**

Worm's-eye of the Florey Building,
Queen's College, Oxford

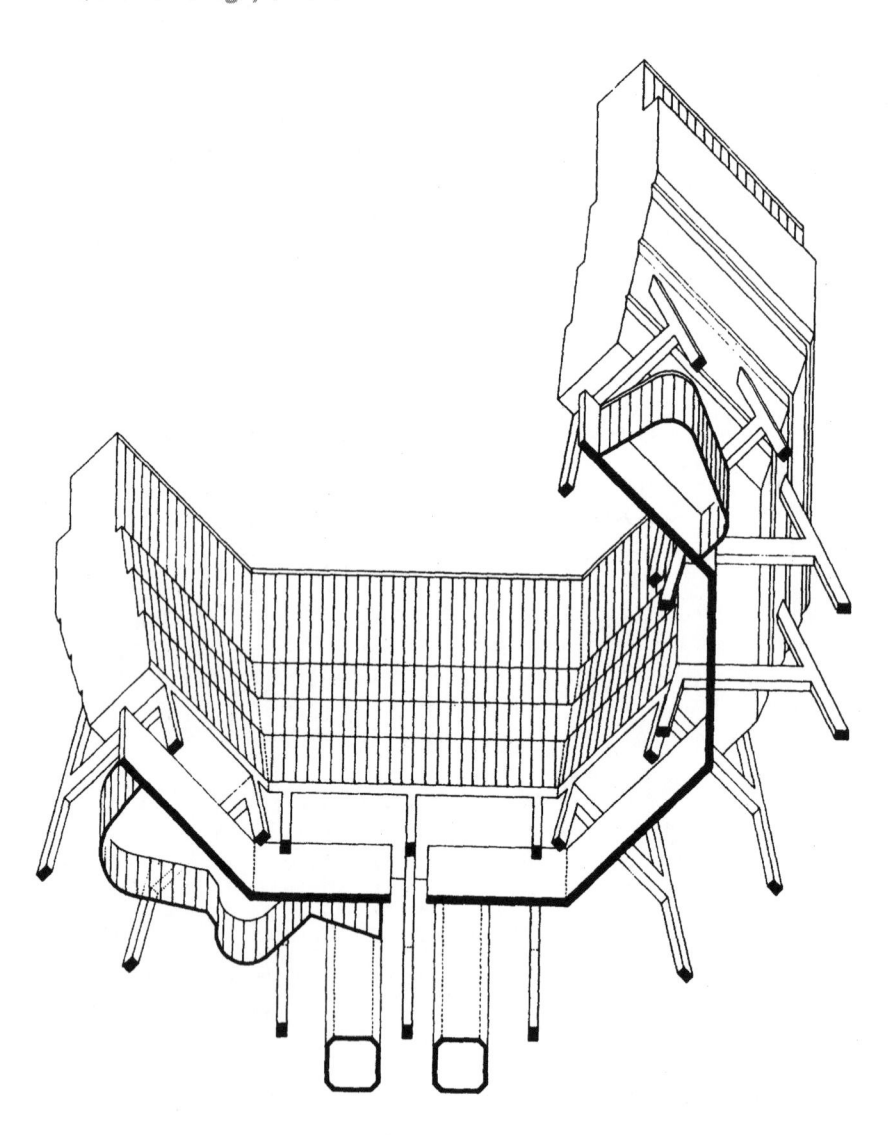

**69** | Iconic pictures

The most extraordinary latter-day evolution of the classical orthogonal architectural drawing type. The worm's-eye or up-view axonometric has a peculiar and specific culture: somewhere between an abstruse geometrical puzzle – where the form of the building would seem to be generated by the compositional demands of the drawing (though in fact they were originally retrospective accounts of existing buildings) – and a child's drawing, or a diagram of a toy.

In *Big Jim*, Mark Girouard's account of James Stirling's life and work, Girouard describes the evolution of this drawing type, specifically identified with Stirling, and notes its precedents in the line drawings of Le Corbusier's work (and in the Smithsons' 1953 down-view axonometric in their competition entry for Sheffield University). Girouard says that this drawing of the Florey Building, a students' hall of residence for Queen's College in Oxford, was drawn post-construction by Leon Krier, then working for Stirling, in about 1972. Girouard says:

> The line-only drawings, especially the axonometrics, are in themselves beautiful objects. They have the purity of ideal Platonic form, existing outside time and space. Their value as icons was first exploited to its full extent by the *Architectural Review* in 1972. The worms'-eye view of the Florey Building is printed white-on-black on the cover of the November issue, which featured the Florey and the Derby designs. 'AR' is printed in red above it. It makes a sensational cover, presumably designed by Bill Slack, the *Review*'s Art Editor. The same axonometric reoccurs black-on-white, on the cover of the RIBA catalogue ...
>
> The drawings tell with especial strength and beauty in the catalogue, where they could be printed on average larger than in the Black Book and where there were no photographs to compete with them for attention. James Gowan wrote angrily to the RIBA to complain that several of the earlier drawings were by him, and were not acknowledged as such. Krier also had cause for complaint; the acknowledgement opposite the title page, 'To Leon Krier for his work on the drawings, catalogue and exhibition' would cause no one to realise that at least 60 per cent of the drawings had been actually drawn by Krier in the previous few years – indeed most of them in the previous few months. One could say, though, that Krier himself was caught up by the fascination of establishing Jim's image, to the extinction of everyone else's.[12]

It's interesting to note that the worm's-eye form is always indisputably attached and credited to Stirling, just as Joseph Michael Gandy's painting of Soane's projects are seen as an authentic and essential part of Soane's oeuvre. This idea of collective (and sometimes individual works) being properly credited to a single designer, whoever actually drew them, is an inherent part of architectural culture, perhaps with its roots in Renaissance artists' and sculptors' studios.

Drawn post-construction by Leon Krier

**ZAHA HADID**
The Peak

Zaha Hadid shot to fame in 1982–3 with her international competition-winning scheme for The Peak leisure club in Hong Kong, a project that was never built. The definitive reason for this explosion on to the world architecture scene was the paintings – huge, spectacular, coloured paintings that reinvented Suprematist geometry for the Deconstructive age; high-code art objects in their own right.

In *Zaha Hadid: The Complete Buildings and Projects*[13] Aaron Betsky writes:

> Her winning entry for the Hong Kong Peak competition proved to thousands of architects and design students (including this author) that the techniques she had been developing were a new form of architecture. Situated at the highest point of the site as well as of all of the programmes that jettisoned the mundane demands of existence in favour of a purely hedonistic collection of forms ... it pulled the very peak apart, so that we, like latterday Titans, could do battle with it ...
>
> her drawings pulled the parts and pieces apart, exploding its site and programme. In one painting, Hadid showed elements of the club becoming part of downtown Hong Kong where the Metropolis' skyscrapers below became abstract planes that rotated, flew and actually turned into the building blocks for The Peak.

In an interview with Alvin Boyarsky, Hadid says of this project: 'I almost believed there was such a thing as zero gravity. I can actually now believe that buildings can float. I know that they don't, but I almost believe it – except when I see my engineer, of course.'[14]

Hadid's paper schemes have always been widely published, and until the present day her built works have been far smaller and far less frequent and have always had to suffer comparison with the spectacular and world-scale view of the drawings. The paintings are part of her design technique: she makes about 200 per project and calls them 'compressed and compacting images – larger than the ideas of the project'.[15]

**ROBERT VENTURI**
Recommendation for a Monument

**73** | Iconic pictures

The quintessential anti-architectural drawing. Robert Venturi's is an architecture of polemic, both in his buildings and his famous books, which are filled with text and images that have overturned the canon of high architecture: the casual Pop-Art views of the Las Vegas strip, with Caesar's Palace appearing as a near-heroic façade but with signs; the 'ducks' and the 'decorated sheds' (described and illustrated in Charles Jencks in chapter 13); the Learning From Levittown study, which illustrated cartoon-strip speech bubbles emanating from the houses. And the slogans: 'Main Street is Almost All Right', 'Ornament is Fine'.

This *Recommendation for a Monument* is overtly un-precious, quickly drawn, based on commercial-style signs (till then considered non-architectural), set against its high-code architectural title, which adopts the conventions of architectural manifesto books and suggests, as they do, that you take it seriously. Yet it also follows exactly – in all but line quality (which anyway resembles the great back-of-an-envelope sketch genre) – the canon of high architecture. This is plainly a Modernist structure (more Gropius than Mies, say). And it is represented, in perspective, as a heroic-view projection, offering both a formal suggestion, an intended symbolic function (of pure Modernist intent in its strict form-follows-function separation of sign from programme and form) and a simply altered architectural framework, one where the billboard sign is part of high architecture, supplying some of Modernism's deficits.

In the text that accompanies this image, the authors write, 'learning from popular culture does not remove the architect from his or her status in high culture', and:

> Irony may be the tool with which to confront and combine divergent values in architecture for a pluralist society and to accommodate the differences in values which arise between architect and client. Social classes rarely come together, but if they can make a temporary alliance in the designing and building of multivalent community architecture, a sense of paradox and some irony and wit will be needed on all sides.[16]

The underlying Modernist purity of the building itself, though (or is it a plinth?), is here made very clear. 'It is all right to decorate construction, but never to construct decoration.'

From *Learning from Las Vegas*

**BERNARD TSCHUMI**
Parc de la Villette

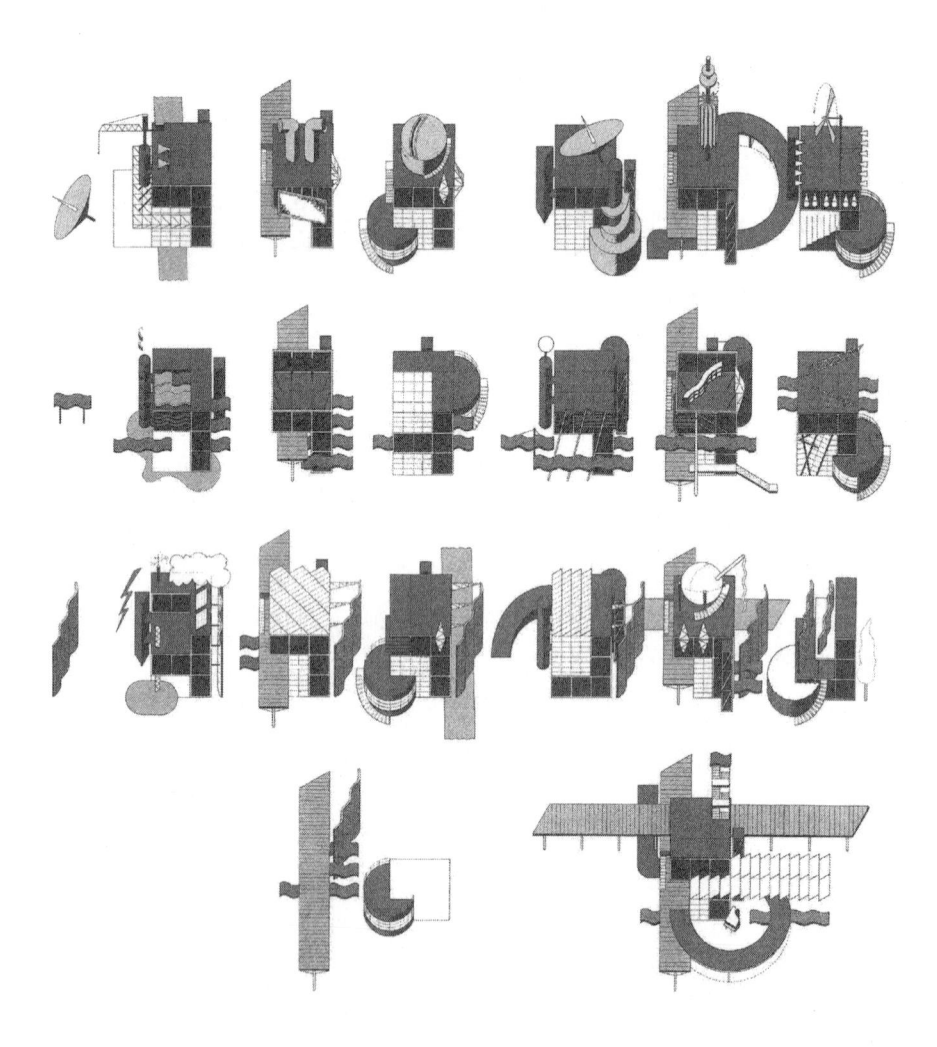

**75** | Iconic pictures

The attempt to draw events as a key part of architectural form became a particular concern during the 1980s and 1990s, with Bernard Tschumi as one of the key players. His drawings include cross-sections of fireworks displays and cartoon strips showing action, section, character and juxtaposition. But his most famous sequence of drawings was for the Parc de la Villette, a competition of 1983 for one of Mitterand's *Grands Projets*, famously entered by many other key architects of the Decon generation, including Hadid and Koolhaas.

It's impossible to pick the definitive image of this project. Tschumi's extraordinary series of exploded, extrapolated, event-driven drawings all manage to convey a particular status of their own. This one can be read as planometric, as icon, as Space Invaders, as chart, as various permutations of a single object, as palimpsest, as 'cinegram'. 'Is the Parc de la Villette a built theory or a theoretical building?'[17] the Tschumi book on the project queries, describing it as an architecture which is 'pure trace or play of language'.[18]

This image is described thus:

> Combination of Folies based on the principle of the *Casa Vide* (the void in each matrix). Each Folie is the result of the intersection between spaces, movements and events. Vertically, organisation of space and movement configurations – Type A: simple Folie. Type B: Folie with gallery. Type C: Extended Folie. Horizontally from the top – First Line: introducing industrial components. Second Line: 'Urban' components. Third Line: 'Nature' components.[19]

Even when it becomes built, as formal language, it is not the form alone which Tschumi wishes to be read. 'I'm upset when the magazines show it all on its own as a piece of sculpture.'[20] His own photos of the built scheme show the pavilions in use and the city in the background – both of which form a kind of pictorial link to the two-dimensional drawn versions, demonstrating constantly changing possibilities of form against activity.

**ANDREA PALLADIO**
Final façade study for San Petronio, Bologna

The classic, exquisite architectural elevation, seemingly innocent and pure in its rational, informative description of external appearance of buildings – 'a picture of the front of a building, set upright and properly drawn in the proportion of the contemplated work', according to Vitruvius[21] – actually has curious implications for architecture. 'The close resemblance between wall surface and paper surface has never been entirely overcome in architecture, any more than has the geometrical equivalence of plan and floor. It is far too convenient,' writes Robin Evans in his brilliant study on architectural representation, *The Projective Cast*. Evans argues that, through the use of perspective, and probably by accident, ways of implying depth in two-dimensional drawings are applied to three-dimensional objects, 'but then interact with the perception of real depth to give more or less of a flutter between the real and the imaginary'. Evans continues:

> The layering of thin parallel planes, already evident in early Egyptian architecture, soon became the governing artifice of the elevation, drawn and built, as can be appreciated from Palladio's last, ingenious design to complete the unadorned brick front of San Petronio, Bologna (1579), or from the façades of his Venetian churches. The effects were obtained by drawing lines on a flat sheet that looked as if they represented something in considerable depth, then building it in limited depth. The result was compaction – architecture as a low relief of its own pictures. The similarity between wall and paper was emphasised, moreover, by the common practice of using a close textured, monochrome facing material such as marble or stucco for monumental buildings, the very colour of which resembled paper. Under these conditions, projectors need not extend very far from the picture to reach the thing pictured, and the imagination of the designer need travel no further than the projectors to envisage what had been designed. Thus limited, architects can cope with space because of a safety factor built into their drawing that protects them from the unimaginable.[22]

**VLADIMIR TATLIN**
Monument to the Third International
(The Comintern)

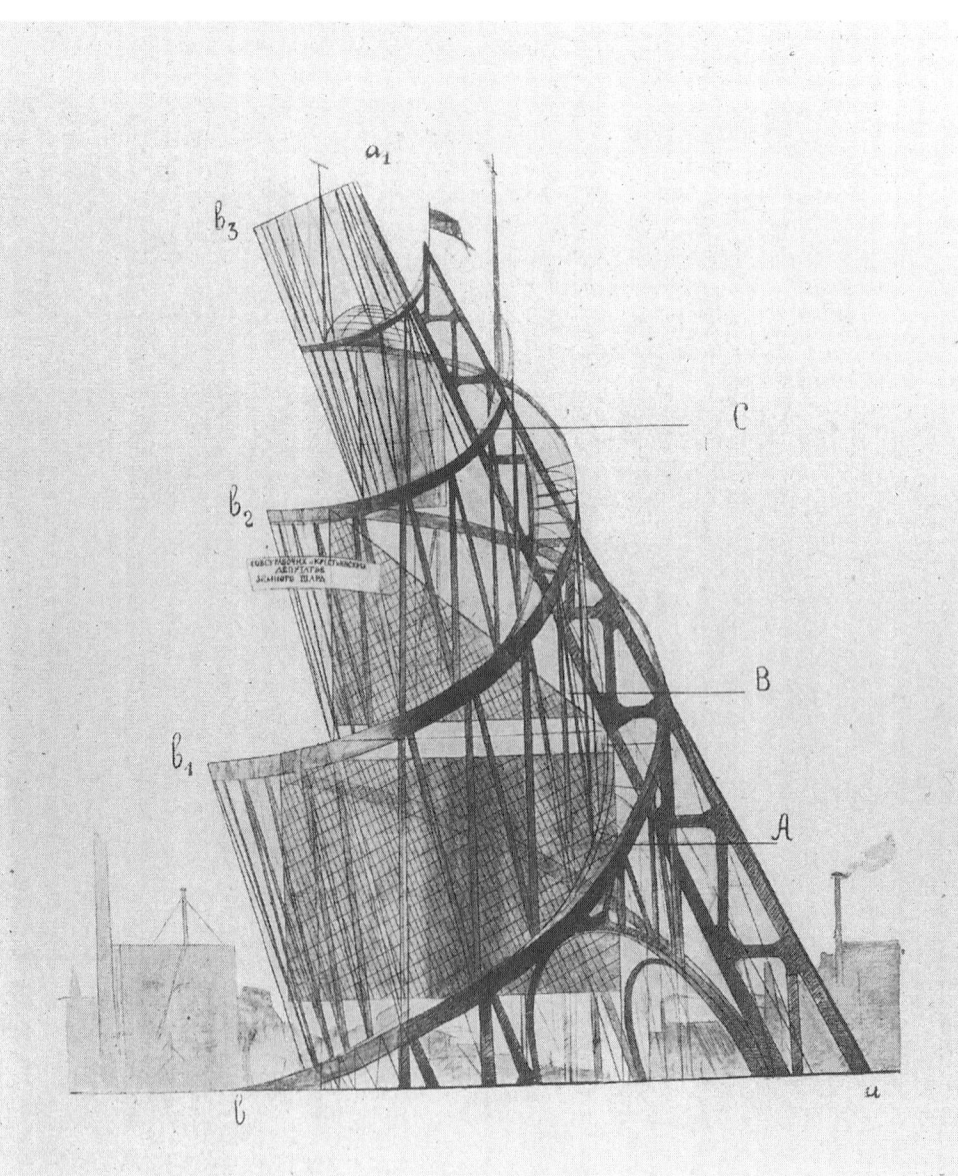

**79** | Iconic pictures

This drawing of 1920 depicts a building that was to be one-third higher than the Eiffel Tower, which the young Russian artist Vladimir Tatlin had seen in Paris six years earlier on the eve of the First World War. This war effectively closed Russia's borders till 1921 and isolated Russian art, which fed on its own creativity through a revolution, a civil war and a blockade.

In spring 1914 Tatlin was still just a painter, and no doubt he visited the Eiffel Tower like any other tourist who has taken the elevators up inside its massive steel framework. Far more immediately influential on his work at that stage was his visit to Picasso's studio, where he saw the painter's first ventures into small constructed reliefs. Returning to Moscow, as one of his young colleagues recorded, he 'talked only about Picassian things', and started assembling bits of found material into three-dimensional works. Soon the scraps of typography and wallpaper that linked the works to Cubism and their Paris inspiration disappeared, and works emerged whose only title was *Selection of Materials* and whose subject was typically some combination like 'iron, zinc, aluminium, glass, stucco, asphalt'. As Tatlin wrote in the manifesto he issued when his model of this tower was exhibited in Moscow, these abstract works of art had enabled him to develop a new formal language that only awaited the 1917 Russian Revolution to give it a content. These works had been 'laboratory models' for artefacts that would now 'change the material forms of our life', and this tower showed their potential to 'stimulate us to new inventions in the work of creating a new world'.

To architects across the world 'Tatlin's Tower' has since become a unique icon of modernity. It offered an image of 'high-tech' architecture long before that phrase was invented, and this from a country which even in the space age was technically primitive, compared with the capitalist West. Indeed, at the time this project was conceived the country was technically on its knees after a decade of war and revolution. But even those to whom its revolutionary content was political anathema have been inspired by its general dynamic and its aspiration to transform technology into an aesthetic medium.

In fact several images of the scheme have circulated to establish the Tower in the mental image-bank of the design community, and this magical drawing that

Side elevation, from Nikolai Punin's pamphlet *Pamiatnik III internatsionala: proekt khudozhnika V E Tatlina*, published by the Fine Art section of Narkompros, Petersburg (sic), 1920 depicts it against the industrial city skyline was not the first to achieve widespread dissemination outside Russia. That role went to a far cruder perspective drawing that was actually traced from a photograph of Tatlin's five-metre-high model. This was seemingly done by a German hand for its first publication in 1922 in the trilingual journal *Veshch/Gegenstand/Objet*, with which the émigré Russians El Lissitzky and Ilia Erenburg celebrated the lifting of the Western blockade of Soviet Russia. From there it did the rounds of leading avant-garde magazines: *L'Esprit Nouveau* in Paris, *Ma* in Vienna and *Zenit* in Zagreb in 1922, then *Broom* in New York and *ABC* in Basle in 1925.

By that time a second, smaller and less refined model was on exhibition among the Soviet official displays at the Exposition des Arts Décoratifs in Paris. Several reconstructions of the original one have been made for major public exhibitions since, notably in Stockholm, London, Paris and, in 1991, as the Soviet Union was collapsing, in Moscow itself. Despite the most scholarly approaches, this has always been a very complex task, owing to the extraordinarily subtle curves that characterise the scheme. Yet even when most degraded, none of these secondary renderings has seriously weakened the iconic power of the scheme or the seductiveness of it as an architectural concept.

In simple terms, the structure depicted here was a steel frame. Slung within the space created by the spiral element were four enormous volumes, each having a pure geometrical form – successively a cube, a cone, a cylinder and a hemisphere – and each enclosed by a double skin of glass forming, as was clearly explained, 'a vacuum' for thermal insulation. These volumes were to house organs of the Third Communist International, popularly known as the Comintern, and would rotate according to the periodicity of meetings of the occupying organisation. The hemisphere on top was a publicity centre, rotating daily, and projecting news by radio, illuminated screens and printed matter into the city and the world around.

The whole scheme must have gone through a vast number of sketches and preliminary variants, but the only known drawings of it are this side elevation and a 'front' view from the left of this image, which does not communicate the composition's dynamic rhythms so powerfully. These two images were reproduced by lithography, each about 20 cm high, in a pamphlet written by Tatlin's great supporter, the art critic Nikolai Punin, three years his junior.

Tatlin himself did not write much, and Punin was generally his mouthpiece. In various official letters and reports of 1918, however, Tatlin had been very explicit about his disapproval of the use of figurative sculpture, and especially of the third-rate works, that were quickly made to replace Tsarist monuments around Moscow and Petrograd under the Programme of Monumental Propaganda, which Lenin personally launched in 1918. These objects were insults to the proletariat, said Tatlin. The 'monuments' erected by socialism should be socially useful structures, not old-style 'art' rubbish. Aesthetically they should attempt some entirely new synthesis of those sensibilities that had previously been compartmentalised into architecture, sculpture and painting. A new society of liberated individuals needed to reconceptualise its material world artistically as well as practically.

What this new 'art' would look like was not clear to Tatlin. Nor, when Punin wrote about Tatlin's first attempts at an alternative 'Monument to the Revolution', in early 1919, was he able to report any details. In an article called 'On Monuments' in the avant-garde's art newspaper *Art of the Commune*, Punin wrote that Tatlin insisted on functional activities embodied in 'pure forms', but still had not resolved the problem of the greater form into which these would be brought together as a unity.

By the end of that year Tatlin seems to have been a bit closer, but still we have no verbal descriptions or visual images of what this Monument to the Revolution would be like. Tatlin was famously secretive, and as the leader of innovation at this time, guru and hero to many of the younger artists, he had good reason. Even as he worked during 1919, official attitudes to the new experimental artists were hardening at the top of the Communist Party: Lenin loathed anything he could call 'futurist', and even his culture commissar, Lunacharsky, was recognising that the initial support he appreciated from these people was becoming a liability as they exploited their public profile. Moreover Tatlin, like several other leading avant-gardists, had indeed welcomed the revolution as an end to the iniquities of the decayed and stagnant Tsarism, but did not necessarily welcome the programme of the Bolshevik party, which finally took over. Indeed, he had been among those who even in early 1918 were still publicly identifying themselves with the Bolsheviks' hated rivals, the Anarchists, whom they finally routed and hoped to exterminate in April that year.

So by 1919 ingratiating oneself with the regime was a good tactic for Tatlin. Still filled as it was with an aspiration to ferment world revolution, the Bolshevik government made great celebrations for the Second Congress of the new international communist organisation dedicated to achieving that end: the so-called Third Communist International. As a lover of change and the creativity of revolution Tatlin would have readily identified himself with Comintern ambitions (though art historians from capitalist America have found it repugnant that their artistic hero should demonstrate such sympathies). Be that as it may, during early summer 1920 all Russian media were drowning in reportage from the two-week Congress, held partly in Moscow as well as Petrograd. In Petrograd its 'enactments' occupied whole areas of the city just as May Day and revolutionary anniversaries did.

Punin's text states quite clearly, 'In 1919 the Fine Art department of [the Culture Commissariat] Narkompros commissioned Tatlin to design a moment to the Third International', and that 'he rapidly set to work and executed the project', which 'he and a "creative collective" worked up in detail and then made a model'. Current scholarship now rather doubts this very early and formal sounding 'commission'. Tatlin had worked closely with Narkompros since its formation and this was probably a post hoc elaboration, now that the scheme had official approbation, on the fact he may have had a subvention of money and resources in order to make the model. It seems more likely that in spring 1920, with a marvellous monument to Russia's revolution under way, Tatlin rededicated it and refined it towards the functions of this world revolutionary body, apparently aspiring to give it a permanent home in Petrograd. As a result, by the time the public, or even his close friends, saw any specific images, this was the project's dedication and the name under which it was always known.

It is interesting to speculate on whether this drawing preceded the model, or was in fact a depiction created after the spatial problems had been solved in timber. We do not have any concrete indications either way, and Punin's explanatory pamphlet does not help. His four-page text describing the halls – their rotation speeds, structure and something of their symbolism – is dated July 1920, but the pamphlet was not published until December, when the model was shown at the essentially national gathering of the Eighth Congress of Soviets in Moscow. During July the 5 m model was well under way. Tatlin and three students were working daily in the Academy of Arts under very primitive conditions. Punin came to help cut timber and zinc jointing pieces about once a week, so he knew it intimately. But the photographs of the work in progress suggest it is being created more through trial and error, guided by Tatlin's hand and eye, than as an exercise in executing drawings. So maybe this image was a post hoc representation made for the publication?

From a poster we do know that the model's three-week showing in the Academy of Arts opened on that year's Revolutionary anniversary of 8 November, and from noon to 4 p.m. Tatlin was present for 'an artistic-political meeting to which trade-union members, soldiers and sailors are invited'. Several handsome documentary photographs were taken of the great model with slogans hanging around it, and there are others extant which include visitors. Like most three-dimensional objects it had 'preferred views'. Its most dynamic and rhythmical view was certainly that looking from behind the great rising diagonal girder, and in one such shot Tatlin, in conversation, stands modestly beside his creation. This key image was the one which went to Germany, probably taken there by Lissitzky, and was traced over to make a stronger image for the crude printing techniques of avant-garde journals.

Within Russia itself, however, this delicate elevational drawing became as well known as the model, both through exhibition alongside it and through reproduction in cruder versions for later shows. Indeed a film sequence, discovered in the early 1990s, shows Tatlin sitting before such a drawing, apparently almost his own height, in the 1923 Exhibition of Artists of All Trends held in Petrograd. In 1924 the present image was reproduced in the seminal text of architectural Constructivism, Moisei Ginzburg's *Style and Epoch*, juxtaposed with a US grain silo derived from Le Corbusier's articles in *L'Esprit Nouveau*. The sequence of influences and mutual inspiration continued; indeed it was to burgeon from then on as the Soviet and European avant-gardes developed their contacts through mutual publication, even when travelling was made difficult by the Soviet regime.

Beyond Punin's slender publication from which this image is derived, whose yellowed paper after 80 years gives perhaps a warmer, less steely impression than originally, the only material to get us one step closer to the actual drawing is a photograph of that drawing, one print of which remains among Tatlin's papers in a Moscow museum. This is free of the annotating lines and letters that Punin added to explain the parts. It is therefore a purer image; but the image we have here, half depictive landscape and half technical abstraction, actually transmits more precisely that ambiguity underlying its conception: is this art or is it engineering? To Tatlin those categories were ceasing to exist. Such was his mastery as an artist that this duality and new synthesis have been felt and understood by later generations across the world, even when depicted in cruder derivations.

In presenting this image Punin wrote that 'the whole form is vacillating like a steel snake held together and united into a structure through one common movement of its parts. By flexing its muscles, its energy seeks escape along that most resilient and dynamic form we know, the spiral.' Many tedious art historical papers have sought to identify 'sources' for that form in everything from the Baroque church to Boccioni's sculpture. None of these accounts for the creative process in which a consummate artist, a musician who evoked tears with his playing of the traditional peasant bandura, a seaman on great sailing ships, a passionate revolutionary, produces a work of art.

**Catherine Cooke**

**FRITZ LANG**
Metropolis

Film and Modernism have been roughly contemporaneous, and the interpretation and criticism of the Modernist city have been one of film's great underlying subjects. Of the films which have been considered specifically 'architectural' – and these always seem be futuristic visions of a great and dystopian city – Fritz Lang's *Metropolis* is the earliest, and the one which established the genre.

This is a futuristic vision of a city transformed into a kind of hell, and yet one that has retained its architectural grandeur and allure; an addictive city whose own scale and momentum, and that of the organisations which run it, reduce its ordinary inhabitants to disempowered, underscaled functionaries. This remains a key argument in all the films deemed specifically 'architectural' that followed it, notably Ridley Scott's 1982 *Blade Runner*. And this image – as so many other aspects of *Metropolis* – typifies many of the characteristics of the whole genre.

Other stills from the film are more expressionist – the patriarch Moloch; the mechanical Babylonian style, again to re-emerge in *Blade Runner*. But this is the picture usually singled out by architects, presumably because of its pure Modernist content. It is recognisably an extrapolation of New York (on which the film was based),[23] and it is recognisably still the period of heroic Modernism, with its cars, aeroplanes flying between the buildings, and its massive, alienating scale. These are all elements (as indeed, was the rooftop fight) which were to recur time after time in city-based films.

Both *Blade Runner* and *Metropolis* were deemed quintessential 'architectural' films during the boom in interest in architecture and film in the late 1980s and early 1990s. At that time, much was written about the similarities of architectural and film technique (the organisation of the architectural promenade, the arrangement of meaningful form, juxtaposition, lighting, etc.), arguments that tended to ignore dissimilarities of technique (film is linear, controlled, edited, single, replicable, narrative, physically unoccupiable, makes its own context, etc.). But it was this content matter of Modernist city dystopia that was the real issue. Such films allowed both architectural enjoyment and criticism of Modernism's partial successes and partial failures – its overscaled quality, the oversupply of nonetheless enviable technology, the extremes of alienation and impotence of its inhabitants, and their individual heroism in the face of this. This picture permits bitter but luxurious enjoyment of the essential, heroic ambiguity of twentieth-century architecture.

**MIES VAN DER ROHE**
Photos of the original Barcelona Pavilion

Designed by Mies van der Rohe, the Barcelona Pavilion was built for an exhibition. Construction began in March 1929 but, due to financial and technical difficulties, not all of the completed building conformed to Mies's design for example, on the exterior side and rear walls, plastered brick painted green and yellow was used instead of green Alpine marble and travertine. In February 1930 the building was dismantled, its various elements dispersed or destroyed. The photographs that established the reputation of the Pavilion only record the parts of the 1929 building that adhered to Mies's design.

It is through the 1929 photographs, rather than the 1929 building, that the Pavilion became one of the most praised and copied architectural projects of the twentieth century. The extent of this copying is due not only to the quality of the design, and Mies's growing reputation, but also the Pavilion's status as an artwork.

The architectural photograph has a number of roles, one of which is to present the building as a higher form of cultural production to defend and promote architects and patrons. Many architectural photographs display similar characteristics, such as perfect climate and no people, because they mimic the perfect but sterile conditions of the artwork in the gallery. Based on art history, architectural histories often discuss the building as an object of artistic contemplation and imply that this is the familiar experience of the building. The photograph acts as the mediator between the writer and the reader, who is encouraged to assume that the experience of the photograph is the same as the experience of the building.

In an attempt to maintain and reproduce the aura of art and the artist, the art institution requires precise codes of behaviour, particularly reverence. Although other experiences are possible, the artwork in the gallery is primarily experienced in contemplation: a form of visual awareness, of a single object by a single absorbed viewer, in which sound, smell and touch are as far as possible eradicated. Protected against heat, light and decay, the artwork is experienced at most a few times. This is not the familiar experience of the building, but for architects the classification of architecture as an art similar to painting and sculpture is socially and financially desirable. To affirm the status of the architect as an artist and architecture as a certain type of art, the experience of the building is equated with the contemplation of the artwork in the gallery, a condition disturbed by the irreverent presence of the user.

Photographs of the original German Pavilion, Barcelona, courtesy of the Mies van der Rohe Archive, Museum of Modern Art, New York

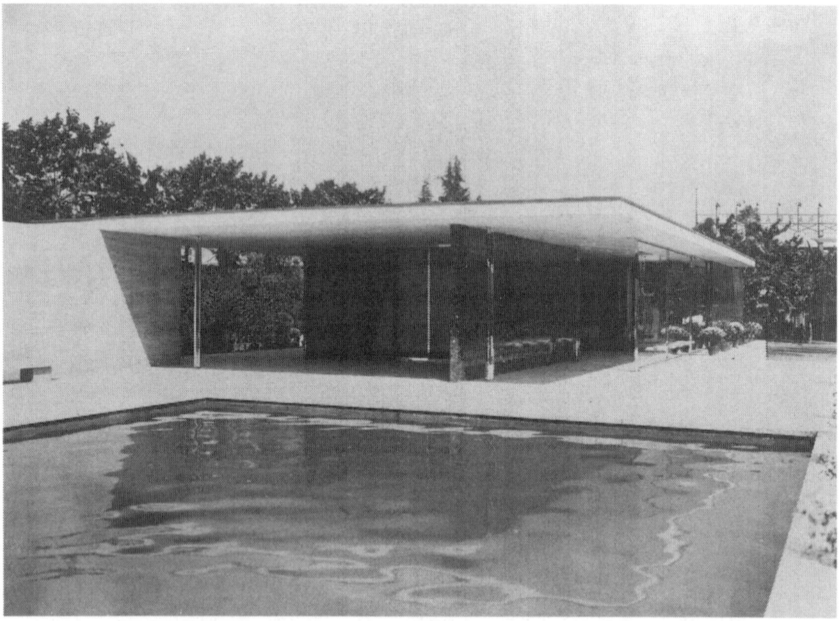

In 1986 Ignasi de Solà Morales, Christian Cirici and Fernando Ramos supervised the construction of a second Pavilion on the site of the first. The subject of the reconstruction is the design as it appears in the original photographs as much as the original building. The 1929 photographs are black and white; those in Solà Morales, Cirici and Ramos's book on the reconstruction are colour. However, the views they show are similar. Solà Morales, Cirici and Ramos state that the purpose of the reconstruction is to allow the building to be experienced once again, but the experience they describe is contemplation, in which the visitor is absorbed by the artwork. They write:

> It is necessary to go there, to walk amidst and see the startling contrast between the building and its surroundings, to let your gaze be drawn into the calligraphy of the patterned marble and its kaleidoscopic figures, to feel yourself enmeshed in a system of planes in stone, glass and water that envelops and moves you through space, and contemplate the hard, emphatic play of Kolbe's bronze dancer over water.[24]

The Pavilion is an architectural icon, not only because it is seductive and much copied, but also because it has most often been perceived in conditions similar to that of the artwork. Between 1929 and 1930 it was an exhibition building to be viewed, between 1930 and 1986 it was known through photographs, and since 1986 the reconstruction's status as exhibit, gallery and historical monument discourages everyday use. The history of the Pavilion implies that contemplation is the experience most appropriate to buildings, affirming the authority of the architect and denying that of the user.

**Jonathan Hill**

## Notes

1. Images from *Blade Runner* and Charles and Ray Eames' *Powers of Ten* were also originally included in the current collection, but had to be omitted for cost and copyright reasons.
2. John Wilton-Ely, *Giovanni Battista Piranesi, The Complete Etchings* (San Francisco: Alan Wofsy Fine Arts, 1994), p. 3.
3. Manfredo Tafuri, *The Sphere and the Labyrinth: Avant-Gardes and Architecture from Piranesi to the 1970s* (Cambridge, MA and London: MIT Press, 1987), p. 42.
4. Tafuri, *Sphere and Labyrinth*, pp. 39, 42.
5. Tafuri, *Sphere and Labyrinth*, p. 41.
6. Beatriz Colomina, *Privacy and Publicity: Modern Architecture as Mass Media* (Cambridge, MA: MIT Press, 1994), p. 3.
7. Colomina, *Privacy and Publicity*, p. 293.
8. Colomina, *Privacy and Publicity*, p. 293.
9. Colomina, *Privacy and Publicity*, pp. 283–9.
10. Daniel Abramson, 'The Bank of England', in *John Soane, Architect: Master of Light and Space*, eds Margaret Richardson and MaryAnne Stevens (London: Royal Academy of Arts, 1999), p. 219.
11. Joseph A. Schumpeter, *Capitalism, Socialism and Democracy*, 2nd edn (New York and London: Harper & Collins, 1947), p. 83.
12. Mark Girouard, *Big Jim, The Life and Works of James Stirling* (London: Chatto & Windus, 1998), p. 195.
13. Zaha Hadid, *Zaha Hadid: the Complete Buildings and Projects* (London: Thames & Hudson, 1998), pp. 9–10.
14. Zaha Hadid and the Architectural Association, *Planetary Architecture Two* (London: Architectural Association, 1983).
15. Zaha Hadid, lecture at the Royal College of Art's Cyberrock series, May 1998. Quoted in Kester Rattenbury, 'Drawing Conclusions', *Building Design* (15 May 1998), p. 32.
16. Robert Venturi, Denise Scott Brown, Steven Izenour, *Learning From Las Vegas: The Forgotten Symbolism of Architectural Form*, rev. edn (Cambridge, MA and London: MIT Press, 1997), pp. 161–3.
17. Bernard Tschumi, *Cinégramme Folie: Le Parc de La Villette*, (Cambridge, MA: New Designs, MIT Press, 1987), pp. vi.
18. Tschumi, *Cinégramme Folie*, p. viii.
19. Tschumi, *Cinégramme Folie*, p. 24.
20. Bernard Tschumi, lecture at RIBA, 20 October 1999.
21. Vitruvius, *The Ten Books on Architecture*, trans. M.H. Morgan (New York, 1914), p. 14.
22. Robin Evans, *The Projective Cast* (Cambridge, MA and London: MIT Press, 1995), pp. 113–17.
23. Fritz Lang, *Metropolis* (London: Faber & Faber, 1973, 1989).
24. I. Solà Morales, C. Cirici, F. Ramos, *Mies van der Rohe: Barcelona Pavilion* (Barcelona: Editorial Gustavo Gili, 1993), p. 39.

Chapter 6
# Think of it as a farm!
Exhibitions, books, buildings
**An interview with Peter Smithson**

*Alison and Peter Smithson (A+PS) are unusual in that they have produced seminal work in all three of the classic grounds of 'high' architectural output: exhibitions, books and, of course, their relatively few but hugely influential and often controversial buildings. The close but varied relationship between their books, exhibitions and their built work has been much debated. For example, their Brutalist housing scheme in London's East End, Robin Hood Gardens, was criticised for failing to meet their own criteria for urban patterns of connections; while their attempts to define in their writing a 'a canon of conglomerate ordering', then expressed in their buildings at Bath University, was deemed as meeting their written criteria but failing to meet the architectural standards of their other projects. ('Time will tell,' says Peter Smithson.) Despite such criticism – indeed, perhaps because of their uncompromising attempts to express and pursue their ideas and beliefs – they remain among the most respected of all UK architects. Kester Rattenbury asked Peter Smithson about the interaction of the different components of their architectural work.*

Peter Smithson: What Alison and I write is for oneself. You write about the insights you have. You think, 'Well, maybe, if they're useful to me, they might be useful to somebody else' – but never intentionally to influence or instruct.

There is an attempt by Max Risselada to put the work – the projects and the competitions and non-built things – together, like the Eames's history charts.[1] Nowhere does it attempt to indicate what is influencing what. People say 'you abandoned your principles at Robin Hood Gardens', because it didn't connect into a pattern as proposed in the books. But the notion was overwhelmed by two things: the noise of the adjacent roads, which meant you had to use the building to protect what space you had; and then, when it was built, the East India Dock was still open – and the river was busy. These influenced the format of the building. There is no sidestepping from the fundamental shift towards specificity (Doorn Manifesto, 1953).

*Kester Rattenbury: The simplest example usually cited for the argument about a disparate polemic between the different sorts of media in which A+PS work is usually the three 'houses' designed in 1955–6: the 'House of the Future', a space-age, plastic-*

*moulded lifestyle exhibition in the Ideal Home show of 1956 that predicted the house and lifestyle of the 1980s; a simple house-shaped frame filled with found objects at the 'Patio and Pavilion' house in the hugely influential 'This is Tomorrow' show by the International Group at the Whitechapel Gallery; and the Sugden house in Watford. Did you find that the argument for these being diametrically opposed was justified?*

No, I don't find any. In the Patio and Pavilion exhibit we made the framework, and the boys [Nigel Henderson and Eduardo Paolozzi] inhabited it. But they inhabited it in a symbolic way. What you have to remember is, the funds for the 'This is Tomorrow' exhibition were £400 for everybody. Therefore you had to beg the material and do what you could. The framework was constructed in the simplest way because, as far as I remember, Theo Crosby talked some plywood company into giving something.

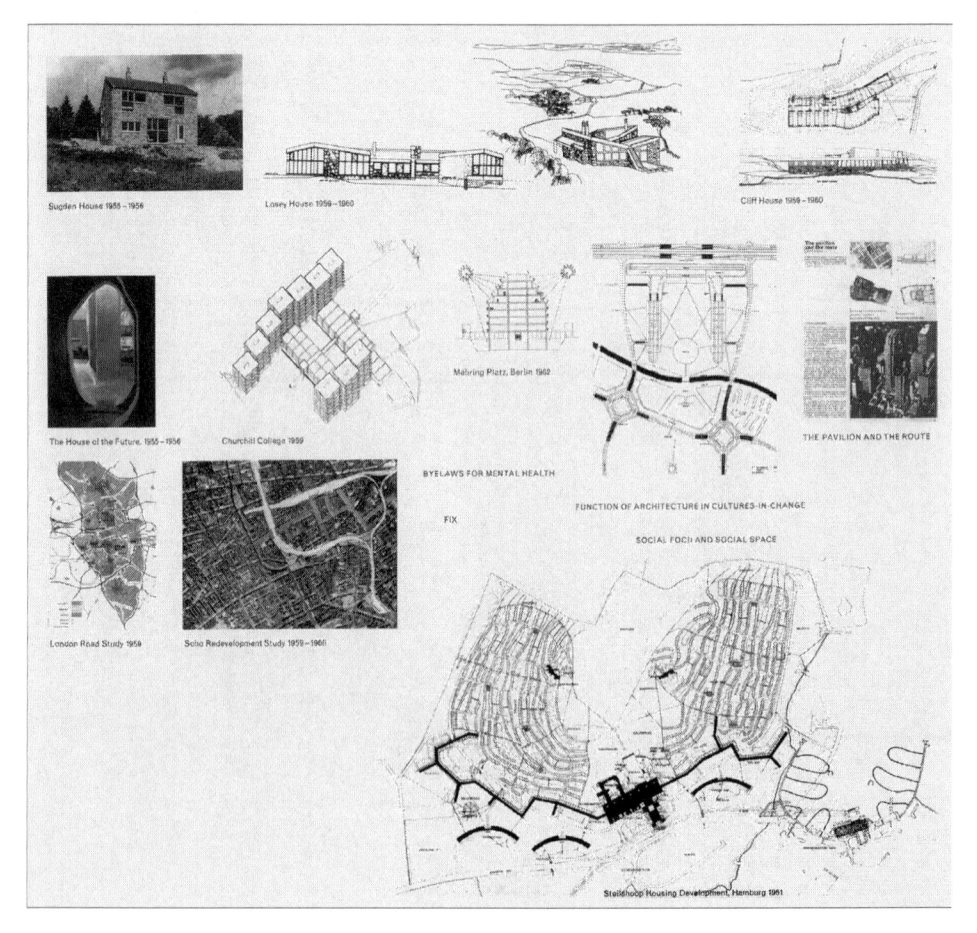

**93** | Think of it as a farm!

We're dealing with a minimum budget to make a framework. That's another overwhelming factor.

In the House of the Future, it was assumed that anything that's in prototype now is likely to be available generally in 25 years. Therefore the content, the equipment, the clothing, etc. were already somehow in development. (Some popular paper recently did an estimate of the accuracy, and it was something like 80 per cent. Eighty per cent of the things that we thought would be available generally were ordinary things now, like deep-freeze vegetables, portable ovens, microwaves – all that stuff, which in the 1950s was in embryo.) Whereas in Patio and Pavilion, Nigel and Eduardo occupied it with symbolic objects of the things we need.

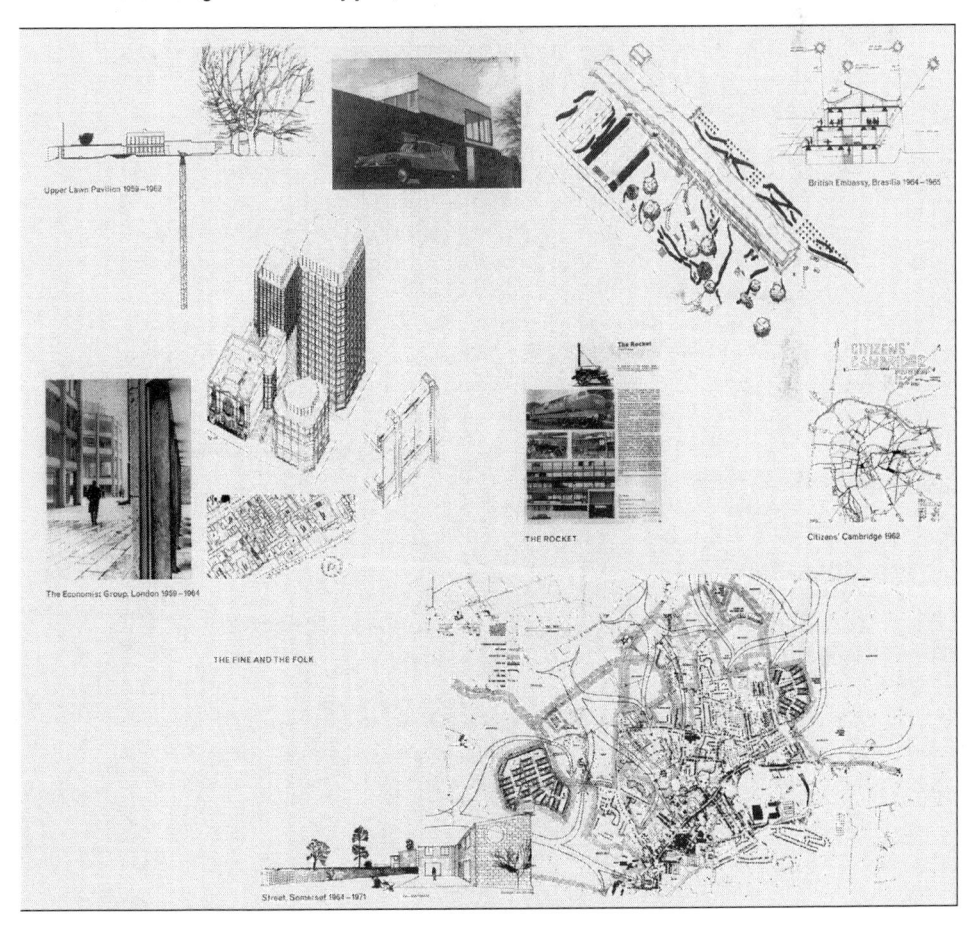

In the House of the Future ... plastic being made of oil – and at that time the cost of oil had gone down every year, and it continued to do so until the oil crisis – therefore the notion of making a house where the matrix was plaster or something heavy, and instead of using cement as a binder you used plastic, seemed reasonable within the twenty-five years – if the price of oil had continued to fall! Certain suggestions for the inhabitation came from us, whereas in Patio and Pavilion nothing came from us. The framework was established, and we went to Dubrovnik while it was being made. There was absolutely no influence on the content. And therefore the relationship between the framework and the occupation itself was absolutely pure – by chance.

I don't see any real conflict between the two; unless you say that in the House of the Future you're trying to deal with what would concretely be available in twenty-five years, where the Patio and Pavilion was a kind of symbolic version. And you could say that that's natural – because one was in an art gallery, and the other was in a popular exhibition hall.

*It's possible to argue that in fact the three houses were counterpoints – though they looked like such different things – or is it that the conditions of designing for a client are so distinct from those of designing an exhibition as to be irrelevant?*

We don't design formally in that way; each is a response to circumstance. Richard Rogers is marketing Archigram. It's a formal language which he's building with; and Foster is the same with Buckminster Fuller – he's using Fuller as a formal source. Well, we don't do that. For better or for worse, to repeat, with us the form evolves out of circumstance.

Now that makes a huge difference, because sometimes it won't succeed, whereas if you're knocking off Archigram you're likely to succeed, since there's a wide band of vocabulary to draw off – that somebody else invented. And time has passed since the sixties. The language, which was then extraordinary – the language of the oil refinery – is acceptable. That's why I use the word marketing: because through some process it's becoming acceptable. You can read that upside down. You can say that the reason why Archigram didn't ever build anything was the opposite: it wasn't marketable. People were afraid of it.

*Yet you have written of designs for exhibitions recurring in later build projects: the Patio and Pavilion frame in the folly at Fonthill, the plan of an exhibition of paintings and sculptures reappearing in the plan of a building.*

Bits of Patio and Pavilion obviously came from the habitations of all of us, but particularly Nigel's. His workrooms and kitchen were like that; the imagery was all over the place. The marketing of the 'as found' was performed by Terence Conran. And of

Nigel Henderson's basement in Bethnal Green (assumed), with print fragments by Eduardo Paolozzi

course that destroys it. He literally marketed where people collected pine cones or baskets. He went to the 'pine cone factory' and bought twenty thousand!

It's like the fake mirrors they have in pubs that are made in Hong Kong or somewhere; advertisements for Guinness from 1910. They have no meaning any more. If you'd found one in a garage, an original, you'd think 'how lovely'; it would move you. But if you've just manufactured it, it loses all meaning. Therefore, you could say that the 'as found' thing moved out, probably into the real art world – but then also found its way out as a product.

We're taking part in an exhibition in Zurich in March called 'As Found'. But we haven't attempted to do any interpretation, and it is in a way terrifying, in handing over all the documents, that you don't know the nature of the interpretation.

*Is it possible to argue that certain sorts of issues are better suited to exhibitions or books than to buildings?*

Well, what we write is an insight gained during construction and by observation – you have intentions, but things happen, and you suddenly realise that what has happened in addition is also interesting. The construction process leads to the insights, which lead to the writing, which leads to more construction. It's a sort of cycle.

I actually never think about what's suitable for exhibitions – except about the format of the exhibitions, and I hate the exhibition that is just magazines stuck on the wall. That is not an exhibition, in my view. Any exhibition has to be a simulacrum of the spatial condition with which it is concerned. To give an example: in the 1940s, Charles Eames did an exhibition on Mies van der Rohe in the Museum of Modern Art, and of course he was able – because Mies had only built about two things in America at that time – to build a room which had some connection with the spaces of Mies van der Rohe. It's possible.

But then, if you were dealing with a less concrete topic like this 'As Found' exhibition, the way they put the images together has to speak about what we were talking about earlier: in what way did that 'as found' thing reflect the culture? It's fifty years ago, there's no possible natural affinity. I was thinking yesterday about war itself. There's a little school on the corner, Bousefield School, where a landmine was dropped on Beatrix Potter's house. How is it that you can train an eighteen-year-old to drop a bomb on Beatrix Potter's house? It's unimaginable. I mean – incredible cruelty propounded as normality. If you can't imagine the condition of that boy who dropped the bomb, you can't also imagine the period of 'as found'. It's just as removed, just as difficult to reconstruct.

*You have said that there are two kinds of exhibitions: the 'emergent', such as 'This is Tomorrow', which you described as being driven by the feeling that 'this is what it is that seems to be needed to be done'; and the 'reflective', a more intellectual reassessment of something which already exists. The books, however, seem even more varied, with a huge range of intentions – emergent, reflective, polemical, eclectic – and ranging from scrapbook to argument to manifesto to poetic, free-form narrative.*

There's only one book which is really, you might say, 'engaged'. It's the book about the Euston Arch. It was absolutely political – because it was Macmillan in the end who made the decision that the Arch should be destroyed, and that was interpreted as, in a way, an act of vengeance. The power of England that materially fruited in the 1880s and '90s was because of the steam engine. And all that invention was from the North; and the Euston Arch brought symbolically – I'm sure the architect had no intention – the new power of the North. And Macmillan represented the traditional power (although he was a working man, you might say, but he married into the traditional power framework). To knock it down destroyed George Stephenson's memory. If it had been a monument to Napier, to a military figure, they wouldn't have done it. That was the Arch. It was the one thing which was consciously political in our life.

*The books are also hugely inventive in their scope: their inclusiveness, their experimental nature. In many ways they prefigure the current graphic-led boom in books as projects, with people trying to reinvent what the architectural book is and what it contains. They include, for instance, fragments of stories, free-form narrative, standard headlamp codes, and they sometimes play with the form of the book itself – the original Euston Arch book was spiral bound in order that it had no set middle or covers.*

Our work life together was commitment: that is, using as a model the working farm. That and good health. Until Alison died, she never had anything wrong with her, never even taken an aspirin. We were capable of sustained effort, particularly her. The working farm is a good analogy; the animals and the children and the work make a whole occupation. Other than that book, one didn't vote, one didn't take part in elections, one didn't join any societies or any of those terrible things. I suppose mostly because if you could join anything it means fully participating, fully engaging. The whole business of Team 10 was like that: it was a life. You'll notice that our children were not born during Team 10 meetings.

*Alison is often quoted as saying, 'A book is like a small building for us', and, 'An architect who cannot build is like a man without arms, almost without identity.'*

Those are good quotes. Our model was Le Corbusier, of course: that is, working in all media. For example, during the '70s, really we hadn't any major constructions from finishing Robin Hood Gardens and St Hilda's till the first little building at Bath. We probably did half a dozen competitions, books written, films made – all preparing yourself in some way.

The one occasion where I was personally affronted by criticism was when the Economist Building was finished, and in one of the Sunday papers a reviewer called Iain Nairn said: these architects have not built anything for ten years, and the building shows it. Now that ten years was filled with conscious preparation – and unconscious preparation. For instance, examining the way metals behaved in high pollution in American buildings – the metals of the Economist Building are all stove-enamelled finish on top of the metal in order that it shouldn't corrode. By the late '50s, the early buildings of Mies and Skidmore Owings and Merrill were all heavily corroded – I give you that as an example. In my view the Economist Building represented the outcome of ten years of speculation and investigation. The reviewer was not competent to see that. Like I said, that Archigram was unmarketable; the Economist Building was unmarketable. It had things in it, observations, that were strange. It had disciplines that Iain Nairn could not understand.

When Skidmore did the alterations, and converted some of the spaces into

American spaces, they didn't know what they were destroying, because those fiddly English spaces that we worked were something different to American spaces. They were European.

*The variety of work must have both shaped your careers and, in a way, made you more liable to criticism. How did this position affect you?*

Alberti also wrote books about cooking. I assume, because he was a courtier, a church civil servant, he felt he had a moral right to write about anything: composition, perspective, being keen on Brunelleschi. Therefore, in any one decade, probably since the middle of the nineteenth century, there's been a book about Alberti. Because people like reading; they don't like looking at buildings. There have certainly been five books about Alberti in the last ten years.

Alberti comes into it because he was a very diversified writer. And maybe there is a common factor. I don't know enough about him. Did he have a long life, for example? Say five realised buildings. Only one drawing exists. You could say Le Corbusier was a prolific writer – but the books were absolutely contained within the discipline – even to the wallpaper. There were no books on cooking or childcare and rearing … . We're encouraging architects to write books on bringing up children.

As an apropos of that, somebody came round and asked whether he could make a reprint of the children's book we did for Peter Cook when he was at the ArtNet gallery. It was called 'The Story of the Tram Rats', a handwritten book, with text by the children and illustrations by the children, and a bit of text. To be prolix in this way – maybe like the Euston Arch, it was circumstantial; the Tram Rats were the traditional, never-ending, children-at-bedtime stories. There were readings of it at ArtNet, with recorded tram noises as the background.

And that leads you to the end where you can see that from the kind of family that Alison and I have, it's got its own rules, separate to society, where the bond is so strong that it makes outside things unreal. I mean, like the Party in the '30s, it is a completely separate world. The politics of the world outside had no meaning whatsoever. It's a kind of conspiracy. Therefore, in a way you're immune to criticism.

## Note

1   Max Risselada, 'Chronology', *OASE* 51 (June 1999). A collection of images of diagrammatic and built projects, large building proposals and urban studies, accompanied only by identifying captions.

Chapter 7
# Diagrams
Interactive instruments in operation[1]
**Ben van Berkel and Caroline Bos**



Architecture still articulates its concepts, design decisions and processes almost exclusively by means of a posteriori rationalisations. The compulsive force of legitimising arguments still dominates contemporary debate, even though it only represents a limited interpretation of the complex web of considerations that surrounds each project. Yet for the most part we cannot bear to analyse our own internal discourse for fear of disrupting the notion of the eminent utility of our projects and thus precipitating their disappearance.

    The dependence of architects on being selected for work should not be underestimated. Inevitably, our strategies, our formulations and the ways in which our interests evolve are related to this dependence. Since architecture – at least in the open, democratic, Western society in which we work – now results from a highly institutionalised, cooperative process in which clients, investors, users and technical consultants all take part, it is natural and right that architects strive to be reasonable, responsible partners in this process and condition themselves to think and to present themselves in a way that will persuade others that large investments can be safely

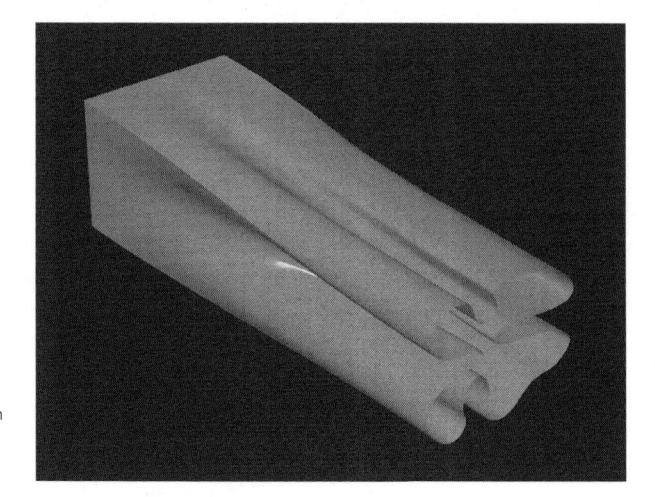

UN Studio, from blob to box and back again

entrusted to them. The frustrating result is that there is hardly any real architectural theory to be found, despite the diversity of practices at work today and despite a hugely expanded volume of architectural publications. There is only after-theory.

The pressure of rationality is such that architectural theory is streamlined toward a moment of compelling logic, in which factors of location, programme, routing, construction and anything else that plays a role in the origination of a design are directed toward the triumphant conclusion that the particular design under discussion is the only objectively justifiable one. The demand to present the 'right' solution, even when the contents of that concept have become very uncertain, propagates architecture's dual claims of objectivity and rationality. Like a door slamming shut, the barricade of retrospective justification roughly blocks the view of what went on behind it.

## Architecture as social discursive practice

Looking into diagrammatic procedures is one way to partially open that door and to dislocate the protective and constrictive barriers that architecture has raised to hide its vulnerable centre. As one of the many techniques used by architects to advance their ideas within the development of a design, a diagrammatic technique presents an opportunity to examine the social-discursive aspect of architectural practice from within.

Discourse analysis is a relatively new approach being used in the humanities. As a method it combines insights from text analysis, argumentation analysis and historical research.[2] Discursive practices have been defined as persistent patterns of discourse management. Their function is to regulate production, consumption and distribution of texts within a particular field of interest. Discursive practices cannot very well be seen as separate from the social framework in which they take place, which is why we refer to them as social-discursive practices. The dependent position of architecture within the economic system generally puts a disproportionate emphasis on arguments of persuasion, which are only a small, externally orientated part of the social-discursive practice of architecture. The challenge for the next generation of architects is to acknowledge and analyse the internal discourse, which from a social-discursive viewpoint is far more comprehensive than the methodological process that is the basis of current design practice, and to find a theory of the real in that.

Dismantling the scaffolding of rationality and objectivity is risky. The process might appear to imply a renunciation of all claims to any measurable, quantifiable worth. If we reject the predictable, rational interpretation of 'winning schemes' as competitive fictions, what standards do we then apply to judge architecture if we don't want to end up with a lame 'anything goes' conclusion? The answer must lie somewhere in the vast field between the poles of objectivity and subjectivity, between relativity and rigidity. The method by which architecture makes use of the intense fusion of

**101** | Diagrams

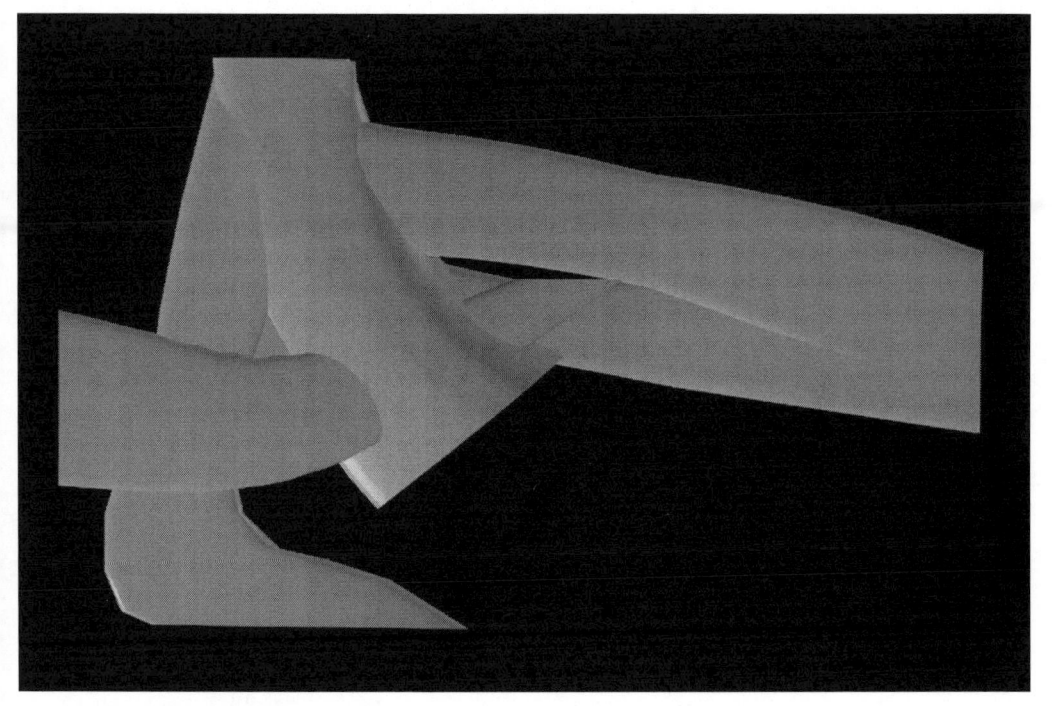

UN Studio, station area, Arnhem – spatial flow

information within a diagram is located somewhere between those poles. It would seem that it is not even fixed in one specific place, as the meaning of the diagram is not unequivocal. There are different interpretations of the diagram, which occupy different positions on the sliding scale between subjectivity and objectivity. Some of the interpretations explored most thoroughly in recent times have been the philosophical implications of the diagram, its imagery and the ways in which it instrumentalises concepts of organisation.[3]

## The meaning of the diagram

The specific meaning of the diagram in relation to architecture has been coloured by our knowledge of Bauhaus methods. But let's forget about this; the Modernist diagram has nothing to do with our subject, as a quick glance at the diagrammatic practices of Gropius, Mies van der Rohe and their students makes clear. To see architecture as a built line diagram is practically the reverse of our position. More to the point is the general understanding of the diagram as a statistical or schematic image.

In its most basic and historical definition, the diagram is understood as a visual tool designed to convey 'as much information in five minutes as would require whole days to imprint on the memory'.[4] Diagrams are best known and understood as reductive machines for the compression of information. When the informed reader consumes a specialist diagram, the effect is like that of a self-inflating life jacket: a small package that grows to full size in the time it takes to exhale a breath of air. But diagrams can also be used as proliferating machines. This is how architecture today interprets their use, thus transforming the diagram's conventional significance. When read architecturally, the diagram, which is often a bland, blank, blinding image, is never fully understood, or rather, its full meaning is not allowed to break through. A diagrammatic practice pursues a proliferating generating and open instrumentalisation in architecture.

Architecture focuses more on the reading and consumption of diagrams than on their labour-intensive production. The condensation of knowledge that is incorporated into a diagram can be extracted from it regardless of the significance with which the diagram itself was originally invested. The specific information contained in the diagram is discarded; that is not what architecture is after. For architecture, the diagram conveys an unspoken essence, disconnected from an ideal or an ideology, that is random, intuitive, subjective, not bound to a linear logic, that can be physical, structural, spatial or technical. In this regard, architecture has been encouraged by the writing of Gilles Deleuze, who described the virtual organisation of the diagram as an abstract machine.

## Deleuze's abstract machine

Deleuze helps us understand ideas by giving examples: thousands of them, so that our minds continuously swing back and forth between the abstract and the real. Architecture similarly oscillates between the world of ideas and the physical world, thus his writings seem to hold a highly specific meaning for architecture. We make extensive use of Deleuze's writings for this text, but are not out and out Deleuzians; our reading is specifically architectural.

Deleuze offers at least three versions of the diagram: via Michel Foucault, via Francis Bacon and via Marcel Proust. We do not make a distinction between the three diagrams in order to demonstrate some disparity between them, for there is none. Instead of recognising three 'versions' of the diagram, we should instead speak of moods or tonalities, for what strikes us is that three deeply significant aspects of the

**103** | Diagrams

diagram are conveyed in three very different modes. In each case, the diagram has a different meaning and corresponds to a different stage in the process of understanding, selecting, applying and triggering Deleuze's abstract machines.

The first stage of the diagram is associated with Foucault, through whom we learn to understand how the figure of the diagram is not representational; this is the crisp, dry, intellectual argument. In the second stage, through Bacon, we live through an artistic struggle; as we mentally take up the paintbrush we simultaneously engage in an earthy and lighthearted, playful debate about the selection and application of the diagram. In the third stage of the diagram, through Proust, the interaction of time and matter is introduced, without which there can be no transformation. Here the argument takes a literary and musical turn; refrains in music, literature and psychology are taken to create a lengthy and intricate narration culminating in the invention of faciality.

For Foucault, Jeremy Bentham's 1791 plan for the Panopticon is 'the diagram of a mechanism of power reduced to its ideal form … a figure of political technology'.[5] It conveys the spatial organisation of a specific form of state power and discipline. The arrangement of the Panopticon is the expression of a number of cultural and political conditions that culminate in a distinctive manifestation of surveillance. It incorporates

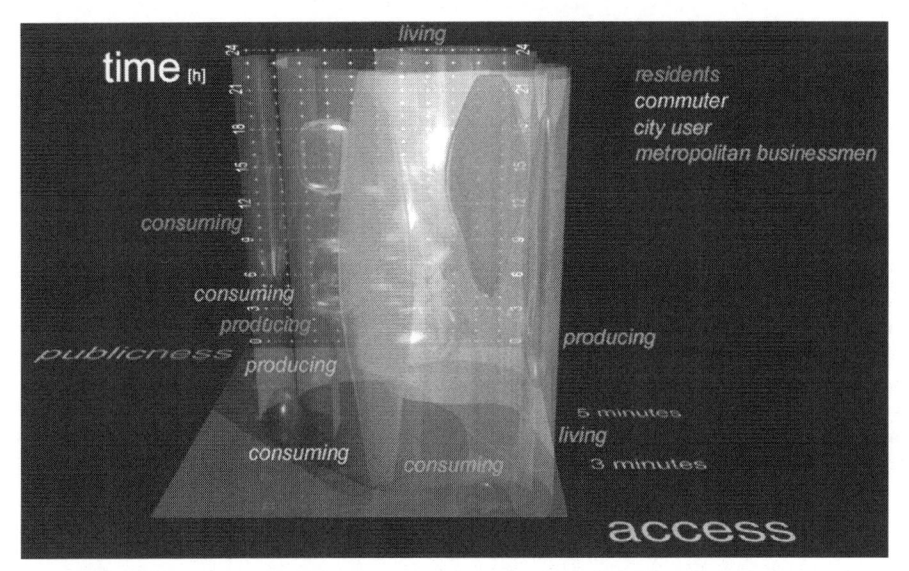

UN Studio, IFCCA (International Foundation of the Canadian Centre for Architecture) competition for Penn Station, New York

several levels of significance and cannot be reduced to a singular reading; like all diagrams, the Panopticon is a manifold. Typically, when a diagram breeds new meanings these are still directly related to its substance; its tangible manifestation. Critical readings of previous interpretations are not diagrammatic. Put in the simplest possible terms, a diagram is a diagram because it is stronger than its interpretations. Although Foucault introduced the notion of the diagram as an assemblage of situations, techniques and functionings made solid, he put the emphasis more on the strategies that form the diagram than on its actual format. He isolated the 'explicit programme' of the Panopticon in the context of his concept of repressive hypothesis; the concept of repression was his real protagonist. Deleuze reverses the agenda and zooms in on the configuration and working of the diagram itself.

Deleuze recommends that Foucault be read not as a historian but as a new kind of mapmaker. For him, the diagram is interesting not as a paradigmatic example of a disciplinary technology, but as an abstract machine that '[makes no] distinction within itself between a plane of expression and a plane of content'.[6] Diagrams are distinguished from indexes, icons and symbols. Their meanings are not fixed. 'The diagrammatic or abstract machine does not function to represent even something real, but rather constructs a real that is yet to come.'[7]

Without this crucial intervention, Foucault's diagram quickly deflates under pressure. The explicit programmes selected by Foucault were never directly or completely realised as institutions because the diagram is not a blueprint. It is not the working drawing of an actual construction, recognisable in all its details and with a proper scale. No condition will let itself be directly translated into a fitting or completely corresponding conceptualisation of that condition. There will always be a gap between the two. For the same reason, concepts such as repression and liberation can never be directly applied to architecture. There has to be a mediator. The forward-looking tendency of diagrammatic practice is an indispensable ingredient for understanding its function; it is about 'the real that is yet to come'.

## Tools against typologies

Deleuze has contributed to the insight that the relentless intrusion of signs and significations can be delayed by the diagram, which thereby allows architecture to articulate an alternative to a representational design technique. Previously, if the concepts of repression or liberation, for example, were introduced into architecture, a complex formal expression of this concept would be reduced to a sign with one clear meaning, which would subsequently be translated back into a project.

This reductive approach excluded many possibilities in architecture. While concepts are formulated loud and clear, architecture itself waits passively, as it were, until it is pounced upon by a concept. A representational technique implies that we converge on reality from a conceptual position and in that way fix the relationship between idea and form, between content and structure. When form and content are superimposed in this way, a type emerges. This is the problem with an architecture that is based on a representational concept: it cannot escape existing typologies.

An instrumentalising technique such as the diagram delays typological fixation. An experimental or instrumental technique does not proceed literally from signs. If aspects such as routing, time and organisation are incorporated into the structure using an instrumentalising technique, concepts external to architecture are introduced into it rather than superimposed. Instances of specific interpretation, utilisation, perception, construction and so on unfold and proliferate application on various levels of abstraction, liberating the design from a tendency toward fixed typologies.

How this is done is a trivial question for many techniques, but a vital one for what we call an instrumentalising technique. The role of the diagram is to delay typology and advance a design by bringing in external concepts in a specific shape: as figure, not as image or sign. How do we select, insert and interpret diagrams? This is where Deleuze's second diagram comes in, the diagram of the painter that 'is a violent chaos in relation to figurative givens, but is a germ of rhythm in relation to the new order of painting'.[8]

Where architecture seeks to resist building typology, painting confronts the perpetual fight against 'clichés, clichés!' as Deleuze exclaims, seemingly as desperate as any of us at the ludicrous inevitability of triteness. 'Not only has there been a multiplication of images of every kind, around us and in our heads, but even the reactions against clichés are creating clichés.'[9] Deleuze describes how, to escape this, Bacon works random smears into his paintings, blind marks that insert into the work another world: a zone of the Sahara in a mouth, somewhere else the texture of a rhinoceros skin found in a photograph.

The selection and application of a diagram has a certain directness. It involves the insertion of an element that contains within dense information something that we can latch on to, that distracts us from spiralling into a cliché, something that is 'suggestive'. In architecture, instead of a smear of paint we use technical manuals, photocopies of paintings or random images that we collect to suggest a possible virtual organisation. These diagrams are essentially infrastructural; they can always be read as maps of movements, irrespective of their origins. The diagram is not selected on the basis of specific representational information. It is essentially used as a proliferator in a process of unfolding.

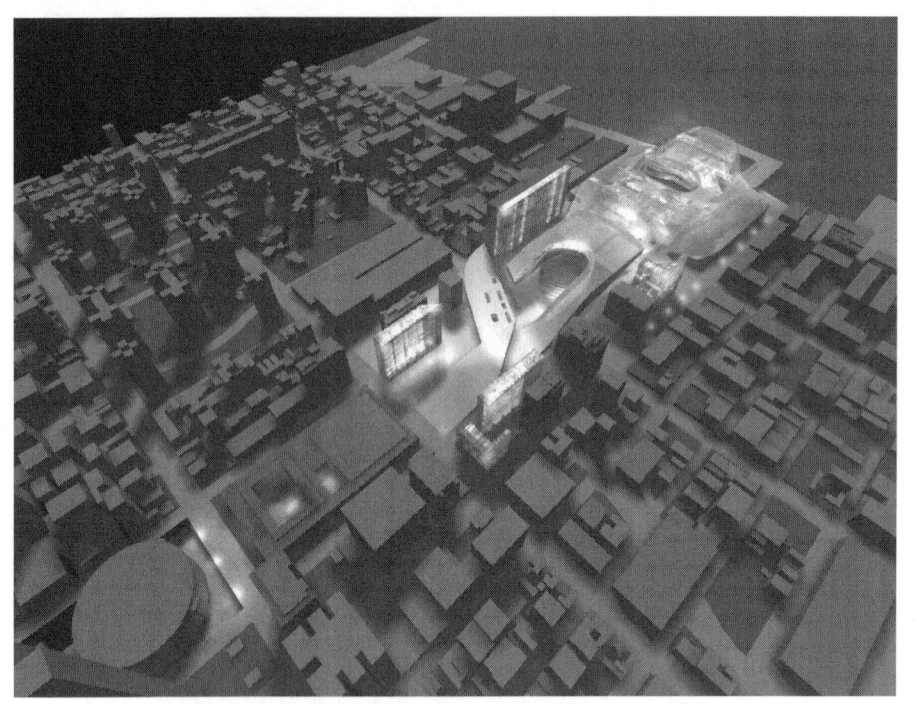

UN Studio, IFCCA – Penn Station, New York

### Instrumentalising the diagram

It is significant that Bacon did not apply his diagrams to his paintings in an unmediated way, as in the collage, but rather instrumentalised or effectuated them in the medium of paint. At this point the third meaning of the diagram, which confirms and facilitates the previous two, emerges: the triggering of the abstract machine. The abstract machine must be set in motion for the transformative process to begin, but where does this motion originate? How is the machine triggered? What exactly is the principle that effectuates the changes and transformations that we find in real life and real time? Furthermore, how can we isolate this principle and render it to the dimensions that make it possible to grasp and use at will?

Deleuze offers an indication by pointing at the novelistic treatment of time. Through Proust's novel run, for instance, long lines of musicality, passion, picturality and other narrative lines that coil around black holes within the story. The black holes are a literary construction that enables change. If there were no black holes for the protagonist to fall into, the landscape of the narrative would be an unrealistically smooth and timeless plane, which would make it impossible for the hero, whose character and adventures are formed by this landscape, to evolve. The landscape of the story, the black holes and the character become one – neither completely subjective nor objective – in order for the story to move forward. The narrative is constructed and read like a face, its intensity, passion and expressiveness fused into an indissoluble composition. Together, the black holes and the landscape form the abstract machine of faciality.

## Faciality: the operational dream

The question is: how could this novelistic device to propel things into motion be meaningful in architectural practice? Can architecture also use the concept of the black hole/surface to develop an apparatus for triggering the effect of transitions in time? One of our current projects is structured as a diagram of faciality. The master plan for the station area of Arnhem consists of bus terminal, underground car parking, office buildings and a train station, all parcelled out to different owners. Previous urban designs for the location have proved the impossibility of accommodating all of the programmatic needs in a cumulative manner. Our research therefore focuses on finding the holes – that is, the overlapping areas of shared interests where one layer of the landscape falls into another one. In the Arnhem project, pedestrian movement, which is the one element shared by every party, forms these holes. Movement studies form a cornerstone of the proposal. The analysis of the types of movement includes the directions of the various trajectories, their prominence in relation to other forms of transportation on the site, their duration, their links to different programmes and their interconnections.

From these motion studies the station area gradually begins to emerge as a landscape of interrelated movements. The holes in this landscape create a system of shortcuts between programmes, a hybrid of a centralised system and an exhaustive pattern of all possible connections. A year into the project, the topology of relations finally demands the introduction of a diagram that encapsulates the technical/spatial organisation. A diagram is never a totally serendipitous find; as part of our search for a new way of understanding the station area we had begun to study mathematical knots with the idea that a landscape with holes could also be perceived as a knot of planes. The diagrammatic outcome of this is a Klein bottle (overleaf), which connects the different levels of the station area in a hermetic way.

The Klein bottle is as deeply ambiguous as it is comprehensive; it stays continuous throughout the spatial transformation that it makes to go from being a surface to

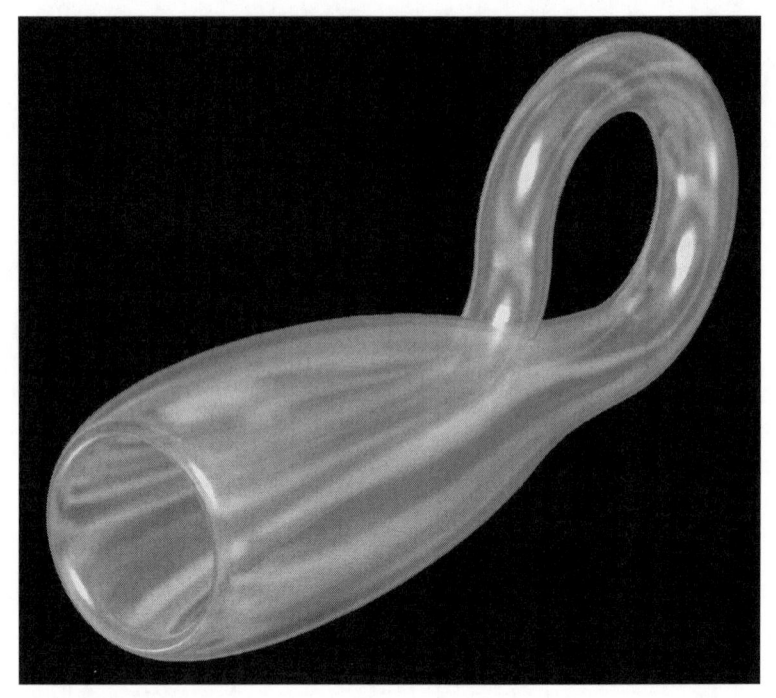

UN Studio, Klein bottle

a hole and back again. As the ultimate outcome of shared, motion-based relations, the Klein bottle is an infrastructural element in two respects: pragmatically and diagrammatically. As a concept, the Klein bottle has come about as a result of studies of shared, interactive, local conditions. As a diagram, the Klein bottle becomes an actor in the interactive process as it begins to evoke new, more specific meanings at, for instance, structural and spatial levels.

Focusing the design on shared concerns means that relations form the parameters of the project, instead of the optimisation of individual data. This generates new possibilities that no single, individual interest could have engendered. The project is pragmatic in the sense that it deals emphatically with real social, economic and public conditions, but, crucially, this is an interactive pragmatism. Utilitarian needs are not met in a reactive way but are drawn together and transformed, which inevitably leads to the renegotiation of the relations between the parties. This approach implicitly endorses a certain policy by centring on collective interests. The project is not an unprincipled opportunist response to what is being asked, which is in any case impossible in a large-scale, multi-client project of considerable complexity. Neither, however, is there a preconceived idea of urbanism that precedes the specificities of location, programme or users. Instead, the project emerges interactively.

The abstract machine in motion is a discursive instrument; it is both a product and a generator of dialogical actions which serve to bring forth new, unplanned, interactive meanings. Discourse theory introduces the notion that meanings are not transferred from one agent to another but are constituted in the interaction between the two agents. Likewise, the architectural project is created in this intersubjective field. Diagrams, rich in meaning, full of potential movement, loaded with structure, turn out to be located in a specific place after all. Understood as activators that help trigger constructions that are neither objective nor subjective, neither before-theory nor after-theory, neither conceptual not opportunist, the location of the diagram is in the intersubjective, durational and operational field where meanings are formed and transformed interactively.

## Notes

1. First published in *ANY* 23, ed. Cynthia C. Davidson, guest eds Ben van Berkel and Caroline Bos. This reprint appears courtesy of Ben van Berkel and Caroline Bos and of Cynthia Davidson, Anyone Corporation, New York.
2. We are indebted to Jaap Bos for drawing our attention to the social-discursive approach in his doctoral thesis, *Authorized Knowledge* (Utrecht, 1997), which deals with the discursive history of Freudian psychology. See also N. Fairclough, *Discourse and Social Change* (Cambridge: Polity Press, 1992).
3. Examples: Gilles Deleuze, *Foucault*, trans. Seàn Hand (Minneapolis: University of Minnesota Press, 1992); Gilles Deleuze, *Francis Bacon: Logique de la Sensation* (Paris: Edition de la Différence, 1981); Greg Lynn, 'Forms of Expression', *El Croquis* 72:1 (1995).
4. J. Krausse, 'Information at a Glance: On the History of the Diagram', *OASE* (SUN Nijmegen, 1998). Krausse here quotes William Playfair, architect of the contemporary diagram, whose book *The Commercial and Political Atlas* (1786) introduced economic curve diagrams and bar charts.
5. Michel Foucault, *Discipline and Punish: The Birth of the Prison* (New York: Vintage Books, 1979).
6. Gilles Deleuze, *A Thousand Plateaus*, trans. Brian Massumi (Minneapolis: University of Minnesota Press, 1987), p. 141.
7. Gilles Deleuze, *Francis Bacon: The Logic of Sensation*, trans. Daniel W. Smith (unpublished manuscript), p. 55. [Since the original publication of the present essay, this has been published (Cambridge, MA: MIT Press, 1992).]
8. Deleuze, *Francis Bacon: The Logic of Sensation*, p. 55.
9. Deleuze, *Francis Bacon: The Logic of Sensation*, p. 49.

Chapter 8
# The height of the kick
Designing gameplay
**Philip Campbell**

I don't remember a time when I wasn't hooked on the small screen. Any kind of moving image – and bang went my attention span. It seemed like a natural progression, slipping from performing in front of the packed stands in 'Daley Thompson's Decathlon' to designing the packed stands themselves. The energy of concept design translated well into the electricity of computer-aided design. Then the computer took over. When I looked, the world in the box was living, breathing, yelling out its tangible 'completeness'. That's when 'concept proposals', 'site analysis' and 'project mock-up' lost their allure. Simply, and suddenly, I was participating, in real-time.

Putting a little perspective on it, the validity of the computer-generated world cannot be compared to the complexities of the real world. Once past the relative-importance inferiority complex associated with this, there's a lingering longing to embrace the physical world again. I can imagine a future scenario where a generation of computer 'world-builders' break back through the barrier, step out of the rubble of the failed and alienated dot.com kingdom and drag with them, kicking and screaming, a new vision for pure physical existence.

I suppose architectural education, by its very nature, is relatively general: a good grounding for a leap of faith across the fringes of one's primary discipline. Architecture seems to have its fair share of 'jumpers'. Computer-generated worlds and societies need us – to provide their little bits of reality-based magic, the construction of a well-placed order and a viable solution to the conundrum of whether a transvestite caryatid would dress to the right or the left.

So I think I was prepared and cooked. Not bound for the muddy boot, climbin' ladders type of architectural existence, but a widening path to the architectural expression I aspired to: one where an interest in theory and a need for visible results opened up a vast electronic playground. Making a mark was the offer on the picnic table of fabulous electronic things ... another sandy digital Columbus steps ashore. Of course, it had nothing to do with the money, a fear of public speaking, or the complete inability to know a good brick bond when I see one. Especially not the money ...

I got involved with games through a simple head-hunt. I had been working as an architect in San Francisco, executing concepts in never-to-be-seen, faraway places like

Kuala Lumpur and Singapore. It seemed a few flashy conceits and a couple of high-profile twentysomething clients was all it took for the 'computer boys' to get a whiff of you. Apparently, it was fashionable to have an architect on board back then. Lucas had one, so they all had to. Over a crispy battered fish and a two-tone plastic table in some unremarkable restaurant chain I signed my architectural life away. My computer-generated conversation ice-breaker was, 'At least they don't fall down in cyberspace – unless you want them too.' I quickly realised how inappropriate that was. They take their worlds very seriously here.

It seemed all too easy at first. Generally, computer worlds were disorganised and static, and existed only to provide a complementary coloured background to the blood squirting out of the Evil Zombie Tyrant. Some games were artfully produced slideshows, 256 glorious shades of amber, but zero immersion. The technology had simply not yet arrived.

But the dreams were in place, the evocative promise of enormous online worlds. Designers were finding their visions streamlined into a kind of shorthand and had to rapidly learn to translate their language into a few pithy syllables. What developed was less a construction, more a concoction – the basic architectural massing, with applied *trompe l'œil*, combined with the computer games' stock-in-trade: movement and characters. The illusion of life was created with a pinch of motion sleight-of-hand, overly dramatic 'actors' hogging the screen, and the architectural ambience firmly in the background. Sometimes the mix worked. Sometimes the dreams were conveyed, in a few words, by a mere sketch. Pioneering worlds played to lower expectations with a potent potpourri of magical tricks, implied complexity and outright blatant fakery.

Now the technology bar has been raised, and there are fewer excuses. No longer need the architecture be a short summary, a precis to the developing plot. Now it steps out from the wings and plays a vital role. Let's hope the audience hasn't left yet.

Players feel comfortable in tangible space. If their perception of a space is clear, it can lead to a confidence in decision-making. The mind's eye can concentrate on other things – like winning. Designers face a constant battle in their manipulation of the player: when to encourage, when to reprimand, when to reward. Players like to feel clever, and the environment plays a part in this.

So, the designer works with the player's perception of the architectural constructs, the problem of creating the illusion of tangible structure and composition of spaces that does not interfere with, but enhances, gameplay. An illusion of space that can be understood by architectural novices – the public – and that can be created with few polygons within a rigid building system. Hence huge *trompe l'œil* pyramids and cityscapes carefully faded to black or suggested behind impassable barriers.

112 | Philip Campbell

Phillip Campbell/Quantic Dream, Global Location Profile – 'Fahrenheit'

In 'Tomb Raider: Return to Atlantis' the central 'pyramid' area of the Atlantean city had two design components that were additional to the basic necessities of providing good gameplay and being interesting visually. These were maximum visibility of what lay ahead and a logical sequence of 'built' architecture. The players could see the exact structure through many levels of building, and through many layers of gameplay. This gave the players a chance to 'feel clever' by understanding the complexities of the structure and exactly where they had to go. They could make intelligent decisions about the direction they took and get a hint of what they might face. In this case, the placement of a centaur-like creature in the depths of the structure provided an early view of an enemy who 'couldn't wait to meet you'. For the player the question was 'when?'.

Notwithstanding the fact that players can understand a form of architecture alien and unfamiliar to them, the designer must form a series of visual cues that enhance comprehension. By compiling a believable Atlantean architecture from a synthesis of recognisable elements – the notation of doors and windows, for example, or a familiar succession of spaces – it is possible to enhance the gameplay by using the 'known' as a way to delve into the 'unknown'. Rather than being worried about revealing too much information, the designer can use obvious foreshadowing to invigorate and stimulate gameplay response. The ability to clearly divine a possible 'path' through the structure, primarily as a result of a certain legibility in the design, can lead to an event anticipated through time, be it a blood-crazed centaur or other such juicy pay-off.

Conversely, gameplay can also be enhanced by making the player feel uncomfortable. The creation of uneasiness through a succession of spaces or vistas 'tuned' architecturally to 'apocalyptic nightmare' has a more immediate application in a fabricated world. A sense of discord is rarely seen in reality unless it forms a part of the story the architect is telling. A sense of loss or emptiness – as evoked, for example, in relation to the most serious of all real circumstances by Daniel Libeskind's use of fragmented forms, coherent but empty and cold voids in his extension of the Berlin Museum with the Jewish Museum – is an everyday requirement of your typical computer game. The game's manipulative world desperately needs this kind of expertise, a world where the manipulation of space is a primary storytelling device. At present, we rely too much on blatant wordplay for scene-setting, cold expositionary dialogue that emphatically makes a story 'told' rather than 'lived'. Our advantage, though, is that the emotional impact that can often only be implied by the best architecture can be vividly acted out in a game, with a palpable sense of danger, the threat of 'real' death, a life lived at hyper-reality pace. We can carelessly defy gravity and logic in a place where Escher constructions are not merely visual conundrums; they are traversable and habitable.

The ability of designers not just to understand the pure form of their architecture but to comprehend the nature of the 'journey' through that architecture is crucial. The success of the gameplay often depends, for example, on the designer's ability to set up the players' expectations by creating legible space, only to later confound them with a physical change in architectural state. This process, which generally occurs over a period of storytelling time, can also be invoked simultaneously. An environment that oscillates between a reality-based state and a dream-based state has no true parallel in the 'real' world. Here is where the true exploitation of the rules of our fantasy-based worlds can distance us from the hard reality of fact.

Gameplay thrives on interaction. Unfortunately, environments are often an afterthought. The norm seems to be human interaction, *mano a mano*, and it's interesting to see where compromise is made first. Currently, the proliferation of Internet-based 'webisodes' is starting to feed the demand for easily consumable, minimal-download interactive entertainment – with nary an environment in sight. Instead, it always seems to be a combination of characters emoting against a frozen tableau, a panto-painted backdrop. This is the commonsense formula: narrow bandwidth + lowest common denominator, and is probably why most of these 'webisode' productions are ultimately unsatisfying, incredibly static and offer a poor excuse for real interaction. The logic has been firmly locked into the 'campfire' model for dramatic storytelling and the characters try in vain to propel their story along while floating in amorphous, ill-defined 'narrative space'. Anyone who understands the relationship between people and their environment understands the need for that dimension of stimulation.

I always try to visualise my computer creatures moving in a matrix of space, so that what makes up the definition of my interaction-charged beings depends on their exact relationship with their immediate surroundings. It's like a heightened form of the pure physical relationship between, say, my head and a concrete beam when they collide. Not only must we be aware of the tangible physical properties of our computer-generated objects – collision detection, momentum effects and the like – we must also 'program in' emotional responses to environments and to other characters and objects. Remember, all 'life' that exists in our computer world must initially be 'pre-programmed', or at least based on a rigid set of parameters. Rather than being constrictive, I see this as an opportunity to manipulate these 'living' reactions. It's as if we have been granted the power over every single molecule that exists in our creation. A flick of a pixel here, and Keanu's hand enters the mirror in 'The Matrix'. A chameleon-like change in a yellow room, the Medusa's kiss of stone, are physical deformations that can play out between person and place in our thoroughly calculated environment. Like the 'impossible' occurrences in Flann O'Brien's *The Third Policeman*, it is a slightly surreal way of thinking, but it helps to compose interactive rhythms based on a notion of immediate proximity. Characters truly inhabit their worlds, and the synergy between the elements can be complete. So while the primary interaction may still be leaping from lip-synched mouth to mouth in a neat conversation pair, the environment is always rearing its ugly head and tapping the protagonists on their shoulders.

Proximity generates interaction, and thus gameplay. As is the nature of design, this proximity may be in the form of a beautifully realised piece of built form, or it may be a really deep shadow. Our environments are offering us a context for our interaction.

Memory as a gameplay enhancement can be tweaked by an understanding of the nature of the game environment. As in *Waiting for Godot*, something can be not present and yet always present. A hint of architectural expression can generate that whole familiar–not familiar dimension, from the blatant obviousness of a homely fireplace to the half-remembered mythology of an ancient and unseen Colosseum – the potent combination of an eight-year-old's imagination and an overly fervent bible class monitor. As a designer, I feel it is my duty to poke and prod around the memory of my paying customer, searching for resonance, drawing the couch potatoes forward from their recline and into the interactive world I'm invoking. The magic occurs when the poke of a memory fragment prods the user into a memory-related gameplay moment.

Proximity and memory can be seen to contribute to an overall 'sense of place'. So, while my characters are manfully struggling to emote the narrative to its scripted finale, it's the physical environment itself that helps the interactive story arrive at its final destiny. The very point of 'interactivity' is that there is some kind of ongoing dialogue between storyteller and audience. It's a bungee-elastic, malleable journey that stretches out to its 'side-quest' limits and then snaps back into place for the denouement.

Environments are part of the puzzle that is either meant to be deciphered or is deliberately obfuscated. Both can enhance the gameplay experience; the choice of 'architectural system' is usually dependent on factors totally unrelated to architectural 'desire' – 'engine' technology, latency and optimal end-user CPU processing power, for example. Unfortunately, the *Ten Books on Architecture* begat the *Four Books on Architecture*, which begat the 'Rather Small Pamphlet on Computer-Generated Architecture'. What emerges from the idea of making architectural sense is usually dictated by the demands of the user's technology. When dealing with real-time – and, frankly, the only type of computer time worth dealing with here – we still have a massive technological problem.

Real-time is the ability to generate computer images on the fly, so that environments and their contents are processed as they are actually experienced. This is the only form of computer experience that can come close to replicating the freedom of choice allowed in the real world. Basically, on arrival in your computer environment you can go anywhere and look at anything you choose within the limits of the simulation. This puts an incredible burden on the technology required to generate this, frame by frame, at an acceptable speed of movement. Consequently, even the best proprietary engines in the gaming world today must deal with compromise in the architecture they are trying to represent. Hence the birth of modular systems, the ever-present 'primitive', the segmented curves. There are technologists out there spending lifetimes trying to generate a perfect real-time curve – which puts things into perspective!

Understanding the limitations of your chosen system at least allows you to determine the nature of your architectural compromise. Most game-building tools are based on variations of the generic 3D Studio or AutoCAD-type systems. Shapes, vectors, polygons, whatever the material of choice, can be thrown at your screen until it can't take it anymore, and a Fiat test track becomes a slow boat to China.

The tools used to create 'Tomb Raider' (Core Design and Eidos) are radically different to this norm and employ a system that warms the cockles of my architectural heart. A unique 'sculpting' approach actually turns what appears at first to be completely restrictive into a gameplay-enhancing triumph.

The world of 'Tomb Raider' is generated around a shorthand of four-sided and three-sided polygons. Anything away from this norm, be it Corinthian capital or geodesic dome, must be generated as a separate, specific object and placed in the setting like a prop. These props are limited in number and complexity per deployment. Architectural conceit is limited to this basic recipe, a diet of squares and triangles garnished by an occasional spiral stair, plumbing fixture or glowing lava ball. The diverse locations confronting Lara Croft, including modern-day London, ancient Egypt and Atlantis, are approximated in this fashion and 'wallpapered' (textured) accordingly. Obviously, the texture is made to do a lot of the work.

But here's the twist: the building blocks of this world are proportional to, and respond to, the actual physical dimensions and, moreover, the physical limitations of Lara herself. The entire system is justified by the absolute necessity that it is determined by how far Lara can leap, or swing, or jump … by how far she can see. The length of her stride, whether walking casually or running for her life, establishes the physical dimensions of her virtual playground. More Modulor than modular.

In a typical building-block system, like AutoCAD, the environment is generally constructed first, and the gameplay is threaded through its many apertures, a silver thread of fun. Although the physical representation may be more precise, what tends to happen is that the gameplay thread, the critical path, is the only absolute requirement. This results in a lot of 'dead space'. Space-left-over-after-planning appears; creating design crevasses that open up and suck the player into reboot hell. Remember, critical-path gameplay also includes wondrous vistas, inspirational spaces and the like – the visual requirements of an environment are not necessarily neglected. There's just a lot of non-contributing stuff that our character interface may or may not know how to deal with.

Building the sort of environment in 'Tomb Raider' is like sculpting from the inside out. You get inside a solid lump of matter and hollow out the contents. It's like pressing your hand on one of those pin-boards that leaves an impression long after

**117** | The height of the kick

Campbell/Quantic Dream, Environment Locators – 'Fahrenheit'

your tentative flesh has left it. It's the plasticity of Günther Domenig's Zentralsparkasse Bank in Vienna. (Well, almost.)

In fact, in many ways it's more organic. It grows and multiplies with scant regard for structural engineers or surly neighbourhood watch committees ... No planning permission is required in the Wild West border towns of Cyberspace.

Despite the physical difficulty of architectural representation, the 'Tomb Raider' technology succeeds in its primary objective – that the gameplay creates the environment, and more importantly that the environment creates the gameplay.

Here, then, the relationship is more than just casual. The environment, bound by the Modulor-like rules of engagement, can't help but create gameplay – gameplay that is inextricably tied to the requirements of the player-avatar, Lara Croft. If Lara is satisfied, then by extension the player is satisfied too. Whether the gameplay is any good or not, that's another question. The skill of the designer notwithstanding, all we can demonstrate here is that, in this situation, and with these tools, the environment is forever bonded to the notion of gameplay, and therefore has a profound effect on the interactive quality of the entertainment. Maybe this is one of the secrets of Lara Croft's worldwide success?

Le Corbusier would be turning in his grave if he could see how inherently easy it is to please the 'player/inhabitant'. In our idealised situation, we have managed to create an interactive, Modulor-like solution to the simulated physical needs of the player-avatar. We have satisfied our avatars emotionally, too, because we have established their required emotional needs. If only real life was this simple, then personally moulded habitats would be all the rage.

Primarily, though, in games environments we're dipping into our big bag of 'low architectural conceits'. All that elementary psychology that we enjoyed in architectural school is rampantly having its day. We find our starting point when we've accepted that the major player identifier is the character he or she plays. The player-character is undoubtedly the strongest element in a typical game, whether it be a scruffy private eye or a legionnaire of the Roman Empire. Our first foray as designers of computer experiences must involve the reactions and senses of this character, because it is the direct pipeline to the player beyond. Once the immediate bond is established between player and player-character, be it through an environmentally induced sense of loneliness, a fearful throbbing sound or the splendiferous spectacle of erotic dancing, we can then exploit that connection. We have broken the fourth wall and drawn our audience closer to the screen.

Now, if we are so inclined, we can start to make our architectural conceits work a little harder for us. First, the designer's vanity play has to be taken care of, and if St Paul's Cathedral is to be shoehorned into ten thousand polygons, not to mention the plot, then it must be so. Gameplay now guides our hand, and we must be prepared for any eventuality, because good interaction can only evolve from the maximum amount of choice possible.

At this point, most architectural conceits may apply. Whether it is the primal unity of environment and gameplay, as with 'Tomb Raider', or a historical setting with gameplay transposed, the designer can call upon his bag of tricks to conjure up the required result. He may be a masterplanner, producing an ordered composition and a logical layout that evokes nostalgic memory and an innate sense for the player of what is where. He may be a historical copyist, or completist: La Ville Radieuse never looked so finite. A reference-free Atlantis may be the goal, a new order realised and a tangibly tangy sense of reality. Again, the 'game' is multidimensional; the immersive nature of first-person entertainment can equally be used to credibly tame a charging unicorn or to perceive an architectural surround in all its glory of scale, iconography and rhythm.

Authenticity is next, believe me. The nature of real-world physics is simulated more precisely every day, and currently you are able to vibrate your way in an old taxi up and down the urban hills of San Francisco and talk directly in five timeless languages to the scholars at the School of Athens. Technology now exists that will allow you to smell your cyberspace buildings, an oft overlooked pleasure. Currently all simulated computer worlds have to operate within the same pre-ordained 'system'. It makes no difference whether that world has been fully explored by its creators for its perfection and its imperfection – at present, we are dealing with everything in a known world. No matter that we promise fifty degrees of freedom: ultimately we will have to had considered every possibility, every possible interaction, the physical properties of every object and their relationships to each other. Even our most advanced AI-driven robots need paths and answers for every eventuality. The introduction of real people, in their massive multiplayer droves, into this world raises the probability bar. But we still need to establish a framework for their interaction.

The mad scientist in us takes control and watches the 'perfect' world play out: pre-ordained Chaos versus pre-calculated Order. As creators of this world, we impose conditions that imply a correct solution, visible only to us. Where is Mandelbrot when you need him most?

The scale of architectural involvement in these worlds is directly related to the responsibility of its role, and its necessity. For example, the best-selling game 'The Sims', the latest iteration of the hugely popular Sim City franchise, relies on our familiarity not just with the basics of human life, but with the iconographic nature of familiar architectural forms. The interaction/environment formula varies wildly from project to project, and the skill is in achieving a balance. What good is an accurate depiction of life in a medieval town if it's no fun to interact with? As technology advances, the digital builders among us will simply have a better choice. It's not a question of having more polygons to play with, or better lighting effects. It's simply that we will be able to choose how we balance our interactive worlds.

Perhaps these 'interactive games' that we are playing out are doing more than simply pleasuring us, taking us from Level A to Level Z with a simple bit of computer-generated horseplay. Perhaps, as we slip from screen to widescreen to virtual reality to theme park reality, we are acting upon the true primal nature of wish fulfilment. As our toolkit grows ever more sophisticated, as our simulated realities become more and more immersive and interactive, aren't we tapping into something fundamental about our continuing lives?

It seems obvious that a honed and perfected digital 'lifestyle', coupled with hyper-real levels of communication, must eventually leak out into our 'real-world' desires. The ease with which we build a digital impression of ourselves, move through our ideal landscapes, face up to and tear down our terrors and inhibitions. The way we find love on the Internet – our idealised notions of ourselves are going to demand more 'on the outside' …

So, all the movers and shakers, the manipulators, the builders, the shapers of our planet, will find themselves responding to a new set of criteria, a new type of audience demand, a newly interactive public. Ultimately we may see an architecture that acknowledges this new breed, understands the notion of our double lives and finally comes to terms with our heightened perception of what constitutes our existence. Shouldn't 'interactive' and 'immersive' be equally applied to our everyday experiences?

For builders of cyberspace everywhere, the technological shackles are slowly slipping off, our powers of creation are becoming manifestly stronger – and with that our responsibility grows. The faceless 2D avatars of the past are transforming into beautiful effigies of real beings, real faces wink and grin, real emotions howl in the dark digital night. We must deal with the transition, transforming the simple online/offline light switch with a delicate touch. Above all, we must be careful that the hopes and dreams, the inspirations and aspirations, the sense of belonging and community that can develop when we play out our fantasies in our ideal online places do not just wither and die in the cold, hard light of reality.

We step out of the vampiric notion of the dark lonely secret, hidden in cyberspace, sadly traversing an empty landscape 'round midnight …

… It's just not like that any more …

We step into the light, that light of reality, bursting with people and places and 'the things we've seen'. Now we wait for the real world to respond …

Chapter 9
# Foto-graph, Foto-shop
David Greene, Institute of Electric Anthropology[1]

In 1974 the Institute presented a seminar at the Architectural Association on the subject of the photograph in the context of architectural education and publishing. This short essay tries to revisit and re-use the text of this seminar and place it within the culture of current design practice. Photoshop, I think, brings a new angle to this. The old text, with new comments, follows.

> It's interesting to note that at the Architectural Association there is a fashion for writing semiological analysis of architecture. I find this intriguing, not because semiology is enjoying a vogue in intellectual circles, but more because what is being in this instance analysed is not the buildings themselves but published photos of the works. The application of semiotics in the architectural arena is perhaps itself open to question, but the apparent acceptance of the photograph as being not a photograph of the building but the building itself is, I feel, perhaps worth a brief comment.
> 
> Firstly, the fact of the photograph does not in itself signify the existence of that which is being photographed, although it may signify the existence of the idea of the object. For example, the picture postcard of the *Arc de Triomphe* is as much a picture of the idea of the *Arc de Triomphe* as it is of the actual object. The fact of the postcard denotes that the *Arc de Triomphe* is an important idea more reliably than it denotes that such an object exists in the form shown.
> 
> Secondly, what one can see emerging is an architecture that only related to photographs of architecture. With reference to this, the history of modern art has often been described as a history of photographs of modern art; and perhaps the history of modern architecture might also be viewed in this kind of way. The influence of the photograph of a building as seen in the magazines is perhaps one that's worth discussing further. It is out of this interest in photos that I am drawn to make a short comparison here between a pin-up, a car and a building.

Photos of these have interesting areas of correspondence; these correspondences could demonstrate that this tradition of architectural focus has given us a kind of architecture as irrelevant as the styling of the car and as culturally and morally empty as the pin-up. I'd like to point out that I present this not as a complete or logical analysis but as a question for comment.

The images I am thinking of are a Ford advert and a piece of architecture (I think by Denys Lasdun), both taken from the *Observer* supplement of 28 April 1974. The pin-up was taken from volume 39, no. 4 of *Men Only*. The first area of correspondence is technical competence: the high quality of the photographs and the quality of printing; the expert placing on the page by skilled graphic designers; the careful selection of the final image to support the claims of the accompanying text.

Secondly, all three are also dynamic objects, in that they are normally perceived whilst moving, or move and change themselves, and yet they are here perceived in a very static and posed way and are just as new. There's not a spot of road dirt on the car or graffiti on the building, and the girl's skin resembles that of a baby. This might be a second area of correspondence, which could be described as aesthetic: a carefully contrived aesthetic stereotype is manufactured. The subtle skin textures and balance of light and shade are matched by the pristine finish of the cellulose on the car and the immaculate shutter marks on the building. (In order to support this image, functional elements are subtly groomed.)

The third area of interest lies within the text accompanying the pictures. A superficial examination will reveal that, first of all, all three make extravagant claims for their subject. All three products are described in an extremely evocative but very vague vocabulary that leans heavily on a dictionary of descriptions whose meaning is open to a wide variety of interpretations. This dictionary of descriptions serves no useful purpose, other than – like the photographic technique – to support the previously mentioned pre-packed aesthetic stereotype. I quote *Men Only* of the girl: 'A certain element of woman's poise and bearing grins through Dulcie Scott as a fresh free and unswerving feminine spirit.' About the building Stephen Gardiner writes, 'The light filters in through secret angled openings, staircases slant and slowly rising steps are greeted by bright green turf, laid neatly between white walls.' And of the car Ford writes, 'All little things, but it's surprising how they strengthen the lines' ... .

It is certainly difficult to deny the centrality of the photograph in discussion about architecture and learning about it. Imagine if we could only pass comment on, talk with reference to and compare buildings one had actually been to rather than merely visited through the photograph.

The presence of these photographs is not particularly a problem. Their proliferation, the startling improvements in techniques of printing, image enhancement, picture quality, etc. – all this is well known, and was so in 1974. What was not actively realised 28 years ago was that technology would present the designer with a tool that could in quite a literal sense create photographs. Photographs of reality and the 'yet to be' become now indistinguishable.

We might speculate on the consequences of the lack of difference between the 'is' and the 'yet to be' within the photograph, and we can examine and talk about the latter in the same way as we can about the former because we are, in both examples, discussing a photograph. We may even be gazing at a moving picture, watching the shadow of a cloud pass across an 'elevation'.

> **photo-graph:** light-drawing. **photo:** *photos*, greek, light. **graph:** *graphitos*, greek, written or drawn in a particular way. **shop:** a building or room for retail sale. **photo-shop:** light sale.

Generations of students and tutors, critics and journalists have been talking about the drawings on the wall in front of them as if they were talking about architecture, or an architecture yet to be, rather than discussing drawings. Now the discussion addresses photographs, and the critics will be unclear whether they are built or unbuilt.

The collapse of geography, time and place brought about by the mobile phone infects the studio and its coterie of talkers and writers. I talk to my friend, but his phone number no longer betrays his whereabouts. I look at his project, and I no longer see a drawing.

> Foto-graph; Foto-shop.

The air mouse, such an innocent and incongruous name for such a potent weapon. The picture grows and evolves on the screen in response to the twitches of fingers and the small journeys of the mouse across its pad.

Consider the flailing body of Jackson Pollock above the canvas on the floor: it is hard to imagine a greater shift in the relationship of the movement of the body and the production of the picture than that between Pollock and the cordless mouse. Pollock took the canvas off the easel and made it horizontal (on the floor); the computer takes the drawing board (horizontal) and places it on the vertical screen but leaves the pencil on the horizontal surface – strange spatial shifts.

Who decided that drawing should be like watching TV?

Pollock does not allow us to forget the substance of the world, his body, the bulk and plasticity of the paint. The similarities in movement are picked up with an absolute difference of substance and message. In the field of architecture, perhaps Brutalism, with its total lack of smooth surface, its essential, substantial roughness, was a similar antithetical reminder or, more, an early warning of the imminent arrival of … air mouse, that untethered creature which when we enter its habitat allows us to forget the substance of the planet, everything that is except for light. Foto-graph, Foto-shop, Light-machine.

People say Archigram's project should have been easier with current technology; I believe it would have been impossible/entirely different/too smooth to do the job. Pollock couldn't fake it, you might say his body, the paint and the canvas blur into one object. No such collisions are possible with air mouse. Faking it is easy. Faking it is all that's left. The space between the body and the picture (if that is what we can call it) is the infinite gap of the digital world.

There has always been a kind of drawing in architectural design that is trying to say 'and here is what it would look like'. The photograph is of interest here because we accept it as usually speaking directly of 'and this is what it looks like'. Photoshop says both simultaneously. Only the small print may advise you of its secrets … 'this may be a computer generated image'.

The perspective and the axonometric, the plan and the elevation languish in the backwaters of the architectural representation industry. We can talk of hardcopy but not the drawing. Design becomes TV. The slightest quiver of the finger on the mouse may only pull down another menu; such quivers of the hand holding the ruling pen would have betrayed the authorship of the drawing.

And we haven't mentioned video. Imagine yourself as a builder. Imagine you build your building from a video. Foto-shop, Light-machine, you have a new job; you make light into substances and events. As a builder you need to attend film school. Are you making a film or a building?

**Note**

1    David Greene and Mike Barnard.

## Part 3
# The reporting of architecture

It's curious how, despite the current fashionable interest in the relationship between architecture and the media, little critical attention is given to the way architecture gets written about. The process by which people and their works are defined as famous may, one has to hope, be connected with their inherent merits. But the media through which this process is achieved are almost entirely architectural publications, especially magazines and books (and, in a somewhat different form, exhibitions and lectures). All these media have their own strong drives and tendencies, many of which have little to do with architectural merit per se. To win contemporary fame and a place in history, architects and architecture have to make it through a highly biased, highly self-referential publication system: typically, works first appear in magazines, and then progress through the equally self-determining world of architectural book publishing.

Of course, these systems vary from country to country and in different circumstances. The UK, uniquely, has not just one weekly 'trade' magazine aimed directly at registered architects but two; both are news-based and heavily funded by product advertising. This is quite different to the situation in the Netherlands, or Germany, or America, or France. The funding structure of the magazines, their circulation and the parties directly interested are different in all cases, as is their relationship (sometimes financial) with the architects whose work they describe, and the output of the magazines inevitably reflects this.

Books too are highly regionalised and specific, with hidden criteria, intentions, constraints and costs – circulation figures, production costs, audiences, timing and so on – interacting or even conflicting with the intentions of their authors. From mainly academic publications like this one, with their tiny budgets, to the big-bucks coffee-table market; from the tourist guide to the polemical manifesto; from the scholarly tome (effectively funded by academic institutions that support their staff to produce them) to 'vanity publishing' and the mass of monographs partly subsidised by the architects themselves – all forms of publishing of architecture have their own criteria and biases. This part of the book takes samples from some of these areas that form the basis of our current definition of architecture and architectural history and examines some of the ways in which they operate.

Pierluigi Serraino and Julius Shulman have discussed elsewhere how the fame of houses of West Coast Modernism depended more on whether photos of them were published than their actual quality.[1] In his chapter Serraino describes Shulman's photographs of Pierre Koenig's Case Study House #22: one of the classic cases of how iconic photographs come to exemplify a particular sort of architecture. Serraino compares the orthodoxy of the classic architectural photograph with the popular photograph – in particular, how different views of the house are targeted at different audiences, and the subsequent adjustment of interpretation that results.

Architectural magazines, like all forms of media, are of course inherently biased. My own chapter, based on research done in the 1980s (before I became an architectural journalist), looks at architectural coverage in national newspapers at a time when both journalists and developers were learning to turn the inherent news bias of that coverage and the aesthetic agenda it established to their advantage. Next, Alan Powers looks at the seminal, famous, long-lasting books that have been critical in architectural history, and finds that a similar mix of personal, professional and accidental forces (intellectual credo and practice brochure) has not just been a modern phenomenon. He also notes a particular curiosity of architectural books: it's necessary for them to have text and an author, but that doesn't imply that people read them.

Charles Jencks takes up a similar theme, but writes from a personal perspective: books are of course an integral part of his ongoing polemic. Arguing that it is publications that give meaning to ambiguous architecture, he describes a history of Post-Modernism in which books, as well as buildings, are seen as the site of a kind of continuing dialogue of development – and where contemporary architects are engaged in putting their own mark on posterity in the battle of the big books.

In all cases books and journalism should not be perceived as passive recipients of representations but as active participants that shape ongoing work and thus, often for reasons of their own, identify and record exactly what is considered to be architecture. Paul Finch's coda to this section uses an A–Z lecture format to add a few home truths about the way the UK publishing industry works.

**Note**

1   Julius Shulman and Pierluigi Serraino, *Modernism Rediscovered* (Cologne: Taschen, 2000).

Chapter 10
# Framing icons
Two girls, two audiences
The photographing of Case Study House #22
**Pierluigi Serraino**

Photographic accounts of architecture for a readership of specialists and for the general public can be strikingly different. Given the same building, two competing forms of depiction coexist in the pictorial reproduction of the artefact: the former is documentary, technical and celebratory; the latter suggests occupancy, consumption and lifestyle.

To examine this dichotomy in representational practice and its consequence in the appreciation of architecture, this essay chronicles the iconographic trajectory of Case Study House #22 in Los Angeles, California, and of its acceptance in architectural culture. This project, designed by Pierre Koenig and photographed by Julius Shulman, acquired an iconic force in West Coast Modernism through a night-view photograph of the living room, which gradually made its way into mainstream architectural culture. The shot shows two women, dressed in white, sitting on a glass and steel structure suspended on a cliff over the Los Angeles lights. For most, this particular print epitomises a glittering period in California Modernism. If today this marker constitutes the defining image of a key building of this time, it is a unanimous consensus that is a relatively recent achievement in the memory of the architectural discipline.

Publications targeted at architects present illustrations that are analytical, abstract, emphatically editorial and self-referential in nature. Their purposes are manifold: to describe and catalogue the geometry of a structure; to inform peers of the latest advances in the discipline; to reinforce the professional identity of designers within the larger population of experts in the building industry; to set normative benchmarks in the value judgement of a particular scheme; and to establish paradigmatic norms of spatial representation. For this specialised audience, architectural photography draws from a repertoire of fixed conventions, crafting a highly exclusive visual rhetoric for architects' own understanding and use. In particular, it often tends to obey the representational principles of architectural drawings. For instance, camera positions are often parallel to the planes of the built form, in mimicry of architectural elevations.

For lay readers, a different set of pictorial traits apply, making architectural photography for the general public a genre in its own right. The migration of a building from a specialised to a consumer periodical entails a dramatic revision of the philosophical underpinnings of a photographic composition. Settings are transformed into

Julius Schulman's photo of Pierre Koenig's Case Study House #22. No girls: the architectural editor's preference was for naked architecture.

displays of objects of desire for the specific class they are geared to. Space is staged to appeal to the palate of the social élite, for whom design is a vehicle for social distinction. The history of architectural photography in the popular press parallels the history of middle- and upper-class taste.

Photography is a flexible field serving large numbers of purposes, where the attitude towards the framing of the scene stems from the intended scope of the coverage. In architectural literature, pictures of all kinds share commonalities that are foreign to other domains. A particular level of description permeates the record of a design. Following the powerful and strict conventions of architectural drawings, architectural photographs display structures devoid of human traces, often captured under fair-weather conditions, in a pristine state untainted by their everyday use. The camera brings perceptual order to what is frequently a chaotic environment.

Traditionally, the photographer gains access to a building once it has just been completed and ideally landscaped, yet before it has entered its normal life cycle in the social and physical fabric of the city. The freezing of this metaphysical condition on the film characterises the bulk of images in design publications.

It follows that architectural picture making raises provocative issues relevant to the absorption of information about 'design' by architects themselves. On one side, photographs serve a documentary function; on the other, they provide the readership with the opportunity for comparative exercises and critical reflection on diverse designs. Decontextualised from their physical adjacencies and severed from the societal circumstances that determined their own production, projects of different scales and types are presented to the reader in publications and reconfigured in a new visual relationship. Such juxtaposition is routine in magazines and newspapers all over the world. Yet the impact on the reader in the value judgement of various architectural propositions should not be neglected.

Pictures bear the interpretative signature of their authors. Through their camera, photographers bring a consistency of visual representation – on which architects capitalise. Photographers craft a pictorial homogeneity among dissimilar spatial configurations. To hire a particular photographer means to buy a distinct 'vision' for the advertising of the designer's work, in the pursuit of media branding. Given a particular assignment, each photographer brings a unique approach, according to the hierarchy of philosophical and aesthetic priorities that he or she brings to the viewfinder.

A case in point is Julius Shulman. The photos of Shulman, who fell into architectural photography largely by accident and became the favourite and most extensive chronicler of West Coast Modernism, have strong and specific characteristics. His frames are characterized by an alignment of architectural elements in a constructed scene and under controlled lighting conditions. Radically, he often uses not only props but people, usually excluded from all architectural photography, and he arranges them to emphasise – sometimes to hide – various aspects of the building: to mimic a cantilever or to hide a shadow. His goal is to suggest occupancy and to activate desire in the viewer for a comfortable lifestyle in a modern home. To file down the sharp ideological edges of Modernism for the palate of the general public, Shulman frames

Shulman's photo of Pierre Koenig's Case Study House #22. 'Two Girls': the photograher's interpretation of both architecture and lifestyle.

together domesticity and steel – such as by placing a cocktail in the foreground of his compositions. 'Wouldn't you like to have a martini here?' Shulman likes to ask when he explains his photographs to viewers.

John Entenza, publisher and editor of the magazine *Arts & Architecture* as well as mastermind of the Case Study Program, an enterprise to publicise innovative modern design to the American scene, first published Pierre Koenig's scheme in May 1959. The project was presented as a steel shelter open to a 240° view of the surrounding panorama. Two overall drawings of the house, an interior close-up and a floor plan, delivered the vision of this modern domestic temple to an audience educated in the tenets of the International Style. In October 1959 the editor printed a progress report of the construction site showing the previously published floor plan and five photographs of the steel framework. In the February 1960 issue, a one-page piece with four recent pictures provided the readers with the latest developments in the assemblage of the structure. These photographs were technical in content – and somewhat analogous in viewpoints to the wire-frame perspectives shown in the May 1959 article.

On its completion in June 1960 Case Study House #22, known also as the Stahl Residence, received an eight-page spread in the pages of Entenza's magazine. Shulman carried out the assignment on 9 May 1960 in the presence of the architect. Koenig remembers that the shooting session took five days. At the time the house was just finished, and its interior was still unfurnished. To meet the deadline for the Arts & Architecture coverage, the Californian photographer did a first whole day of shooting, retaining complete control over the construction of the photographic compositions. Temporary furniture was supplied specifically for the job and arranged by Shulman himself. It is worth noting the presence of the Van Keppel-Green chaise longue outside the house in the lower part of the second photo. That same piece of furniture was already familiar to the readers through the iconic picture Shulman took in 1947 of Richard Neutra's Kaufmann House in Palm Springs, California. Thirteen years separate the two images, yet that same chair was positioned in the frame to send the viewer a message of modern living. Shulman placed the chair out on the patio next to the plant to suggest the inhabitability of the outside area as well as the interior – characteristic of the modern house.

The two women dressed in white, called in for the shoot later in the afternoon that first day, were the girlfriends of two students at the University of Southern California who were helping with the shooting. This image, currently among the most published visions of modern architecture, was to become a template of perception for generations of architects to follow. However, complying with the orthodoxy of his architectural ideology, Entenza instead picked sixteen black and white unadorned photographs from that assignment, leaving out the well-known exposure of what both Koenig and Shulman today call the 'Two Girls'. The visual features of the images in Entenza's selection expressed the minimalist geometry of the artefact, the notion of transparency of the interiors to the distant landscape and the tectonic aspects of the construction. Little can be deduced about the owners, their way of living and their experience with the architecture, let alone the immediate surrounding context. For a

**132** | Pierluigi Serraino

long time, the *Arts & Architecture* article provided the most comprehensive coverage in the specialised literature of Koenig's project.

Later that summer Shulman returned to photograph the house after the Stahls had taken possession of the house and had placed the furniture according to their own liking. On 17 July 1960 Dan MacMasters, future editor of the *Los Angeles Times' Home Magazine,* featured the residence in the 'Pictorial Living' section of the *Los Angeles Examiner,* the Sunday supplement of a newspaper that stopped publication in 1989. The colour version of the 'Two Girls' made its first appearance on the magazine's front cover.

The supplement's five-page description of the project produced a radically different account of its design attributes through the reorganisation of photographic relationships. Many of the pictures exhibit a staged integration of architecture and lifestyle, presenting the design in its socio-physical context. The main points of interest were the users and the activities for which the building was created. People posing while apparently performing daily tasks animate the space, and the beholder is allured by the comfort of modern domestic space. The severity of the steel lines is balanced by the arrangement of items and commodities, which elicit ease of use as well as a way of living. The building functions more as the backdrop to the unfolding of family life than an artefact on its own terms. Hints, such as particular magazines, gadgets and fashionable commodities, are consciously disseminated within the frame to engage the observer in a game of psychological reconstruction of the before-and-after of that exposure. The reader's consumption of that photograph was not only a way to enter into a privileged community, but also an opportunity to indulge in a form of virtual voyeurism. As newspapers and their Sunday supplements are not listed in the architectural databases, this publication quickly became invisible to architects, disappearing from the professional radar screen.

That same year the colour version of 'Two Girls' was accorded a first prize in the colour category of the American Institute of Architects' 1960 National Award Competition for Architectural Photography. This recognition granted the image large-scale circulation in periodicals and newspapers throughout the country. On 25 December 1960 the real estate section of *The New York Times* published a black and white version of the photograph on its front cover. The dramatic illustration was pointed out as a felicitous blend of architectural and contextual information. In February 1961 the *AIA Journal* made the picture the first image in its four-page report on the photography competition. The colour image reappears in the February 1961 issue of the *National Photographer,* a magazine geared to photographers, as part of the news about the AIA award. That same month the house was shown with a short descriptive text in the pages of *Sunset,* a monthly periodical on West Coast architectural culture for lay readers. In this instance the residence was part of an advertisement for the products of Bethlehem Steel. The selected picture, driven by the sponsor's interests, displays in the foreground the metal decking and the I-beams. Case Study House #22 was later featured in the *Arizona Republic* newspaper on 17 December 1961.

In 1962 Shulman published his first book, *Photographing Architecture and Interiors,* under the sponsorship of the Whitney Library of Design. The publication was a primer on camera and darkroom technique as well as an exposé of Shulman's approach to architectural photography. In the middle section of the book, the black and white and the colour versions of the 'Two Girls' are placed next to each other on a double-page spread to demonstrate the disparity of their visual impact. In March 1962 Peter Blake, architect and at the time chief editor of *Architectural Forum,* wrote a four-page article on the Stahl Residence for *Holiday* magazine. In that instance the colour image reveals a slight variation from the black and white twin image: the girls have switched seats, yet the composition and lighting are clearly the same. In this first round of publications, the last appearance of the 'Two Girls' composition was in the February 1963 issue of *Designers West,* a magazine popular among interior designers. Here the photograph was published as part of an interview with Shulman on how to harness the language of photography for the promotion and advertising of products of the building industry.

In the architectural press, it was Esther McCoy who wrote, in 1962, the first comprehensive account of Entenza's experiment. The book, *Modern California Houses; Case Study Houses, 1945–1962,* showcased the canonical work of the Modernist pioneers using many of Shulman's photographs. Case Study House #22 was there, illustrated just as it was in *Arts & Architecture.* The same choice of photographs was made in the 1977 reprint for a local Los Angeles publisher.

Following these first three years of the project's existence in the pages of architectural and general periodicals after the 1960 shooting, a first long period of absence from the media ensued. In the late 1960s Reyner Banham, British architectural historian and critic, undertook what was later acclaimed as a classic in the literature on the built environment and the urban culture of Southern California, *Los Angeles: Architecture of Four Ecologies.* When Banham visited Shulman's studio to ask for material for his book, the photographer presented him with, among much other material, the shot with the two girls. The volume was published in 1971. In the concluding chapter, Banham argues for the stylistic contribution of Los Angeles to the Modern Movement in the United States. Koenig's project is positioned between the work of Charles Eames and the production of Craig Ellwood. Banham's book provided the first critical introduction of the spectacular night image to a readership of architectural adepts.

This brief literary resurrection of the photograph was followed by a second, longer period of editorial oblivion. In 1981 Paul Gleye produced *The Architecture of Los Angeles,* an influential outline of architectural movements in Southern California. Case Study House #22 reappears in one image, one that matches the photo on the opening page of the 1960 article in *Arts & Architecture*. It was only in 1985, when architectural historian Mark Girouard's *Cities and People: A Social and Architectural History* was published, that the picture was brought once again to the readership's attention. Although the intellectual focus of this book was on urban environments in Europe and in the US, the black and white exposure with the two girls was used as the pictorial prelude for the concluding reflections on modern cities. Those years marked the beginning of a renewed interest in post-war architecture of Los Angeles.

Inevitably many of these publications tapped into the archival sources of Julius Shulman, considered the most authoritative photographic recorder of 50 years of West Coast Modernism. Sooner or later the authors were introduced to that image, which would find its way in the pages of their volumes. The 'Two Girls' in black and white opened the chapter on the 1950s in Sam Hall Kaplan's *L.A. Lost and Found: An Architectural History of Los Angeles*, printed in 1987. That same year, Dominique Rouillard reprinted, in black and white, the cover of the 17 July 1960 *Los Angeles Examiner* 'Pictorial Living' section in his *Building the Slope: Hillside Houses, 1920–1960*. The catalogue of the exhibition organised in 1989 by Elizabeth A.T. Smith at the Museum of Contemporary Art in Los Angeles, and titled *Blueprints for Modern Living: History and Legacy of the Case Study Houses*, further consolidated in architectural discourse the 'Two Girls' as representative both of the house and the whole era. Since then, the frequency of the publication of the image in the literature has increased exponentially with the numerous studies on Californian Modernism and on Shulman's work.

When asked why it took so long for the 'Two Girls' to emerge as the paradigmatic illustration of Case Study House #22 in the design debate, both Koenig and Shulman maintained, in informal talks, that the times were not ready for that shot. In those days the Modernist ideology seemed to inhibit pictorial interpretations of buildings aimed at pleasing the popular taste. Hardliners were likely to deem that type of photography too ephemeral to serve the timeless values of the modern revolution. A Cartesian zeitgeist informed the elitist vision of how architecture was to be reproduced and expounded in the media: abstract, positivist, empty, unaffected by the state of affairs in the world, mimicking the formalities of perspective. The publishing forum certainly subscribed to this theoretical theme and manufactured a specific pattern of graphic representation that is still prevalent in editorial policy nowadays. The Post-Modern age helped to loosen up the inflexible position of the hard-core Modernists, leaving room for alternative readings of architecture. Shulman's rendition of Koenig's project generated a mystique about the post-war period that also brought to the fore a lasting focus on the agency of the photographer in manufacturing a consensus around architects' work and the marketing of their ideas. Capitalising still on the popularity of that image, Case Study House #22 today enjoys the unconditional support of the cultural infrastructure at a global scale.

The 'Two Girls' images are a rare crossover between two independent, almost parallel forms of photographic representation of architecture. Broadly speaking, different attitudes inform the taking of a picture according to whether the receivers of the photographic message are architects or the lay public. When photographers shoot for practitioners, the typical focus is a formal investigation of the artefact; for the general viewers, the tendency is to capture human experience. Each perspective carries its own set of conventions and levels of signification. Objects placed in the frame, for example, provide a sense of scale and are clues to patterns of use for architects, while they become evidence of social status for lay viewers. By staging people, always posed, in the set-ups, the photographer gives dimensional awareness to architects, while offering a societal portrait of the elite to the general spectator.

Whether photographs are used as a vehicle for propaganda, a marketing tool or an educational aid, buildings rely on the technology of photography, and its built-in recording limits, to find their way in the culture of architecture. This diversity of representational approaches – and their internalisation by consumers of design information – might be one of the concurrent causes of the lack of understanding between architects and the general public in architectural matters. Designers indulge themselves in the circular referencing of a repertoire of highly connoted still images of new works. They scrutinise the portfolios of an exclusive group of peers, paying attention to their signature, to what characterises their shaping of space. This mechanism perpetuates a practice of representation that is coded and accepted as legitimate only within the institutional boundaries of the profession. The mass of non-specialists (in other words, the users) absorb and evaluate images of architectural projects within the larger context of their own needs, desires and routines. Unable to partake in the design concerns of the practitioner, these users draw on a literature in which they can easily identify their value structure.

## Acknowledgement

My heartfelt thanks to Julius Shulman and Pierre Koenig for their constant support and help.

Chapter 11
# Naturally biased
Architecture in the UK national press[1]
Kester Rattenbury

> Happily, we can date the birth of architectural coverage in the UK media to a specific moment in time. Unlike the birth of a person, which is becoming a complicated issue of science and law, media coverage of architecture was delivered safely to the RIBA by the capable hands of Prince Charles on 30 May 1984 at Hampton Court ...
> **KR, with apologies to Charles Jencks**

## Making the news

In the tiny, parochial world of national architectural debate, it must have been the biggest event of all time. Prince Charles, heir apparent to the British throne, then considered an unusually mild-mannered and uncontroversial Prince of Wales, used his platform as guest of honour at the 150th anniversary gala dinner of the Royal Institute of British Architects to launch a startling, vitriolic attack on the architectural profession. The speech was headline news, and the British media went wild.

With a battery of instant-fame squibs, he lambasted major projects going through the planning process – a 'monstrous carbuncle on the face of an old and much-loved friend' (ABK's extension to the National Gallery in Trafalgar Square), a 'glass stump, better suited to downtown Chicago than to the City of London' (the Mies van der Rohe office proposal for Mansion House), a 'municipal fire station' (ABK again). More broadly, he denounced an entire profession for arrogantly promoting a failed and unpopular modern language in the teeth of public hostility.

This was profoundly ironic. For years, British architects, stuck in a slough of unpopularity and a thoroughly accepted consensus that modern architecture had definitively failed, had been begging for more media attention. The public simply didn't understand architects, the profession said. More media coverage would present a better and fuller public image, simultaneously informing public debate. Now the profession found itself swamped in media coverage – all of it bad.

Not just that, but the media focused on exactly the problem the profession was hoping they would solve. They portrayed architects as arrogant, out of touch; as

**137** | Naturally biased

The nation's number one architectural critic: Prince Charles with Charles Correa (far right), to whom he presented the 1984 RIBA Royal Gold Medal before turning his guns on the whole profession

crazily constructing an entirely unpopular environment, despite proven failure. Architects were left apologetically agreeing with parts of the criticism, supporting the unwonted media furore in principle – and desperately trying to rebut almost everything the prince said about architecture itself.

Perversely, though, this burgeoning of debate of architecture in the media did seem to prove the very claims of media influence that the architectural world had been making. More media coverage did generate more public debate. It did seem to influence public opinion. It even seemed to play a very strong role in the decision-making process of high-profile planning decisions. It could even be argued that the attack did put architecture definitively 'on the agenda', catalysing – after the first wave of broadly hostile coverage – a steep rise in media and public interest in architecture and design throughout the 1990s, culminating in a great wave of home makeover shows and fly-on-the wall studies of the ups and downs of building projects, from a self-build housing co-op in Brighton to Tate Modern.

But this boom in media coverage was not driven by the self-promotional or altruistic desires of the architects who had sought it. It was driven in the early stages entirely by the prince's newsworthy status and the spectacular way, in media terms, he set the story up. It would have been equally newsworthy had he attacked lawyers or dentists. And, bizarrely, it defined the prince as the nation's number one architectural critic – and, at the same time, as the voice of public opinion, a one-man vox pop, an untested and specious but highly influential position which he occupied without question for the best part of a decade.

But nor, in the longer term, did the effects on the media follow the prince's agenda – despite the string of speeches, his book, the TV programme and various articles that followed.[2] Initially, these were taken very seriously. But the media were interested in his agenda for its newsworthiness, and slowly and increasingly they reinterpreted the subject in its own terms – many of which turned out to be, coincidentally, more sympathetic to the profession. The sudden shift of architecture to centre stage and its evolution as a media subject – with all the effects and shifts in the chimera of public opinion that followed – was almost entirely driven by the values of the media.

## The myth of the critical media

It was not surprising that architects looked to the media to help sort out their public image. Aside from the problem of attempting to disentangle media coverage and 'public opinion' (often treated as interchangeable), the news media have – and had more strongly in the early 1980s – a kind of moral halo relating to their informative and educative potential and to the questionable but persistent myth of their critical role. It is still common to hear that the media represent the voice of the people, that they challenge and check people in positions of authority. It is worth saying at once that this view has almost no support in any serious research of the time.

There is a profound difference between how journalists tend to describe their work and how media researchers describe it. Journalists and media producers see themselves as independent, autonomous people, collaborating to produce information based on news values generated by public demand and what the public deems significant (politically and socially important events), and having a duty to criticise and challenge the establishment.

While there is truth in this, such a role is highly circumscribed. Researchers, with a more objective approach, a far less glamorous forum and a much smaller audience, describe the media as essentially part of the establishment they claim to criticise, with institutional, commercial and personal interests all more or less invisibly inhibiting the desire, ability or even imaginative framework for criticising the establishment, except in minor, exceptional and (usually) the most famous cases.

Although their arguments vary, researchers describe the media as a nexus of systems and values that almost inevitably produces a limited, partial and biased world view. And this view is one which, while offering a superficial, token and occasional challenge to the various forms of power, in most cases stealthily and consistently promotes the interests of the power base. Real instances of active criticism on the part of the media – though highly visible and memorable when they do occur – only indicate a gradual shift in the nexus of systems and values. More often, though, criticism is effectively token: a show of silk whiplashes that masks an actual reinforcement of prevailing power.

## 'You can't do architecture on TV'

Prince Charles made his speech in a British media culture where architecture was definitely not sexy. In the early and mid-1980s, most national papers – even some of the quality press – did not employ an architectural correspondent, and regular reviews of buildings appeared to be substantially less frequent than opera reviews. TV, often described as the 'ideal' medium for architecture because of its visual information, and which did produce occasional specialised programmes and series, treated it irregularly and seriously. It was common to hear quoted the words of the veteran broadcaster, the late Huw Weldon: 'You can't do architecture on television.'

But this lack of overt or official scheduling of architectural coverage in the media masked a mass of coverage of architectural subject matter by other names. Newspapers, in particular, provided a stream of regular and highly organised coverage – but as news or under property, housing, conservation, lifestyle or development tags, each having its own strong, well defined and consistent characteristics. The range of subjects is in itself revealing (the lack of structured emphasis on social issues, for example).

Within this coverage, and usually firmly pigeonholed as an arts issue, was a tiny core of specialist 'architectural' coverage. In the 1980s this was produced by extraordinarily few writers and exclusively in the quality segment of the national press, though the same few people also appeared as pundits and presenters on radio and TV programmes. Though it was volumetrically tiny, this was effectively the whole of specialist architectural coverage. And however broad-ranging the actual writing might be, the subject – firmly defined by the press's strict sectional structure (news, reviews, sports, politics, etc.) – was almost always treated as an aesthetic issue, rather than being a matter principally of, say, social concern.

A systematic search through a year's coverage of architecture in six UK national papers also identified some astonishingly strong assumptions.[3] Development was good, home ownership was good, conservation was good – and, interestingly, architecture was good, though this made a far weaker showing. The reverse assumption, the widely held myth that architects were unpopular or that modern architecture was a failure, was only reflected slightly in the coverage. These assumptions, extraordinarily pervasive, was never analysed or contradicted in any substantial way.

Moreover, as you would expect from media research, these assumptions belied strong, if occasionally conflicting, support for the establishment. Conservation was the profound cultural embodiment of established and traditional values; development and individual home ownership were booming parts of booming Conservative policy. This despite the fact that half the newspapers sampled were 'left-wing'.

But this set up a particularly curious framework for the coverage of architecture. Effectively, with scant organised coverage of architecture as a core subject area, the agenda was determined by a scenario in which conservation was pitted against development – just the sort of conflict favoured by news values. And when specific battles flared up – or were represented – along these lines, the architectural core agenda, as managed by these few architectural writers, was brought in as mediator on almost entirely aesthetic terms. Aesthetics or architectural quality was always to be used as the deciding factor in press opinion.

This added up to an intriguing picture: the aesthetics of architecture, as managed and represented by a few specialist correspondents – as the mediator in competing forms of highly established and powerful interests.

## A landscape of loaded opportunities

It is hardly surprising to find that this was a situation available for exploitation, and the market in the mid-1980s was wide open. With limited coverage – but small numbers of people taking any direct interest – the possibilities for influence were eccentric but powerful. What media research calls sources – organisations and individuals who feed the news and inevitably try to shape it to their own ends – were few, highly disparate and, in some cases, very effective.

This was certainly not true of the official architectural bodies. ARCUK, the UK's official architectural registration body, had almost no public profile and no publicity mechanism. The RIBA, effectively a voluntary professional club, but with a much higher public profile, in 1986 showed far less media savvy than it does now, and made relatively scarce showing in the newspaper coverage of the year. Indeed, actions such as electing Rod Hackney, praised by the prince, as its president, suggested that, if anything, the profession's agenda was being set by the media.

Nor were architects themselves yet very effective as sources. In a whole year's coverage, the numbers of mentions of architects were very small. Rod Hackney, with his royal media leg-up, managed to poll 31 mentions in the sample of a whole year's coverage in six national papers – the highest count. Rogers, Foster, Wren and James

Stirling came after Hackney. Rolland, the RIBA's president at the time, had only five mentions – less than 1 per cent.[4]

To put this in context, 1986 was the year in which the Lloyd's Building, the Hong Kong and Shanghai Bank and the Stuttgart Neuestaatsgalerie – all major, established, newsworthy buildings for big institutions – were completed, with the huge 'New Architecture: Foster Rogers Stirling' exhibition at the Royal Academy – a radical expression of arts establishment confidence in contemporary architecture, given the assumed climate of opinion – timed to coincide. These events, unusually at the time, did get coverage (but nothing like the volume of coverage they would have got in 2000, when even the Stirling Prize was broadcast live on prime-time TV).

The RA show was actually a turning point. Set against the still-current consensus on failure of architecture, it was a huge and calculated show of confidence in modern architecture (managed, incidentally, by two journalists: Simon Jenkins of *The Times* and Deyan Sudjic of the *Guardian*). It did mark a shift in what was deemed public opinion, and it did establish the new star system that continues to dominate the mainstream media's coverage of UK architecture in the new millennium – the stars being the iconic, newsworthy representatives of the profession.

In the 1986 sample, however, 36 per cent of the architects who received more than ten mentions were actually dead, historical figures being, on the whole, far better known than living ones. A whole raft of other figures made no significant showing at all, despite the emergence of several new waves of design styles and trends, such as deconstruction, then booming in the design press and eminently 'newsworthy' in designerly terms for its physical drama alone. Le Corbusier's paltry four mentions speaks for itself.

## An unusual level of influence

Specialist journalists in all types of subject areas tend to have a high level of belief in their own autonomy. But they are, as media research shows, not only compromised (like all journalists) by the values of the media they work in and by a strong, shared mutual agenda, but also (like lobby correspondents) by a powerful dependence on the people and institutions they're reporting on – because they need them as a regular source of information.[5]

This is hardly good grounds for impartial reporting in any case. But architectural journalists were,[6] in terms of media research, not only extreme in the extent to which this operated, but almost unprecedented – in terms of media research – in the extent to which they deliberately used this system.

This is an exaggeration of normal specialist journalist tendencies. Architectural correspondents believed they had more freedom than other journalists, often because their editors knew so little about architecture. But analysis of the survey of newspaper coverage showed that they stuck even closer to the strict demands of general news values and the editorial policies of their paper than in the general run of non-specialist coverage about architecture. Perhaps lack of editorial subject expertise made it more essential to conform to strict news values to make sure the stories 'made the papers'.

But beyond this, the world in which the journalists operated was tiny. Architectural journalism even now does not necessarily or ideally provide a full-time day job, and is often dovetailed with several other activities: teaching, PR, working for practices, working on exhibitions, writing books, etc. All this tends to compromise impartial reporting, as working relationships and friendships are built up with the architects you are writing about. It was – and still is – a career structure centred on a small, tight series of social and working networks or relationships. This is, of course, not overtly expressed in the written articles or declared as an interest, but it inevitably affects the coverage. It's a classic media effect – but in architecture it's unusually extreme.

But this heightened version of a normal specialist bias producing a tightly managed, narrow agenda with large levels of unseen influence was, in the 1980s, put in the shade by a very specific and deliberate use of it. SAVE Britain's Heritage was a campaigning group of conservation journalists who had a virtual monopoly on specialised architectural coverage in UK newspapers during the mid- and late '80s. The editor of *Country Life*, the architectural correspondent of the *Daily Telegraph* and the *Financial Times*, the anonymous 'Piloti' in *Private Eye* (the satirical magazine that was a major source of gossip for all other journalists) were all leading members of SAVE, as were other leading architectural writers. These weren't papers with the highest circulations, but they had a particular status as source material for other newspapers – and indeed for powerful institutions and the 'great and the good'.

The SAVE campaigners were unusual in analysing their position and using it deliberately to admirable effect. They had begun as outsiders in the '70s after the demolition of the Euston Arch and were instrumental in saving the seventeenth-century Huguenot weavers' area in Spitalfields on the edge of London's big-bucks financial district. By the '80s, many of their arguments had been won, and their technique was immaculate.

As they were all friends and co-members of SAVE, consensus was frequent and easily established. It was, of course, almost inevitable that their highly significant and influential articles – all aimed at the decision-makers – would argue the same points, though with different voices and bylines, and with no apparent connection between them.

Given the tiny volume of specialised architectural coverage, what looked like a national consensus, as far as the normal media understanding went – comprising the opinions of almost the full range of independent specialists – was in fact the organised

**143** | Naturally biased

Scandal, controversy and disaster. Architects thought that these kinds of newsworthy images were the only thing that got the media interested. In fact, openings, exhibitions and launches were far more frequent subjects.

opinions of a very small group of people. The high quality of the writing and the usual policy of allowing the art critic free aesthetic reign ensured the status of their views. They skilfully pulled off a series of media coups and may in fact have been key in establishing a broad underlying consensus on conservation as an inherent part of the assumed 'public opinion'. It was a feat that media researchers at the time considered unprecedented.

## Other voices

Despite what looked like a fairly random and sparse group of 'architectural sources' using the media to put across their views, many people were making active use of the state of media coverage of architecture in the '80s, and in increasingly sophisticated and organised ways. But this shift in awareness and sophistication actually operated against the more 'oppositional' sources – and increasingly reinforced the influence of big and powerful organisations.

Despite disingenuous claims about the impartiality of news values, the vast majority of 'events' that sparked media coverage of architecture were *organised*, and usually by those with the money and influence to do so. Openings, exhibitions and launches of buildings overwhelmingly outweighed disasters, controversy and scandal. These of course were planned events arranged by big institutions.[7] The received wisdom among architects concerning news coverage of their subject – that it only showed buildings falling down or being blown up – was way off the mark.

There were, however, a number of 'oppositional' sources – usually pressure groups that were actively using the media to pursue some kind of campaign – the quintessential example of public action through the media. But in the architectural coverage of the time, the most visible of these oppositional voices was the Prince of Wales. His deliberate use of 'shock tactics', in media terms (making an unexpected statement), was consistent with his odd role as self-appointed representative of public opinion. His views, usually phrased in well-chosen, soundbite quotes, were widely repeated in controversial cases such as Paternoster Square, the National Gallery and the Mansion House schemes – and apparently or allegedly (this would be well-nigh impossible to prove) swung many decisions in controversial planning cases round to his side.

But Prince Charles, a quintessential establishment figure, was of course hardly a true representative of 'oppositional' campaigning. It was exactly his establishment position that brought him his media platform and punch. And in many cases his role as people's champion was, arguably, massively compromised by this position. He could not, for example, attack the developers of Paternoster Square for overdevelopment – as some people believed he would have liked to do – only for the style of the architecture. (The Classical redesign that he backed was in fact of a far higher density of commercial use than the previous, more Modernist development had allowed.) Nor, of course, was he likely to speak out on behalf of those trying to stop the demolition of listed buildings at Covent Garden when the developer was the Royal Opera House, of which he was the patron. He had powerful influence, generously given and heavily curtailed by his extraordinary establishment position. But during the '90s he was also handicapped, in media terms (in the middle of the decade, at least) by continuing to say the same thing. As the '90s wore on, the media agenda – increasingly favourable to new development and new architecture – overtook him and left him behind.

## The battle to the strong

Prince Charles and specialist journalists were key but maverick players in a significant change in the activity of the sources in the mid-'80s architectural coverage. This change was the shifting power play between (normally local) pressure groups that sought to use the media to change policy or decisions on specific issues or projects and major property developers. Developers also sought media support for their activities, but by attempting to engineer positive coverage from positions of influence – using 'editorial influence', effectively covert, rather than staging newsworthy events or overt campaigns. Indeed, their activities were often said to be connected with suppression of media coverage, and hence were difficult – especially if successful – to trace or assess.

During the 1960s and 1970s, some of the independent pressure groups had, through extraordinary and determined campaigning, won some significant policy battles. Many were still active in the '80s, during the period of this study; but as developers grew more sophisticated and large-scale commercial development became more established, their ability both to get coverage and to score any influence was waning.

High levels of direct influence were often cited as reasons for the failure of media events staged by pressure groups, a claim that is difficult to test (for example, the non-appearance on television of filmed coverage of the invasion by a flock of sheep of a meeting at an early stage in the Canary Wharf development). Nonetheless, the opinion of the veteran protest group leaders was often that developers were getting more sophisticated and more influential in pulling the media round to their side.

A very specific factor certainly swung the support of the specialised media increasingly behind the developers. The mid-'80s saw the growth of the sophisticated developer patron – Peter Palumbo, Stuart Lipton, Trevor Osborne and others – who began to actively seek world-class architects and artists for their schemes. This managed to shift their role in architectural coverage from mere 'commercial developers' to admired patrons. It also, significantly, tended to mean that the core agenda of specialist coverage was inherently in favour of their developments.

The most famous and revealing examples of this shifting power play in the mid- to late '80s were concentrated in two big cases.[8] One was a campaign that lasted throughout the 1980s. The Covent Garden Community Association, the architect-led group that had so famously and successfully campaigned in the '70s to prevent the demolition of Covent Garden to make way for a major inner city road, now fought the extension of the Royal Opera House via further development of shops. Commercial development had been tightly limited by the area plan that had been set up after the association's initial successful campaign to protect the buildings and the inner city residential and working community.

This extraordinary campaign involved many of the key sources – specialist journalists, the Prince of Wales, architects and major developers – and explains a large amount of the use of media in such complex and influential cases in the late '80s. But it is particularly interesting also in comparison with the other huge case, which preceded and to some extent prefigured it. This case also involved many of the main issues and players: developers, the conservation lobby, specialist journalists, the Prince of Wales, architectural quality, development policy, principles of conservation. This was the massive, long-running set-piece battle of development versus conservation that ran from the 1960s to the '90s in the City of London: the Mansion House redevelopment.

## St George and the dragon: Mansion House

In 1962, Peter Palumbo, a young developer with a powerful and sophisticated taste for modern architecture, had bought a site by the Mansion House, near the Bank of England, and commissioned Mies van der Rohe, one of the world's greatest modern architects, to build what would have been the architect's first building in the UK. It was to be a classic Miesian steel-and-glass office tower, set in a plaza formed by clearing some of the Victorian buildings on the site. The plaza would thus be framed by the Mansion House itself, which was designed by George Dance, and by other Lutyens, Dance and Street buildings: an unusually distinguished architectural ensemble. A poll of public opinion showed 70 per cent in favour of the scheme. Planning permission was granted – conditional on Palumbo buying the rest of the site.

But that took twenty years. By then the UK was at the height of its reaction to all things Modernist – and high-rise in particular. Mies, from being one of the greatest architects in the world, was now considered beyond redemption. Moreover, the conservation movement, now extremely influential, was rallying around the preservation of the remaining Victorian buildings on the site. When Palumbo reapplied for the planning permission, which had expired, it was refused.

Palumbo appealed against the rejection, and a public inquiry was called, which started in April 1984 and lasted almost three months. It was a set-piece battle of its era, with national and specialist press in attendance – indeed, the weekly trade paper *Building Design* ran a regular column from the courtroom.

Each side brought forward a large number of expert witnesses. The conservationists argued, as Marcus Binney (SAVE's chairman) reported in *The Times*, that the

**147** | Naturally biased

Mies van der Rohe's original, never-to-be-built Mansion House scheme for Peter Palumbo. This photo shows how the scheme would have opened up a new plaza, framed by the distinguished buildings around it.

building would be 'neither novel nor innovatory, inappropriate for its site and would be deeply unpopular with members of the public'.[9] And that it would involve demolition of a group of listed buildings, some admittedly 'mediocre', but which taken together made up a part of the medieval street pattern of the City of London and an essential part of its fabric. They also argued passionately that, whatever the quality of the new building, the principle of conserving listed buildings was sacrosanct.

Against this, Palumbo and his supporters argued that the demolition of 'second rate' buildings would enhance the better buildings on the site, that the new buildings would be 'a masterpiece of the modern movement which would be one of the most thrilling perspectives in the city', and that the preservation of the existing group of buildings under these circumstances would 'put the City of London in pickle as a Dickensian Disneyland'.[10]

As a set-piece battle, this had intriguing characteristics. Both sides were trying to pull in as many establishment figures as they could to their side (Foster, Rogers and Stirling all supported Palumbo, for example) – and not always as expert witnesses. Palumbo's appeal to Mrs Thatcher to intervene was 'exposed' by the conservation journalists as a devious move, while they themselves overtly publicised their own telegrammed appeal to the Prince of Wales in Venice to intervene on their behalf:

'British architecture needs your help ... The Mies van der Rohe stump is likely to be approved by the government ... another word from you, Sir, at this crucial time, could help save London.'[11]

Interestingly, media supporters of both sides also sought, to different extents, to cast themselves in the weaker and more romantic role: the role with particular popular and media appeal. Martin Pawley, the *Guardian*'s correspondent, one of the few architectural correspondents not in SAVE and who supported the Mies scheme, noted 'the defence of Victorian architecture by women of 35 or under' as adding the 'damsel' into the George and dragon scenario. Revealingly, he added his own romantic, post-Ayn Rand version of the other side: 'the young patron, the dying architect, the great city, the malevolent critics, the final masterpiece ... an architectural epic ... I could not see how the conservationists, who were clearly having an adventure of their own, could fail ... to be moved by the romance of this.'[12]

Perhaps the role of the damsels in representing SAVE had an additional interpretation. With the exception of Marcus Binney, chairman and editor of *Country Life*, the journalists on SAVE, though all established architectural historians and writers, did not, it seemed, appear as witnesses in court. Critically, this meant they were able to go on reporting the case as specialists without calling their affiliation into question.

The Mies scheme was refused permission in April 1985. But if Palumbo had been determined to win before, he was more so now. He commissioned James Stirling to design another scheme, and reapplied for planning permission with a smaller volume of demolition. He was again refused planning permission. And the case again went back to a public inquiry.

Palumbo himself acknowledged in an interview that the Stirling scheme was not nearly such a good building as the Mies building.[13] But it was far more applicable to the 'consensus' of opinion of its times. This is something of a curiosity: Stirling, though great, was a 'difficult' architect, and this was by no means his best building. But his Staatsgalerie in Stuttgart was seen as friendly and popular, and the new building was loosely Post-Modern, with historical references, and followed the medieval street lines. It is easy to imagine that Palumbo was playing a clever end-game with public opinion.

Whether the economic, political or planning mood had changed, or the relative merits of Palumbo and the conservationists to establish themselves as representatives of the mood of the age or of public opinion; whether Palumbo had become more sophisticated in handling the media, whether Palumbo had become more influential (he had become head of the Arts Council in 1989); whether the conservationists were suffering a media backlash because of trying to run the same media campaign twice – the outcome was different. The quality of the building, apparently dismissed in the earlier inquiry, was overtly taken into account as a 'material consideration' in determining that the listed buildings might be demolished.

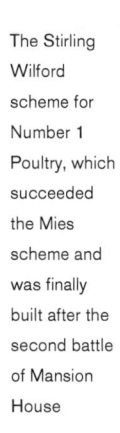

The Stirling Wilford scheme for Number 1 Poultry, which succeeded the Mies scheme and was finally built after the second battle of Mansion House

Historically, there is not much question that Palumbo's assessment is right. The Mies scheme – especially in its planning and opening up of a real plaza in the City – was of exceptional quality; the Stirling – though its rooftop garden has extraordinary and surreal qualities – does not have the same urban scope and does not, of its kind, hit the same architectural heights. But it was, absolutely critically, deemed more acceptable of its time. Palumbo's matching of the type of architecture to the perceived spirit of the age got the scheme through planning on this attempt. The conservation issues were, in principle, almost exactly the same.

In a last lovely twist, Palumbo preserved the cupola of the demolished Mappin and Webb building that was at the heart of the site. It now sits, like a traitor's head on a spike, in the garden of the Farnsworth House, Mies's masterpiece glass house in Plano, Illinois, which Palumbo owns.

## David and Goliath: the Royal Opera House

The Mansion House affair was a staged set-piece battle that was re-enacted over a shifting political and architectural culture. The Royal Opera House case, which overlapped with it, continues and expounds its description of the same terrain.

In 1986, the Royal Opera House announced its plan to build an extension of its backstage facilities on land that had been granted to it in 1974 by the Labour government. To fund this, it proposed to build a substantial commercial development – shops, offices and an underground carpark – as well as the backstage facilities and only 13 extra seats for the auditorium. The development was to be designed by Jeremy Dixon, with Bill Jack of BDP, in a manner partly Modernist, but with a deliberately part-historicist exterior that completed the colonnade on the north side of the plaza. All this required a specific 'relaxation' of the Covent Garden area plan, which restricted commercial development. It also required permission to demolish twenty buildings, five of them listed, including the Grade I dramatic iron-and-glass Barry structure, the Floral Hall.

The proposal was submitted for planning approval, but was hotly opposed by the Covent Garden Community Association, the local campaigning group that had so successfully opposed demolition of the market for a six-lane motorway in the 1970s. The CGCA argued that the proposal was counter to the intention of the gift of the land for arts purposes and that it breached the area plan, which specifically restricted commercial development and protected the conservation area. The Opera House argued that it was the only viable way to fund the extension of backstage facilities, and that the scheme was good in itself, 'repairing the urban fabric of the square'.

From the start, this case involved a bundle of contentious issues. The ROH had been heavily criticised for its elitism, its huge proportion of Arts Council funding and its high ticket prices. The area was enormously popular and well known, and the campaigners were veterans: a known pressure group with some good journalistic contacts, dealing with a major scheme and challenging a famous institution in a very well-known location, and who were prepared to work fiercely and determinedly at their campaign.

But the ROH was at the very heart of the establishment, and as such it already had control of all of the key weapons available to both sides in the Mansion House case. Its patron was the Prince of Wales, so there was little chance that the CGCA would win his significant support (in fact, they did write asking for a meeting, but their request was turned down). Lord Sainsbury, the leading client-developer and supermarket owner, was at the head of the ROH board. The head of the National Trust was its director-general. And one of the key architectural critics, and SAVE's leading light, was its architectural adviser. The powerful conservation lobby was clearly unlikely to side with the protestors.

Moreover, the ROH was able – and well-informed enough – to use the ultimate weapon for ensuring good coverage: the commissioning of an architect likely to get the critics on its side. Indeed, the then press officer of the ROH described, in an interview, the choice of Jeremy Dixon, a contextual Modernist with excellent historical credentials, liked and respected by architectural critics, as containing 'a degree of cynicism'.[14]

Westminster Council deferred granting permission, asking for more information to be 'absolutely sure that the commercial redevelopment is the only way of achieving the ROH's aims'. CGCA repeatedly lobbied the Opera House and Westminster, and attempted to get the unlisted buildings on the site listed. The ROH submitted a revised scheme, retaining two of the listed buildings and re-styling the Modernist corner of the proposal in a more traditional style.

Notable among the ROH's publicity was a series of images of the scheme by the artist Carl Laubin. Unlike then-conventional architectural representations, these were paintings that showed the plaza occupied – by street performers, jesters, passers-by. The buildings, though shown in detail, were represented as though in a historical painting – though the painting was set up originally with computer graphics (overleaf). It was an overt presentation to a tradition-loving public, and was a technique that was to be used later in other controversial cases, such as the Classical Paternoster Square redevelopment.

In June 1986, CGCA produced an alternative scheme for the site with a much reduced commercial element, retaining many of the buildings and adding an open-air auditorium. (Later, CGCA 's failure was attributed by one journalist to their not engaging a big-name architect to work up the association's proposals, an interesting and possibly valid comment.) CGCA also lobbied the first ROH outdoor screening – an attempt to mitigate its reputation for elitism by broadcasting the opera live to a free audience in the plaza – with fake programme leaflets. CGCA won a fair amount of press coverage throughout their campaign. Nevertheless, Westminster granted provisional permission for the scheme in June 1987, saying 'the ROH have demonstrated [… that the scheme] represents the only means of financing the essential improvements to the ROH'.

CGCA then took the ROH to court, claiming that the use of commercial development to fund permitted schemes was not legitimate grounds for contravening planning restrictions – particularly as the ROH, rather than the public, would benefit. But the court ruled that the profits were a material consideration. CGCA commissioned a series of financial reports challenging the ROH's financial calculations and calling for a full financial investigation into the scheme. But a subcommittee of English Heritage nonetheless granted conditional approval for the demolition of the Floral Hall, the ROH refused to produce its financial calculations, and the appeal was rejected.

Then on 6 February 1989, the *Guardian* published a front-page, exclusive story, titled 'Opera in Disneyland', quoting leaked documents based on minutes of meetings between ROH and Westminster and between the ROH and its solicitors. These documents claimed that the ROH, while still fighting for the original scheme,

Carl Laubin's computer-generated but historicist paintings of the Royal Opera House redevelopment by Jeremy Dixon, Edward Jones and BDP. The images are eerily similar to the final building.

was planning to abandon it and was considering (among other things) plans for a 'Mid-West Pleasure Emporium' with 'Theme Cafes'. They hoped that the original scheme would get planning permission and that subsequent changes could be treated as 'change of use'. The article also claimed that the documents showed that the government had granted £2.6 million to buy extra land for the revised proposal at a cheaper price than the market value – which went against Treasury guidelines. The PSA objected to the cheaper price, but the Treasury overruled it, the article claimed.[15]

The scoop, by the political journalist David Hencke, made major, worldwide news in the press, radio and TV, and the effects were immediate. English Heritage refused outline permission for demolition of the Floral Hall and recommended that the DoE call in the planning application. Questions were asked in the House of Commons. And still the scheme was not called in.

The ROH continued to revise its plans. The cultural-building-commissioning tide was on the turn – arguably even over this building. The principle of public-private funding for the arts – of art institutions funding themselves off the back of commercial development – had become established. Moreover, it was overtaken by the establishment of the National Lottery, with its specific first remit to fund building projects for arts organisations. The lottery's award of major funding to the ROH allowed the office element to be removed from the scheme altogether. The final scheme, which involved retaining half the Floral Hall, relocated as a first-floor atrium with a mirrored back to suggest its original dimensions, opened in 1999.

The use of the architecture as a campaign tool had been prescient. Funding an arts building from commercial development was potentially still contentious – but not if the building itself was such as to win critical (and presumably, or therefore) public approval. From the original choice of architects to the oil-paintings targeted at the public (though both seemed unnecessarily cautious by the standards of the far more pro-Modernist atmosphere of 1999), the ROH campaign placed itself well to turn the media situation to its advantage.

In effect, CGCA managed a huge delaying tactic – something for which Jeremy Dixon was later to thank them, because the climate and funding situation improved radically for such partially commercial, high-profile arts buildings over the next ten years until the project was finished in 1999.

In retrospect – in media terms – this case could be seen as the turning point of a battle in which the notion of direct action by community organisations became downgraded, or possibly regarded as 'nimbyism', while mixed commercial funding for arts organisations because established, as was the specific use of a specific kind of architecture to ensure a good public reception – through its critical reception by specialist journalists.

### The case for conspiracy theories

In these two cases there is little doubt that media systems did not provide fair, impartial coverage of their subject matter. They provided tools for powerful interested parties to use. This is, of course, linked directly to the workings of power, policy and influence in any era. But though the individual organisations and the nature of the power may change, some version of this intricate network of personal and official connections between the media, individual journalists and individual campaigners seems likely to persist in whatever form is available.

This does not mean that the journalists or the editorial policies of papers or other media organisations are deliberately misleading people. Specialist journalists see part of their job as putting forward their opinion, and they do so. But their opinion is heavily compromised – first by the values of the system in which it is generated, and then by personal or professional constraints within it.

These factors are not usually secret. If a journalist has a particular working or personal relationship with any particular architect – and most of them do, because this is the society in which they live and work – it is usually well known within the small circles in which they operate. It is, of course, not at all apparent to the wider audience. Conspiracy theories tend to evaporate at close quarters. But such theories provide a useful, even essential, framework for recognising the powerful existence and influence of these sorts of patterns in all media output.

**The role of the media**

From the point of view of the architectural journalistic profession, it is hard not to see the publicity of architecture in the UK national press over the last ten years as a massive success story. Effectively, journalists and the media have done some sort of equivalent version of what architects fifteen years ago were saying the media should do. Public consciousness of architecture has been raised. A beachhead has been established whereby modern architecture has become acceptable. Most significant, the media have probably been at least partly complicit in a public confidence that has permitted the major buildings funded by the National Lottery and the Millennium Commission.

But these two cases certainly showed that the media were not an impartial tool for representation and even negotiation of controversial media issues. At all levels, the media have a loaded system of values, tending to cut out some issues and promote others – from the political to the personal. And the reasons for doing this, though often fairly well understood inside the media, at whichever scale, are simply not obvious or easily available to the audience, and the apparent informality and reactive way in which the media work masks what are actually powerfully, naturally biased tendencies.

In the media coverage studied here, we have seen the triumph of the aesthetic, and that is in itself revealing. Architecture, sometimes thought of as the whore of power, is an attractive legitimising front for all sorts of policy. What we have seen in the UK in the last fifteen years is the development of a powerful system with which our professional and aesthetic values – those of the media and those of the architectural hierarchy – totally concur. We like what is beautiful and well made, whatever it is. Social and programmatic issues are put to the back of the debate. While there is a strong argument that this permits a far more liberal, far higher quality architectural situation than has been seen in this country for some time, it is also dangerous. We are tied, more firmly than ever, into the legitimisation of the production of new buildings – which the media are anyway currently slanted to support.

## Notes

1. This essay is adapted from my PhD thesis, *Architecture and the Media* (1990), which I researched at the postgraduate research school in the school of architecture at what was then Oxford Polytechnic, in collaboration with the Centre for Mass Communications Research at Leicester University. In particular, the arguments on media research are taken directly from this original research and expanded much more fully there.
2. The prince's publications were numerous. Principal amongst them were the TV programme *A Vision of Britain* (BBC1, 18 September 1989) and the accompanying book.
3. In my research I looked at every copy of *The Times*, *Guardian*, *Observer*, *Daily Mail*, *Daily Mirror* and *News of the World* published during 1986, and I evolved a detailed coding system to record and analyse all coverage of architectural issues by architectural or any other journalists appearing anywhere in the editorial section of the paper. In the light of what is to follow, it is worth noting that the mainstream left-wing papers are actually over-represented here, so the analysis is not merely a sample of a press which is – and was more so in the mid-1980s – volumetrically right-wing.
4. The poll included key design figures who were not architects as well as those who were and were as follows: Hackney, 31 mentions; Rogers, 27; Foster, 21; Wren, 21; Stirling, 19; Adam (historical), 19; Lutyens, 12; Palumbo, 12; 'Capability' Brown (landscape), 11; Terence Conran, 11; Mies van der Rohe, 11; Barratts (house builders), 10; Farrell, 8; Casson, 7; Burton (hist.), 8; Dixon, 8: Inigo Jones, 6; Nash, 6; Powell & Moya, 6; Sam Webb, 6; Robert Venturi, 6; Raymond Andrews, 5; Barry (hist.), 5; Rolland, 5; Wyatt (hist.), 5; BDP, 4; Leon Krier, 4; Le Corbusier, 4; CZWG, 4; Mackintosh, 4; Michael Manser, 4; Humphry Repton (landsc.), 4; Travelstead (dev.), 4. Thirteen other names had 3 mentions; 26 names had 2; and 188 other names had 1. The privileging of news over architectural values is seen most sharply in the different coverage of Mies and Le Corbusier: Mies, though less fashionable at the time, was 'in the news' over Mansion House; Le Corbusier was not.
5. Jeremy Tunstall's *Journalists At Work* (London: Constable, 1971), though now 30 years old, was a key source for this part of the work. Other key sources included Steve Chibnall's *Law and Order News: An Analysis of Crime Reporting in the British Press* (London: Tavistock, 1977) and Philip Schlesinger, 'Rethinking the Sociology of Journalism: Source Strategies and the limits of Centrism', in Ferguson, *Public Communications: The New Imperatives* (London: Sage, 1989).
6. In all, 36 people were interviewed, of whom 20 operated as architectural journalists in some way; others represented source organisations such as the major institutions mentioned and pressure groups. Eleven were regular contributors to the national press at the time of the study.
7. The actual figures for the most frequent 'activating events' were: opening of building, 10.2 per cent; sale of building, 9.6 per cent; pressure group action, 7.4 per cent; planning permission, 6.2 per cent; scheme announcement, 5.8 per cent; exhibition, 5.6

per cent; and so on. Disasters (treated as a broad term) accounted for only 3.3 per cent and was twelfth on the list. Most stories were regular or deliberately organised official events.

8   These case studies were developed through wider examination of press coverage of the cases in question and other documentation (letters, etc.) relating to them, along with detailed interviews with many of the key figures.
9   Quoted in Jan Burney, 'Mansion House Diary', *Building Design* (13 July 1984).
10  Quoted in Burney, 'Mansion House Diary'.
11  'The End is Nigh', *The Architects' Journal* (15 May 1985), p. 4.
12  Martin Pawley, 'Of Mies and Men's Inspiration', *Guardian* (13 August 1984).
13  Interview with Peter Palumbo, the Arts Council, 6 June 1989.
14  Interview with Ewen Balfour, ROH, 23 May 1989.
15  David Hencke, 'Opera in Disneyland', *Guardian* (6 February 1989).

Chapter 12
# The architectural book
Image and accident
**Alan Powers**



The printed book was used to communicate architecture as soon as it became available in the late fifteenth century, and is still being used today. Its dominance may be threatened by new types of medium, but some of its characteristics are likely to be copied in the other media that may replace it. For the time being, no other medium confers such intellectual respectability, whatever its shortcomings may be for communication.

If books have influenced the way that architecture is perceived and discussed, then architect-authors in turn have made interesting experiments in making books. This essay concentrates on the genre of book in which a body of design by an individual or a practice is presented while it is still current, partly no doubt for self-promotion, but also for other motives. An architect will often have a message to deliver in relation to the work, ranging from a complete theory of architecture to a subliminal gloss. The hybrid nature of these books allows of emphasis falling towards theory or practice record, but in the most notable examples, from Palladio's *I Quattro Libri* to OMA, Rem Koolhaas and Bruce Mau's *S,M,L,XL* (1995), there is a remarkable consistency of intention.

Such works are not as common as might be supposed, for many architects choose never to make the transition into making books, or lack the opportunity. The existence of such books has, however, strongly influenced the way that architectural history has developed.

Palladio's *I Quattro Libri dell'Architettura,* published in Venice in 1570, came nearly a hundred years after Johannes Gutenberg's first printed book. Prior to it were printed editions of Vitruvius, Alberti and Serlio, but while in some ways impure in its content, it presented a new mixture of fact, imagination and record. It was not Palladio's first book, as he had already published his guide to the antiquities and churches of Rome in 1554. He had also been familiarised with the process of producing illustrated books when preparing the illustrations for Barbaro's *Vitruvius* of 1556. Like Serlio's text, the written part *of I Quattro Libri* speaks with the voice of the practitioner addressing his fellows, although in such a way as to benefit the patron as well. Its theoretical assumptions are more implicit in the contents and layout than explicit in the words of the text, and in this way it exemplifies aspects of the architectural book

Title page from Palladio's
*I Quattro Libri* (1570)

Johann Bernhard Fisher von Erlach, Dinocrates, Colossus of Mount Athos, from *Entwurf einer historischen Arkitektur* (1721)

that have persisted to the present: its basis in executed work and its close relationship of text and image composed in spreads or on a single page.

The *Quattro Libri* also edits the visual information about Palladio's villas by showing them in idealised form as completed structures, when many had only been partially built, and others, such as the Villa Sarego near Verona, were never intended to extend as far as the woodcut illustrations indicated, even if they had been completed. The text slides over these inconsistencies without commentary. Some aspects of Palladio's work, such as his churches, are completely omitted, while works of antiquity, or buildings emulating them, are included, such as the plate in book IV showing Bramante's Tempietto of San Pietro in Montorio.

The printed record of Palladio's work has therefore taken on a life of its own, inevitably far more potent than a few dozen buildings in the Veneto could ever be. Its wide dissemination made it a model for architectural publishing, particularly in the English-speaking world. Its form was not imitated exactly, but this creation of a world that is imaginary but still rooted in reality is part of the fascination of architectural books, particularly those that allow fact and fantasy to exist side by side. The category of book that presents an architect's work alongside text or images to suggest what the work could become, beyond the boundaries of space and economic reality, extends the range of architectural creativity.

*I Quattro Libri* offers a seductive combination of text and image, of the real and unreal. Other types of book have historically included records and restorations of antiquity, manuals of the orders, pattern books, books of imaginary designs, and purely theoretical texts, including editions of Vitruvius. Sometimes these genres are mixed with each other, perhaps with the intention of inserting an architect's own work into the canon of history, as was done openly in the fourth book of Johann Bernhard Fischer von Erlach's *Entwurf einer historischen Architektur*, 1721, in which his own designs are shown in the context of the wonders of the ancient world and a remarkable range of images of Islamic and Chinese architecture, the first of their kind to cross over from topography to architectural literature. As Hanno-Walter Kruft writes, 'Fischer's concern was … to create a Holy Roman Imperial architecture for the Hapsburgs in which history gave his own designs legitimation and continuity.'[1]

Many of the architectural books which have become historical reference points were less the result of careful planning and forethought than of accidental collaborations between different parties. Architects themselves are seldom natural authors, and the subject itself, from Vitruvius onwards, tends to pull in so many contrary directions that books were prone to inconsistencies unless their content was carefully controlled. The editor or licensed interpreter became an important if sometimes shadowy figure in the process of creating the idealised reality of the book. Francesco Borromini's *Opus Architectonicum,* apparently prepared in 1658, although only published in 1725, 58 years after Borromini's death, had a text 'ghosted' by his friend and architectural patron, Father Virgilio Spada, even though written in the first person.[2] Sir Christopher Wren's *Parentalia* was edited by his son for posthumous publication and is heterogeneous in content, including biography, theory and verbal and visual descriptions of projects.

Architectural books usually contain a mixture of text and illustration, which is a hybrid way of conveying information, allowing for an interesting slippage between the two components. This was furthered by the nature of printing techniques that, until very recently, favoured a separation of text and pictures, whether the plates were engravings or photographs. Palladio's *I Quattro Libri* used woodcuts for printing the illustrations, and although these were much cruder than the copper engravings that later became universal, owing to their finer quality of line, they had the advantage that the pictures and text could be printed together in one operation. The engraving of plates was an expensive investment, but they had a long life and could also be issued independently of the book. For anyone wishing to skip reading the text, they certainly offered an attractive experience of browsing.

The complex pre-publication history of the most famous eighteenth-century architectural book, *Vitruvius Britannicus,* shows how architectural polemic and commercial opportunism could operate hand in hand. Although the Scottish architect Colen Campbell is famous as the author of the first three volumes, published between 1715 and 1725, Eileen Harris and Nicholas Savage have demonstrated that he was not involved until a late stage, when the book (conceived more as a topographical record than as a collection of designs) was already far advanced in the hands of three publishers.[3] The announcement of the imminent publication of Giacomo Leoni's first English translation of *Palladio* then threatened to make much of its material seem out of date.

A great investment had already been made in *Vitruvius Britannicus,* and it had to be saved from failure. This was achieved by interpolating the plates of Campbell's pure Neo-Palladian designs at significant points in the course of the book, so that, for example, the plates of Wanstead House appeared immediately after the designs of Inigo Jones. The new style affected not only the architecture itself, but also the conventions for its presentation. Orthographic projections alone were acceptable, and perspective plates already engraved of Greenwich, Castle Howard and Chatsworth were displaced into Volume III, even though the elevations and plans of these buildings appeared in Volume I.

Harris and Savage take their detective work further in positing that the lack of engravers' names on the plates in the first volume was the result of the need to employ a larger team of engravers to work at speed in getting the new plates finished, so that the name of the engraver Henry Hulsbergh was deleted from the other plates in case the haste should look too obvious. In addition, Campbell contributed an introductory text which castigated the Baroque and whetted readers' appetites for the plates of Inigo Jones's Whitehall Palace in the second volume, published in 1717. This was important because of the hope that the accession of King George I in 1714 and the formation of a Whig administration in 1715 might bring about the building of a new royal palace in London. The strange discrepancy of the third volume, which combines plates of Campbell's work with plates of gardens with which he had no association or polemical engagement, is explained by Harris and Savage as the result of Campbell being superseded in the Palladian fashion by Lord Burlington and William Kent.

Inigo Jones, whose designs in Burlington's collection were prepared for engraving by Kent, and published in 1727, was the great posthumous publishing success of Georgian England. The *Designs of Inigo Jones*, in two volumes, was published only for subscribers, contributing the quality of exclusivity that invested architectural publications as 'positional goods'. Burlington inserted plates of his own designs for Chiswick House and the Dormitory at Westminster School, showing, as *Vitruvius Britannicus* had done, that editorial juxtaposition could be more effective than verbal argument in asserting genealogical affinities between Jones and those who wished to see themselves as his rightful successors.

In eighteenth-century England, with its emergent consumer culture, architectural books can be divided into two classes: on one hand the expensive and luxurious productions which would boost an architect's reputation among potential patrons, and on the other the pattern books and manuals which were designed not only for cheaper production, but in order to contain exactly the 'how to do it' information that was required by builders. Batty Langley, one of the most prominent authors of pattern books, complained that William Kent's *Designs of Inigo Jones* and James Gibbs' books were 'no more Use to Workmen than so many Pictures to gaze at; not so many Rules, or Examples to work by, or after, unless to such who understand the architecture thereof, as well as their Authors who design'd them'.[4]

Gibbs bridged the two worlds of architectural publishing in Georgian England, since his selection of ornamental parts of buildings – notably doorcases, window surrounds and chimneypieces, some of them derived from Inigo Jones – provided exactly the kind of material that was required for reprocessing in the pattern books. Gibbs was the only architect to make a substantial sum of money from architectural publishing in this period.

Robert Adam, coming in a later generation, was acutely conscious of the making and marketing of his professional image. Publication was not necessarily the best way of achieving this, however, since it might make an exclusive style too easy to copy, even though it provided status and advertisement. His early career is full of plans for a project commissioned in 1769 from the draughtsman Charles-Louis Clérisseau and his cousin William Robertson, the author, rather than created by himself, even though his name was prominently displayed. Since the end of the Seven Years' War in 1763, travel in Europe and the Mediterranean was much easier, and expeditions to record ancient sites became competitive. The history of the visit to Spalatro and the subsequent scramble to publish illustrate the symbolic importance that books acquired in the Neo-Classical period, perhaps the first occasion when claims to architectural scholarship might have a direct impact on the success of a practice.

While the Spalatro volume was far from being a work of disinterested scholarship, being at least as much a way of 'positioning' the Adam brothers in the contemporary architectural polemics concerning the respective merits of Greece and Rome, it was not a book of their actual work, something which Robert Adam, the leading brother, had long been reluctant to produce. When he and his brother James came to publish their *Works in Architecture* in 1778, they were responding to a crisis in their own careers. They had announced such a book several times, but explained their reluctance to actually proceed with it in terms of the loss of exclusivity which it might imply. Sight of their drawings, in the gloriously coloured original, was a privilege reserved for potential clients only. Furthermore, Robert believed that English engravers were inadequate for the task; or perhaps, as Harris and Savage suggest, he was afraid that unauthorised copies of the images would be made as they passed through the engraver's shop.

Harris and Savage explain that the announcement of the publication of *Works in Architecture* came at a time, in 1773, when the brothers, a threesome including John Adam, were faced with bankruptcy following the run on Scottish banks in 1772 and their over-extended credit on the Adelphi scheme. The latter burden was relieved by their expedient of a lottery for the unlet houses in March 1774, but, as Harris and Savage write:

> Any non-financial benefit to be gained by publishing the Adam firm's designs was something about which Robert at least would have needed convincing, and it is not improbable that he was only persuaded to venture on it in earnest by his brothers impressing upon him that here was an asset, like their collections of antiquities and old masters, on which they could sit tight no longer.[5]

The book that resulted was published in instalments, partly because the engraving of more plates, more commonly financed by advance subscriptions, would have delayed its object of immediate effect. The whole procedure is symptomatic of the growth of what the historian Neil McKendrick has identified as the first consumer culture in the second half of the eighteenth century.[6] There was no skimping on the book itself, however, which in the quality of its images (apart from the quality of what they represent) remains one of the most alluring ever published, reflecting as it does their Roman friend Giambattista Piranesi's new standard for atmospheric perspective rendering on a

Gateway to the Admiralty, Whitehall, 1760, from *Works in Architetecture of Robert and James Adam*, Vol. I, part IV, 1773

copper plate, as much as for giving extra liveliness to the rendering of the details, some of them at full size, which contrast with the broader views in each set of houses presented. The plates which Piranesi himself etched in Rome of the entrance hall and antechamber at Syon House take their place among the works of London engravers.

The texts accompanying the plates appear to Harris and Savage as outdated and platitudinous. However, in the opening page of text some five hundred words of main text are sufficient to generate at least two thousand words of footnotes, extending over onto the verso, in a manner that in our own time we might recognise as a sort of hypertext, particularly given the more conversational tone of the notes in contrast to the formal statements of the text.

If the Adams's *Works in Architecture* is a book to dream with, how much more so is Claude-Nicolas Ledoux's *Architecture Considerée sous le Rapport de l'Art, des Moeurs et de la Legislation* (1804), a work planned well before the French Revolution of 1789, but taking its rhetorical quality from that event, which had destroyed Ledoux's practice and might easily have taken his life. The text of Ledoux's book has a reputation of unintelligibility, being similar to the contemporary works of the English poet-painter William Blake, and perhaps better deserved. It might be unkindly described as the first example of genuinely pretentious theoretical writing by an architect, and as such, the precursor of many others.

Ledoux's book seems to signal a substantial move from text to image, of a kind that we have subsequently come fully to accept as natural for architectural books, although it occupies a strange transitional place where a theoretical statement is demanded by the visual material, even if its intellectual consequences are then evaded. As Allan Braham says, the text is strangely at odds with Ledoux's practical and businesslike manner as an architect.[7] The plates, too, have been misleading, in that certain of his early buildings, such as the château of Benouville near Caen, were revised by Ledoux for the engravings, some 35 years later, to appear more Neo-Classical than they were when built. The best-known plates are those for the Ideal City of Chaux, a development from Ledoux's actual project of the Salines Royales at Arc et Senans, in the Jura. Had Ledoux's contemporary Étienne-Louis Boullée published his own *Essai sur l'Art* at the time, it would have demonstrated the possibility of personalised visionary writing grounded in more approachable and reasoned theory and linked to a body of design, presenting a much greater integration of text and pictures than Ledoux's work.[8] Boullée's essay instead remained among the considerable body of unpublished texts in architecture until 1953.

The early years of the nineteenth century in Britain were remarkably productive of architectural books and show the growth of the architectural community beyond its exclusive circle of the eighteenth century. Technology assisted the process, and the content of the majority of architectural books responded accordingly by abandoning the difficulties of theory and using reproductive techniques that would produce the most seductive images of architecture. The subject matter was exclusively domestic, and the target audience was the client, aspiring to gentility, or possibly downsizing from the responsibilities of aristocracy by building an elegant retreat. As John Archer writes of the first of these books, John Plaw's *Rural Architecture,* 1785, 'A thin quarto containing brief descriptions and aquatinted illustrations of villas, cottages, and other small dwellings, it differs markedly from other contemporary publication types.'[9] This launched the genre of the 'villa book' as a recognisable type. Archer also comments on the close link between print medium and content in Plaw's book:

> His generally symmetrical façades, embellished with Neo-Classical ornament, gain added depth and texture because of the wide range of tones and shades made possible by aquatint. Perhaps not coincidentally, his plates were the first in any British architectural book in which landscape was an important part of the entire composition. Aquatint facilitated portrayal of varied textures and shadings in trees, shrubs, lawns and stones, which correspond with similar textures and shadings in elements of a building, thus establishing close relationships between a house and its surrounding landscape.[10]

**165** | The architectural book

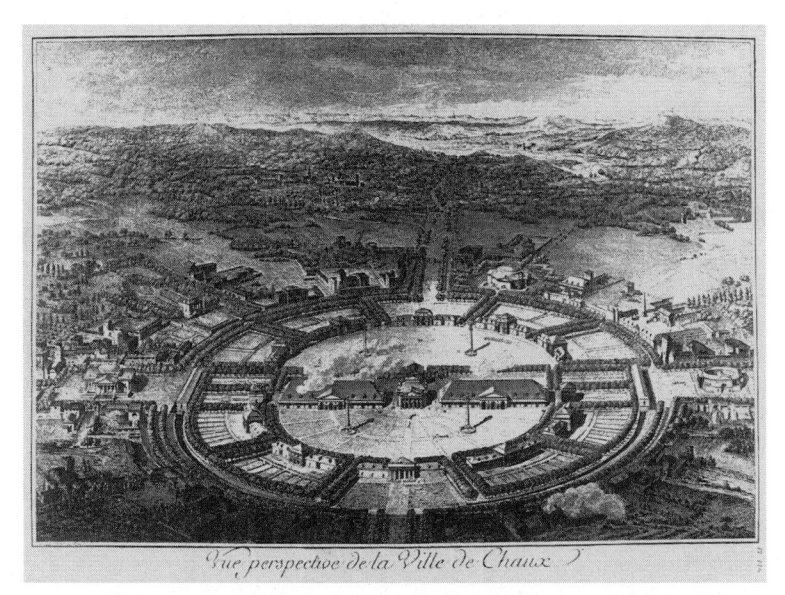

C.N. Ledoux, aerial view of the city of Chaux, from *l'Architecture* (Paris: Edition Ramée, 1847)

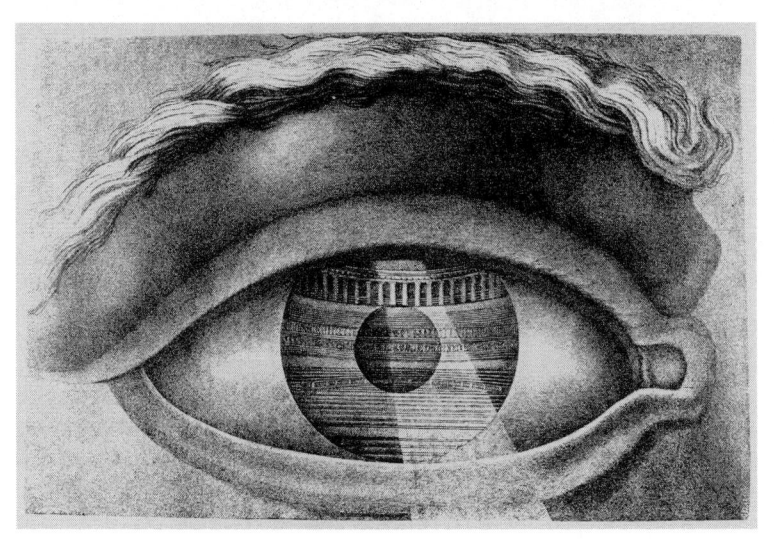

C.N. Ledoux, Besançon, 'Coup-d'oeil générale du théâtre', from *l'Architecture* (Paris: Edition Ramée, 1847)

Humphry Repton, who was himself an accomplished watercolour artist, used books more creatively, perhaps, than any other architect. That these were unique books (Repton's well-known 'Red Books') prepared for clients as a means of presentation of a set of proposals for a country house and its estate, did not diminish their effect. His production of these books began in the late 1780s and continued up to his death in 1818. One must presume, from the success of Repton's practice, that it was an effective method. The relatively small scale, naturally in landscape format, was suitable, perhaps, for passing round a drawing room, and was seemingly angled towards women's involvement in the decision-making process. The books' realistic presentation and the winning *coup de théâtre* involved in lifting the overlaid flaps to reveal a transformed scene correspond to the earliest precursors of the cinema, in the form of devices such as the painter Philip de Loutherburg's *Eidophusikon*, of 1781, a performance of dissolving landscape views with music and sound effects.

The serial nature of books helped Repton to build up a narrative sequence, usually starting with an approach to the estate, then drawing nearer the house, and finally considering the views back along the route and over the immediate surroundings. While rewarding his patrons with this private performance, Repton also understood the value of wider publicity, and between 1789 and 1809 he contributed a series of vignettes of country seats to *Peacock's Polite Repository*. This was an almanac, published annually, and was part of a genre that fuelled middle-class aspirations and consumption. It is therefore fitting that Repton's name, representing almost a brand in landscape and architectural practice, should have been recorded by Jane Austen in *Mansfield Park*.

J.B. Papworth's *Rural Architecture* (1818), was still recognisably in the same genre as Plaw's pioneering work, but included hand colouring. His aquatint plates had been issued during 1816 and 1817 by Rudolph Ackermann in his magazine, *Ackermann's Repository,* and then gathered together in book form. The *Repository* included many coloured plates, as well as real samples of dress textiles, and as such may indicate a turn towards feminisation in architectural publishing, although one which A.W.N. Pugin, both of whose parents worked for Ackermann, did his best to reverse through his own architectural theories and publications from the 1830s onwards.

The picturesque quality of the English villa books seems to have been transferred, to some extent at least, to Karl Friedrich Schinkel's *Sammlung Architektonischer Entwurfe,* also a serial publication, issued between 1819 and 1840. Schinkel's book was one of the first architectural volumes to use lithography, the printing technique that replaced the earlier methods during the course of the nineteenth century. Lithography was favoured by artists for its ability to capture the

**167** | The architectural book

J.B. Papworth, 'A Cottage Orné designed for an exposed or elevated situation', from *Rural Residences* (1818)

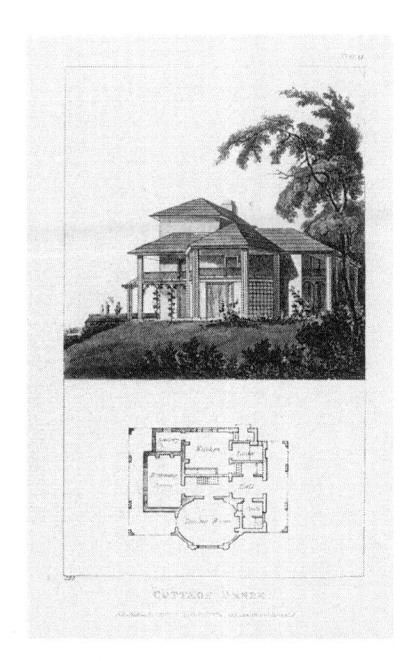

Karl Friedrich Schinkel, perspective of the upper gallery of the Altes Museum, Berlin, from *Sammlung Architectonischer Entwürfe* (1819–40)

spontaneous stroke of the pen, brush or crayon, as seen in the caricatures of Honoré Daumier. These were possible because they were drawn directly onto the lithographic stone, whereas even aquatint required a craftsman's interpretation of an original, through a series of acid bitings of the plate, giving only an illusion of continuously graded tone. Curiously, the artists who drew Schinkel's designs used lithography as a technique of pure line, with results that could equally well have been produced by engraving; but even though the graphic style is cool, the careful rendering of nature and the animated figures create warmth and atmosphere. The plate of the view from the portico of the Altes Museum, Berlin, exemplifies the way that the figures themselves take the eye from point to point as one follows their gazes and gesticulations. Schinkel's early experience as a theatrical designer, and the effect on him of the popular dioramas of the period, had prepared him in the use of compositional framing and illusions of perspectival depth. In theory, the plates of the *Sammlung* would have lent themselves to hand colouring, but there is no evidence that this was ever considered.

The *Sammlung* is primarily pictorial and descriptive, and Schinkel reserved his theoretical text for an unpublished *Architektonischer Lehrbuch*. With the breakdown of the unity of Renaissance theory in the long-drawn-out gestation of Neo-Classicism from Perrault to Schinkel, one might see a parallel separation between the picture book and the theoretical text. Perhaps their alliance had only ever been opportunistic, yet it presupposed a direct rapport between theory and practice. The apparent lack of demand for books of architectural theory, compared with visual sources, meant that many treatises, such as Sir John Soane's Royal Academy lectures, remained unpublished. The historical awareness that came with Neo-Classicism and the Picturesque resulted in a new genre of books of architectural history that were neither records of archaeology nor reconstructions in the manner of Fischer von Erlach.

What is surprising is not that the Renaissance model of the architectural book should have lapsed, but that it should have revived in the twentieth century. There is probably some association with the need to market architecture both as a cultural desideratum and a luxury commodity, for which Frank Lloyd Wright's *Wasmuth Portfolio* could serve as an example. The work was commissioned by the prolific Berlin publisher Ernst Wasmuth in the year 1909 – coincidentally a turning point in Wright's career. Characteristically, he altered the terms of the commission so that his portfolio should exceed in luxury and scale the other examples in the series *Sonderheit der Architektur des XX. Jahrhunderts.*

Wright was already well versed in printing techniques and in the value of the published image. With its subtle use of coloured papers and inks, the Wasmuth portfolio has some aspects of a fine book of the Arts and Crafts period, with its beautiful and easily read drawings, by no means unlike Schinkel's in their graphic style and emotional pitch, offering worlds into which one can enter. The larger portfolio, with an introduction written by the English Arts and Crafts architect C.R. Ashbee, was published in 1910, followed by a more popular book with photographic illustrations in 1911.

The publication as a portfolio rather than as a book could have been a historical phenomenon at any period. It was popular in French publishing in the 1890s and 1900s, and offered advantages to the producer, in saving the cost of a binding, as well as to the user, who could take individual images to the drawing board or wherever else they might be required, without the inconvenience of a whole book. Portfolio publication makes sense for large format works, where the conventional folding of a printed sheet into signatures would in any case not apply. More particularly, it encourages a diversity of paper types, since there is less of a pretension to unity. Despite these potential freedoms, portfolio publications tended to retain most of the other characteristics of books, with a title page and a section of text preceding the plates, so that if bound they would appear as books.

Portfolio publications crossed the boundary between the mainstream of art and architectural publication and the avant-garde of the early twentieth century, with its primary devotion to the magazine as a form of expression. The effect of these intersections can be found in the protean publishing career of Le Corbusier, who of all architects of the twentieth century succeeded in making books work for him, professionally and ideologically. He was initially well schooled in the world of the avant-garde magazine with his work with Amedée Ozenfant on *L'Esprit Nouveau,* from 1920. Le Corbusier became specially adept at using typography as a form of expression. Artists and poets associated with Cubism, such as Guillaume Apollinaire and Blaise Cendrars, had given a lead in novel presentations of text on the page. In *Calligrammes,* 1916, Apollinaire challenged the limits of letterpress typesetting, while Cendrars's *La Prose du Transsibérian et de la Petite Jehanne de France,* 1913, broke with the limitation of the book page and adopted the form of a scroll to indicate the stream of consciousness, with abstract decoration by Sonia Delaunay. Le Corbusier's techniques were never as radical as this, but he used effects of juxtaposition, headlines and slogans with special skill, perhaps learned from advertising. *Vers une Architecture,* 1923, whole pages of which were lifted from *L'Esprit Nouveau,* uses its photographic plates to amuse and surprise.

In *L'Esprit Nouveau* in 1924 Le Corbusier expressed his enthusiasm for the review *L'Architecture Vivante,* founded and edited by Jean Badovici in the previous year, defending its serious publication of 'the interior life' of buildings by means of plans and sections, in protest against which Badovici's non-professional subscribers were rebelling. In 1927 Badovici, through his publishers Albert Morancé, also began to publish portfolios dedicated to the buildings and projects of Le Corbusier and Pierre Jeanneret, a series that extended to seven volumes up to 1937.

Although these inevitably cover much of the same ground as the series of Le Corbusier's *Oeuvre Complète,* issued by the publisher Girsbirger of Zurich from 1933 and subsequently maintained continuously in print, they are much rarer. The verbal content included texts on various theoretical and topical issues, as well as descriptions of the separate projects. The illustrations are mostly of building projects, although the first plate of the first portfolio is a close-up of a passenger aeroplane. There were a surprisingly large number of construction photos of the early villas, showing the concrete blocks beneath the render coat.

The plates were printed by photogravure on a substantial smooth card, resulting in a soft-toned reproduction with good focus, similar in quality to the trance-like realism of pre-1914 architectural photography when printed by similar methods. Thus, even in an age of increasing mechanisation in the printing of pictures, it was possible to turn a more highly skilled technique to the representation of an architecture that was enjoyed by a privileged few, even though its rhetoric directed it towards the masses. Equally remarkable were the colour plates, produced by the *pochoir* technique long popular in French publishing, in which colour washes were applied by hand in flat areas through stencils. It was possible to mix an exact colour this way and also to avoid the use of a coated paper, and as such may have been seen as more satisfactory than the alternative technique of 'process' blocks for colour reproduction, using a dotscreen and a build-up of separate colours to make an optical mixture.

This technique had been successfully practised by German publishers before the First World War and was used for some of the plates in M.H. Baillie-Scott's book *Homes and Gardens*, published in London by George Newnes in 1906, but it was liable to darken and coarsen the colours. In the Le Corbusier portfolios of *L'Architecture Vivante*, the coloured plates appear only in the first portfolio, with one interior of the Maison La Roche coloured over a black and white photograph, and plates of Pessac and other projects for which axonometrics in line are coloured to show the architectural use of coloured surfaces. The Pessac plate subtly includes white, applied to the cream paper, to give extra emphasis to the building surfaces.

The *L'Architecture Vivante* series, with the boards of its portfolios covered in bright Corbusian colours, is therefore pleasingly archaic and luxurious in its style, in contrast to the much more modern techniques familiar from the *Oeuvre Complète*. The latter has received little attention as a publishing phenomenon in its own right, but it may be appropriately paired with Palladio's *Quattro Libri* in its achievement of canonic status, its wide diffusion and its mixture of theory and an illustrated narrative of projects.

Similar, too, despite the apparent objectivity of photographic presentation compared with Palladio's wood engravings, was the degree of *post factum* correction of the material to suit the architect's vision of the way things ought to have been, including in Le Corbusier's case the omission of a substantial amount of early design work.

Adopting the format of a landscape quarto, Le Corbusier and his editors developed the magazine presentation of *L'Esprit Nouveau* with layouts of text, pictures and drawings that still seem very contemporary. The visual repertoire of the earlier journal was expanded with a widely flexible grid for placing the photographs and text, sometimes involving 'bled' images, but not invariably. The typographic style, equally, contrives when necessary to speak with different voices, with descriptions, reprinted text, and reproduction of text from other publications in differentiated style. The result is, even more than Robert and James Adam's *Works in Architecture,* a form of hypertext, in which a sequential reading can be replaced by a journey forwards and backwards through the book, picking out individual items of interest.

The communicative strength of this series of books can be measured by their longevity, and by the way that no need was felt to update the basic concept right up to the end of Le Corbusier's career. Even the binding of rough unbleached linen, with the blocking in packing-case letters, has a timeless quality. All volumes but the second were edited by Willy Boesiger, the exception being the work of Max Bill, a young Swiss designer and architect who had studied at the Dessau Bauhaus. Swiss internationalism may have been responsible for the trilingual texts, which are incorporated painlessly in the books.

The example of the *Oeuvre Complète* has inspired other architects. Alvar Aalto issued three volumes on his work in similar format, chosen too for Sir Leslie Martin's *Buildings and Ideas 1933–1983* (Cambridge University Press, 1983). The series of volumes, *Buildings and Projects: on the work of Norman Foster,* designed by Otl Aicher and published by Watermark from 1991, while portrait rather than landscape, adopt something of a magazine character, in which the voices of other critics and authorities are carefully orchestrated to produce an accumulation of approbation. Foster's more recent conspectus, *On Foster ... Foster On* (edited by Deyan Sudjic, Prestel, 2000), is more verbal, while carrying images on a CD-ROM inset into the front board of the book.

A book can serve as well as anything as a carrying case for a CD, but books as a means of communication seem so far relatively unthreatened by the digital media. No doubt this could change, but paper publication seems still to retain some of its cultural associations with intellectual probity, and the 1990s saw an increasing number of collaborations between architectural practices, independent authors and publishing houses involved in producing monographs on the history of a practice up to the present. These are almost invariably funded by the practices concerned, and the editorial content is therefore strictly controlled. This close involvement has plentiful historical precedent; and, if frustrating in terms of objectivity, it is not necessarily to be deplored, for the presentation can be its own form of text. Colour printing has been less advantageous for the quality of the architectural book, however, since the unity of text and image can never be so complete, despite recent attempts to make the text less boring by rendering it illegible.

Perhaps the most remarkable of Palladio's children in this respect is Rem Koolhaas, whose reputation was to a large extent launched with the book *Delirious New York* in 1978. His book *S,M,L,XL,* designed by Bruce Mau and published by 010 of Rotterdam in 1995, was originally highly priced, adding to its allure. In the terminology of its title, it is both large and small, having a page size scarcely more than a novel, but a bulk and weight exceeding most architectural monographs. Its heterogeneous contents invite comparison with other media, such as film, television, confessional audio diary or a series of lectures. The book is physically conventional, but it seems to depend on the conventions of book making in order to have something to subvert, for the alternation of colour and black-and-white images and spreads, and the changes of typographic style are more like an overgrown magazine. Yet there are many sub-themes and apparent jokes running through it, like an architectural version of Lawrence Sterne's eighteenth-century novel of the absurd, *Tristram Shandy* (1759–67), which uses graphics when words fail.

Koolhaas was a student at the Architectural Association from 1968 to 1972, extending into the period of chairmanship of Alvin Boyarsky, from 1971 to 1990. Boyarsky loved books and was personally responsible for much innovation in architectural publishing, inventing or adapting new forms of presentation, such as the 'Folio', a form of portfolio presented in the kind of boxes made for sets of LP records, themselves on the verge of obsolescence. Daniel Libeskind's *Theatrum Mundi*, 1985, was the first of this series. The culture of the AA became very book-minded at this time, and the present status of books as appropriate artefacts for architects to be involved in was probably the result of this freewheeling creativity, which was linked, as ever, to a sense of career-building opportunity.

In an interview in 1990 Boyarsky complained of the indifference of most publishers to the specificity of the material they produced in the field of architecture. Most AA publications were effectively exhibition catalogues, and Boyarsky said, 'Aside from selecting the exhibition material and the contributors, I'm also involved in the design, the writing or interviewing, selecting the paper and so on, so it becomes very intimate. Obviously, there must be room in this world for contributions that are intense, close up, and heartfelt.'[11] The interviewer asked Boyarsky whether the boom in architectural publications was leading to 'a new form of consumerism, because of its over-emphasis on photography', and he replied, 'Our publications state a case for important ideas people are working on that we believe will become eminently relevant. So that it's not just a way of creating more noise or photographic substitutes for architecture.'

Books frequently parade in borrowed garments of learning and insight, but better this than a loss of belief in the value of ideas. Static though they may be, printed words that are combined with images still appear to offer a medium for architectural expression.

## Notes

1. Hanno-Walter Kruft, *A History of Architectural Theory from Vitruvius to the Present Day* (London: Zwemmer, 1994), p. 184.
2. See Paolo Portoghesi, 'Opus Architectonicum, del Borromini', in *Essays in the History of Architecture presented to Rudolf Wittkower* (London: Phaidon, 1967), pp. 128–33.
3. See Eileen Harris (assisted by Nicholas Savage), *British Architectural Books and Writers, 1556–1785* (Cambridge: Cambridge University Press, 1990).
4. B. Langley, *City and Country Builder's and Workman's Treasury* (1740), p. iv, quoted in Harris, *British Architectural Books*, p. 61.
5. Harris, *British Architectural Books*, p. 84.
6. See N. McKendrick, J. Brewer, J.H. Plumb, *The Birth of a Consumer Society, The Commercialisation of Eighteenth-Century England* (London: Hutchinson, 1983).
7. Allan Braham, *The Architecture of the French Enlightenment* (London: Thames & Hudson, 1980), pp. 159–60.
8. Boullée's text was first published in English as *Boullée's Treatise on Architecture*, ed. Helen Rosenau (London: Alec Tiranti, 1953). The first French edition was *Architecture Essai sur l'Art*, ed. Jean-Marie Perouse de Monclos (Paris: Hermann, 1968).
9. John Archer, *The Literature of British Domestic Architecture 1715–1842* (Cambridge, MA and London: MIT Press, 1985), p. 29.
10. Archer, *Literature of British Domestic Architecture*, p. 31.
11. Interview with Alvin Boyarsky, *Design Book Review* 18 (Spring 1990), reprinted in Robin Middleton (ed.), *The Idea of the City* (London: Architectural Association, c. 1996), pp. 225–30.

Chapter 13
# Post-Modernism and the revenge of the book
Charles Jencks

## Background: remembering Amnesia

Gore Vidal, expert at hitting exposed nerves, calls the USA 'the United States of Amnesia'. Americans are encouraged to forget their past as quickly as possible, the argument goes, so that a corporation or politician can sell the population something it already has. In order to oil the wheels of production and consumption, the modern world demands a succession of new revolutions that no one notices are really old ones. In architecture, the 1990s saw the fifth version of minimalism produced in the twentieth century, typified by the work of John Pawson for Armani, Jigsaw and Calvin Klein. What did this outburst of tabula rasa signify – spiritual haute couture, boutique Cistercianism, or something else?

Inevitably these blank slates were pristine enough to receive any projection. In art, the modern blank canvas has always been suggestive, so that we might forget we saw it in, for instance, 1918. In architecture the dumb-box made different by some unusual material is the perfect expression of the beautiful economic engine rolling on its way. Modernism prospered on this truth, and so it became the obliging background for corporate branding. What starts in heaven ends on Bond Street.

Pathology? Among the several ills that modern architecture suffered during its brief reign as the dominant mode of building in the West – from the late 1920s to the early 1960s – was the loss of historical consciousness. This was a self-inflicted wound that was due to the strictures of such architects as Walter Gropius, who banned architectural history from the Bauhaus. Le Corbusier proclaimed, 'The styles are a lie', and any modern architect who was caught dropping an historical reminiscence was condemned as a pasticheur, reactionary or something worse. History was put into the footnotes.

How did this situation come about? A brief caricature supplies one answer. Nikolaus Pevsner, the English promoter of Modernism, tells a version of the story in his *Pioneers of the Modern Movement* (1936). Tradition and historical styles led, in the case of the Foreign Office competition, to compromise, deceit and toadying to the establishment. The resultant 'comedy', when Sir George Gilbert Scott gave up his

Ruskinian faith in the Gothic style in order to get the job, was so immoral that it led to the idea that architects should not engage stylistic matters at all. Style was disputatious, corrupting and to be avoided. Hence the new architecture was to have either no style, or else the universal one that Walter Gropius and the Pioneers had discovered.

In 1941 Sigfried Giedion told another version of this story in *Space, Time and Architecture:* 'the demand for morality in architecture' was a call by architects for independence. They must become like doctors, rise above society and the client and assert their specialty, their professional expertise, and purge society of its falsity of forms, its historicist wrapping paper. By the 1920s modern architects had come to believe that the plurality of styles and all the clutter of memories and associations that came with them were unfortunate bric-a-brac that had to be swept away if one were to create with a fresh mind. For them, as opposed to architects in most ages, traditions were fetters, not preconditions for creativity. They put architecture on a diet, shrunk the normal house by half, scraped off the ornament and symbols and, as Le Corbusier and Ozenfant declared, started 'the vacuum cleaning period of architecture'. Thus the origin of Minimalism, in its first of five incarnations.

But here lay a strange difference from other Modernist practice. The flight of architects beyond recognisable symbolism and culture differed from mainstream practice, which was – in the guise of Joyce, Eliot and Yeats, or Dadaists, Surrealists and Picasso, or Heidegger and the Existentialists – critical of mass production and mass culture. Architects, by contrast, had to become ultramodern in transcending the status quo, and this meant convincing themselves that design could be, like mathematics, a-cultural and un-historical.

The result of this doctrine soon became apparent. From New York's Park Avenue to central Hong Kong an abstract architecture popped up, shorn of location in place and time, an architecture of amnesia. It is practically impossible to remember as far back as the 1960s, but then there were many attacks on what Norman Mailer called these 'empty landscapes of psychosis'. They were mounted by films such as *Fahrenheit 451,* by writers such as Lewis Mumford, by *New Yorker* artists such as Saul Steinberg and by urban critics such as Jane Jacobs. The average modern housing estate in London, Brasilia, Chandigarh, or La Défense in Paris – or on the outskirts of Moscow and every capital city in the world – had suffered a cultural lobotomy. Architectural forgetting became a chronic condition.

In the brief summary that follows I will discuss the five main stages of architectural Post-Modernism, from 1960 to the present that reacted to this, illustrating the argument with books that carried the message.

Architecture as a sign system is ambiguous, as Umberto Eco pointed out, and in order to be understood its message has to be supplemented by other signs. Indeed, as semiotics (the theory of signs) began to show in the 1960s, all media of communication are subservient to words. Architecture stays in one place, while its meaning travels between the covers of books. Magazines may spread the word faster, but it is confirmed by the book. The medium that McLuhanites predicted for obsolescence also stamps in the electronic message, gives it authority and permanence. In an economy where the image and the brand dominate short-term memory, the book has a special place. It lasts, like a monument. It endures and becomes the marker for long-term memory – that is, considered thought.

Verbal and written language are imperialistic, cannibalistic, they eat all the other media at a sitting. Visual, tactile, environmental languages including nature have to be made semantically precise by words. It is true that architecture communicates purely architectural ideas, and that any building refers to others. There are architectural conventions that carry meaning – a Doric column, an I-beam, a hamburger stand – but architecture is not finished until the captions are written, and this is why architects, as other artists, become people of the book. Indeed, architects such as Le Corbusier and Rem Koolhaas achieved their following first through writing, then through building, and it is their writing that ends up as scripture. One may deplore this, one may aver that architecture cannot be reducible to words (as indeed it cannot), but then one will be using words to say this.

Because every generation forgets the battles of its parents, one has to be reminded that Post-Modernism constantly attacked cultural amnesia throughout its forty years of development. Of course, there is much more to its agenda than the question of historical consciousness, as I will summarise in a note at the end, but this has been one of its recurrent themes, as mediated by the printed word itself, the focus of this account.

## First critique: complexity not simplicity

Inevitably the beginning stage of Post-Modernism, from 1960 to 1972, was a reaction against the destruction of the historical city. Jane Jacobs wrote the first attack on reductive Modernism and the manifesto of the nascent movement in 1961, entitled *The Death and Life of Great American Cities,* and subtitled *The Failure of Town Planning*. As architectural manifestoes go it was non-visual and ended up as a cheap paperback, still in print after forty years. It relied on arguments coming from systems theory and on watching how cities actually worked. Here she states a principle of what was later to become the 'Post-Modern sciences of complexity' when she pointed out, in conclusion, that the city is not only a statistical problem of 'simplicity' or 'disorganised complexity' but also one of 'organised complexity' like those of the life sciences.[1]

In this first period of Post-Modernism, driven by the counterculture and its myriad battalions – 'advocacy planners', feminists, black power enthusiasts, minorities of all types – Modernism was seen as representing the power structure, a bland, commercialised middle class and bureaucracy. Accusations came from all quarters: corporate America had built the downtown in a Modernist mode, Walter Gropius had sold out the integrity of the Bauhaus and designed a squat, clichéd headquarters for the Pan Am corporation, and so much modern art had degenerated into a bland backdrop, a *genre-de-vie*. Modernists had not fought battles over the previous century to make the world safe for Lever Soap and CBS, the reduced, sleek towers of the fifties and sixties, so the reaction against these typical headquarter buildings came from within the Modern Movement. In that sense, *Post*-Modernism has always been another word for critical Modernism: that is, Modernism looking back at its own success and the problems this has caused.

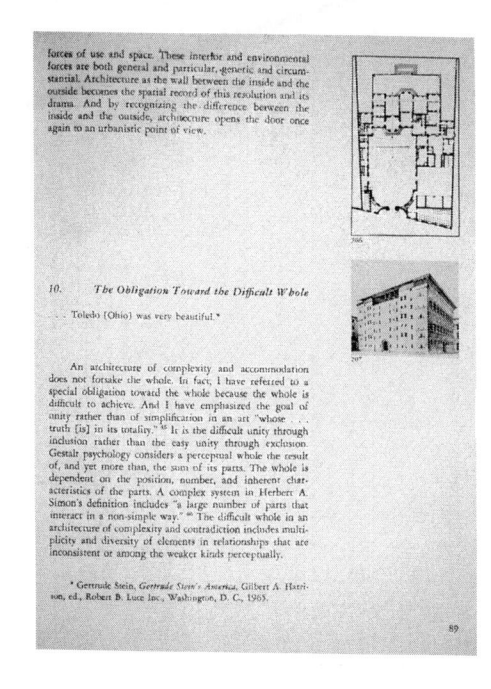

Robert Venturi, *Complexity and Contradiction in Architecture* (Museum of Modern Art, 1966). 'The Obligation Toward the Difficult Whole' became the obligation to face the complexities of contemporary life, not suppress elements of this for the sake of an aesthetic or ideological interest, and nonetheless make some kind of unity from the heterogeneity.

In 1966 Robert Venturi wrote the second manifesto of the fledgling movement, *Complexity and Contradiction in Architecture*.[2] Here the argument was conducted like a slide lecture, which resulted in tiny photos being crammed into the margins. This cheap paperback, aimed at students, was puffed by the historian Vincent Scully as the worthy successor to Le Corbusier's *Vers une architecture* – as a gentle, not aggressive, manifesto. Instead of being analysed in any depth, buildings from different

**178** | Charles Jencks

Robert Venturi and Denise Scott Brown, Medical Research Building, UCLA, Los Angeles (1989–92). Modifying the surrounding medical building type – a tall, flat, brick box with loft space – the Venturis made a virtue of its flatness by exaggerating the window-wall plane, intoduced subtle ornamental rhythms, and inflected the building at its corner and base for contextual reasons. The UCLA bear (the high-flyer) and writing on the wall, completing this inscribed slate, show the lessons of Las Vegas coming home to roost on its parent, LA.

periods were used to illustrate a point such as 'The Obligation Toward the Difficult Whole'. From then on different architectural histories – and in particular the Mannerist, Baroque and Edwardian periods – were open to influence contemporary work. Historical consciousness returned to help the architect solve problems, among them the contrary pressures exerted by the interior function of a building and the exterior urban landscape. Venturi showed that Borromini and Lutyens had successfully resolved these contradictory forces, leading to buildings that are full of surprise, ambiguity and wit. For the next fifteen years this book influenced students and nascent Post-Modernists. Its negative side only became apparent in the 1980s, when too many buildings were smothered with too many allusions; but Venturi and his wife, Denise Scott Brown, carried out their programme of a complex architecture with restraint and appropriateness. Ornament, allusion and geometrical innovations were given a contextual relevance.

## Radical pluralism = radical eclecticism

The second stage of Post-Modernism, from 1972 to 1978, was built on the protests of the 1960s, but it translated them into a philosophy of cultural pluralism. The eclecticism that Nikolaus Pevsner had deplored flooded back in the design and art worlds, especially with art of political movements such as feminism. In architecture it ranged from the ad hoc assemblage method of Lucien Kroll to the radical eclecticism of James Stirling. Hybrid, mixture, polyglot, mongrel, collage, juxtaposition, inclusion – these were the key words. They reflected a basic shift in global communication, the acceptance of all cultures and periods as equally valid and their mixture as relevant. Counter to Ruskin or Pevsner or the Modern Movement or the Design Council or the Queen, for that matter, there was no true style for any period. Did anything go? Not quite; distinctions were to be made, but they focused on how germane languages of architecture were to the various languages that local people were speaking – and, in whatever mode they were talking, one thing was obvious: it was not Esperanto. The International Style might be fine for international businessmen, but it was not deep enough in reference to engage a world media culture, now a richly diverse one.

In the Stuttgart Museum addition of 1977, Stirling juxtaposed several different styles, or 'language games', as Jean-Francois Lyotard, the philosopher of Post-Modernism, might call them: Classicism, Modernism, vernacular and high-tech – and some strident green paint and dayglo handrails that jarred the senses into action. Typically the languages divided into low and high art forms, a double-coding that acknowledged the gaps between different groups of city dwellers.

The American critic Paul Goldberger called the AT&T building the first 'masterpiece' of Post-Modernism, but in important ways that building misunderstood what it was all about, and Stirling's Stuttgart shows why. At his museum the styles are not resolved into a synthetic totality as they are at the AT&T. Rather, they are placed in extreme tension with each other to underscore the heterogeneity of society, the pluralism that acknowledges no single discourse as dominant. The 'tensed field' of juxtaposed styles was an idea shared with Post-Modern literature, especially the novels of Umberto Eco and Salman Rushdie, which were equally eclectic. A new understanding was thus reached. Oppositions between languages and different viewpoints can actually create their own particular kind of meaning – even *are* the meaning – and one could say that the significance of Stirling's Neuestaatsgalerie, ultimately, was the new *episteme* of pluralism itself. In effect, the building represented the fragmentation of taste cultures, with conflict and enjoyable difference becoming the subject of the architecture.

My writings, naming Post-Modernism in 1975 and defining this pluralism, may also have helped catalyse the second stage and could even have influenced Stirling, with whom I was in constant discussion. I had written several articles showing how his

Late-Modern Olivetti building failed to communicate as intended, and we exchanged views on the need for metaphor and multiple-coding. (He disagreed with the former, but accepted the latter.) It is hard to gauge one's own contribution, and in the case of Stirling there is no doubt that Colin Rowe and Fred Koetter's writings on *Collage City* were of great importance.

James Stirling and Michael Wilford, Die Neuestaatsgalerie, Stuttgart (1977–84). Languages of architecture, appropriate and jarring, are played against each other to heighten the perception of difference and architecture as language. High-Tech lighting rails are used as signs showing visitors how to walk through the building, while classical languages, including the Egyptian, are used in functional ways – ironic reversals of customary usage.

*The Language of Post-Modern Architecture* went into multiple editions and many languages, and its third edition (1981) featured a different approach to radical eclecticism than Stirling's.[3] Charles Moore's Piazza d'Italia of 1976–9 was equally a collage of oppositions, again Classical and industrial, but it was more colourful, populist and oriented to street culture. Here was an architecture meant to challenge other

## 181 | Post-Modernism and the revenge of the book

media, and to make use of several at once. Worked out in participation with its users – the Italian community of New Orleans – its modern version of the five Italian orders was both excessive and to the point. It was based on the local context and one of its lively subcultures, those energetic European immigrants competing with the three other main ethnic groups.

Third and German edition of *The Language of Post-Modern Architecture* (1981) with Charles Moore's Piazza d'Italia, New Orleans (1976–9). The Five Italian Orders, for the local Italian community and its mayor, culminates in a restaurant with its neon 'Deli Order'. A combination of Pop Art, supergraphics, pastiche, metallic composite-with-water-spouts – all a knowing take-off of the Trevi Fountain at one-tenth the cost and lacking Rome. Media architecture in the making. *The Language of Post-Modern Architecture* used cartoons, diagrams, evolutionary charts and high-low illustrations to send the mixed message about plural languages. Midway between a book and magazine, it was damned by conservative critics, such as Kenneth Frampton, for too much illustration, but it looks conservative by today's hyper-graphic standards.

The piazza centred on the place where the Italian mayor would address his community each year. Fountains, arcades and metallic-classical Orders surround this point and build up to a crescendo of neon: the wonderfully tasteless joke for a restaurant-to-be, the 'Deli Order'. The knowing irony of using blue neon to outline the perfected proportions of Vignola underlined a Post-Modern dictum of the time. The past, if it were returned to at all, had to be acknowledged as over, as seen from the present. This distinguished it from traditionalism, from the straight revivalism of Quinlan Terry. I put this Post-Modernism formula later, as the litany of Umberto Eco (who had first introduced the idea of architecture as a complex language appealing to different taste cultures):

Post-Modernism is paradox – After Now, Post-Present

Post-Modernism is 'posteriority', after all times

Post-Modernism is time-binding of past, present and future

Post-Modernism is crossing boundaries, crossing species

Post-Modernism is crossing cheeses (gorgonzola + camembert = cambozola)

Post-Modernism is revisiting the past – with quotation marks

Post-Modernism is revisiting the future – with irony

Post-Modernism is acknowledging the already said, as Eco has already said, in the age of lost innocence

Charles Moore, a Yale professor, would probably not have had the bullishness to produce such hyper-Pop without a good deal of contemporary writing behind it. There was Pop Art itself, of course, but more important were Tom Wolfe's hysterical panegyrics on 'electrographic architecture' (the neon sign artists of Las Vegas celebrated in *The Kandy-Kolored Tangerine-Flake Streamline Baby* and more particularly in *Las Vegas (What?) Las Vegas (Can't Hear You! Too Noisy) Las Vegas!!!!*). This was the article that, placed by Robert Venturi's bedside, led to his (and Denise Scott Brown's and Steven Izenour's) *Learning from Las Vegas* in 1972.[4]

Here another plea was made for learning from the past, as well as from Las Vegas, and for creating an architecture that would be inclusive, not just aimed at the professional elite, or 'orthodox Modernists' as they were termed by this team of writers. Their research into the vernacular strip was commendable for opening up the architectural discourse and the first of subsequent sorties made, with the aid of architectural students, into the no-go area of sprawl, crime, sex, commercial vernacular and un-pedigreed architecture. Bernard Tschumi and Rem Koolhaas were to follow suit. Yet, unfortunately, the Venturi team fell into the very Modernist trap they were criticising – exclusivism. Smarting from attacks on their work as 'ugly and ordinary', they decided to embrace these terms as a positive programme, while at the same time rejecting a whole area of communication: what they called Modernist 'duck buildings'. This unlikely nomenclature came from their analysis of architectural symbolism, the idea that buildings communicated either as 'Decorated Sheds' (good) or 'Ducks' (bad). The former were sheds with graphic high-flyers, or appliquéd ornament, stuck on them, and the latter were iconic buildings such as those in the shape of a duck. Modernist buildings were 'irrelevant ducks' because their image was a direct expression of function, structure, space or technique. While their critique of Modernism carried insight, it also contained the seeds of its own destruction.

**183** | Post-Modernism and the revenge of the book

73. "Long Island Duckling" from *God's Own Junkyard*.
74. Road scene from *God's Own Junkyard*.
75. Duck.
76. Decorated shed.

Robert Venturi, the Duck (bad, modern, irrelevant) versus the Decorated Shed (good, appliquéd, clear at 50 miles per hour). The problem? Decorated sheds were not symbolic but 'signolic', a dissociation of the signifier and signified.

Inclusive symbolism must embrace the full panoply of architectural signs, as I was to point out many times, not just applied elements from the reduced spectrum of the ugly and ordinary, not just decorated sheds. Furthermore – and this was much more damaging to their case – a symbol is resonant and has deep levels of meaning and connections with the function of the building, everyday life and the full architectural task (space, structure, ornament). A symbolic architecture is precisely the opposite of what they called it throughout their book. It is tied to many meanings in a multivalent way so that one cannot tell what generated the form: function, space, sign, ornament or technique. As I argued in *Towards a Symbolic Architecture* (1985), their idea of the decorated shed produces 'signolic', not symbolic, architecture. Signs, like the Las Vegas high-flyers or traffic signs, are one-liners that do not engage the rest of the building, and they force a dissociation on architecture. Unfortunately many Post-Modernists learned the wrong lessons from Las Vegas, as far as I was concerned, and produced an assemblage of clichés rather than a resonant symbolic architecture, but the movement continued to move on, in response to these problems.

## Post-Modern Classicism

The third stage of the growing tradition, from 1978 to 1985, saw Post-Modernism go public with the Venice Biennale of 1980 and then turn professional and, finally, corporate. During this period, the ironic Classicism of Venturi, Stirling, Moore and countless others became more straightforward and urban. Its continued quotation marks acknowledged the 'already said'; but its inflation in scale showed it was going straight for the mainstream, and power. Michael Graves's Humana Tower, for the large health corporation in Louisville, was one of its first corporate monuments (*pace* Goldberger) that embraced both Classicism and industrial society.

However, in becoming successful this stage of the movement took on many of the problems that beset Modernism – above all, overproduction, inflation and what is called 'quick-build.' Massive $2 billion buildings were designed, as usual with leviathans, on the back of an envelope. Philip Johnson, who declared himself quite publicly a 'whore' for architecture (he would do a lot to get the job done), was the fastest at work. Even Stirling had been proud of the conceptual sketch of Stuttgart, quickly conceived on the back of his airplane ticket. Cesar Pelli was no doubt the master of this restricted genre – most evident in the fifty-storey Canary Wharf Tower in London's docklands, a building that had, under construction, a velocity of one storey per week and that, finished, makes pleasing proportional rectangles out of a commission that is now fashionable to deplore. (The rectangles are more pleasing the farther one is away from them because of problems of parallax.)

Less speedy and more thoughtful Post-Modern Classical structures were built around the world, epitomising the embrace of the corporate and civic worlds. These buildings are probably too well known to need summary. Suffice it to say that some of the lasting achievements of the third stage of Post-Modernism are evident at IBA in Berlin, the international building exhibition that lasted throughout the 1980s and employed some of the best Post-Modern architects, among them Charles Moore, Hans Hollein, Matthias Ungers and Robert Krier.

If there was one text behind this European urbanism it was Aldo Rossi's *L'Architettura della Città* (1966), and so it was appropriate that Rossi's colourful toy-block Classicism epitomised the planning. The lessons of history drawn upon at IBA concerned not only previous Classical periods but also the historical typology of the city, its streets, its squares, its contained open space, and its common language. All of this was absorbed at IBA, which was certainly the best urbanism built in the 1980s – with the district renewal system of Barcelona a close second. Later, Barcelona in the 1990s under its mayor, Pasqual Maragall, became the exemplar of an enlightened Post-Modern urbanism and, because of the 1992 Olympics, financially viable as well.

The gathering argument of Post-Modernism thus mixed two related motives.

**185** | Post-Modernism and the revenge of the book

Gae Aulenti and Act, Musée d'Orsay conversion, Paris (1980–6). Building as extended text. The train shed, symbol of nineteenth-century power and materialism, meets thirteenth-century cathedral layout in a twentieth-century temple to the contradictions of nineteenth-century art. Diverse timeframes and building types are merged and contested in this double-voiced discourse. The central nave reaches one important station at the transept, left, with the large history painting *Romans of the Decadence*.

First was the search for a viable urbanism that could pull the patterns of city growth into some kind of complex whole that did not destroy that of the past (Venturi's 'Difficult Whole'). Second, the other side of the coin, was the search for a rich language of architecture that could communicate with the diverse population of the heteropolis – the direction towards which all cities in the global marketplace were evolving. The two goals are pulled together in Gae Aulenti's conversion of the Gare d'Orsay in Paris into an art museum and turned into an extended text.

Here she combines three building types that epitomised different periods and that were thought to be incompatible, even at war with each other: the medieval cathedral, the nineteenth-century railroad terminus and today's museum. These were, in effect, three well-known architectural conventions, 'words' that were yoked together as a dramatic narrative explaining the nineteenth-century art inside. For those prepared to read the signs, an amusing dialectic was set up. Marching up the left aisle ('left wing') is the avant-garde we have been taught to love so much; up the right aisle ('right wing') is, inevitably, the reactionary and academic art we have learned to hate (until recently);

while down the central nave, where the trains used to chug in the past and give off puffs of impressionistic smoke, is the florid public sculpture of the nineteenth century.

The procession goes slightly uphill, implying progress, and this pilgrimage culminates first at the 'transept', where one comment is made by a somewhat hedonistic painting titled *Romans of the Decadence:* the sybaritic Romans reminding the spectator of the direction that the contemporary art exhibition opening has recently taken. Finally, after walking over a glass 'crypt', where the bones of nineteenth-century urbanism can be seen, the 'high altar' is reached, where the Paris Opera – ultimate spectacle of the nineteenth century – is placed under a shroud. This is serious opera buffa at its best. Resonant in its symbolism, the old station is now a double-barrelled comment on the role of art today. Art, as everyone knows, is our inadequate substitute for religion, while the new museums, which underwent inflationary growth in the 1980s, have become cathedrals dedicated sometimes to spiritual contemplation, sometimes to Mammon. Inasmuch as the new religion showed more faith in the art market than in culture in general, Gae Aulenti's ironic collision of types is meant both to enhance and undermine this fact. Here again Post-Modernism is a critical Modernism, a double coding that sends opposite messages at the same time.

No wonder several mainstream critics, and Still Modernists, disliked the building so much. All they could see was the heavy Egyptian Classicism, proof that they were still obsessed by the very taboo they affirmed: style. They missed the masterful weaving of meanings and art, the extraordinary subtleties in layering and lighting, the drama of discovery, the dialectic of building types. They also missed the way the Classicism was crossed with the shallow, layered space of Le Corbusier, and actually transformed into a new grammar. But such dismissals of the building – and they also greeted Robert Venturi's extension to the National Gallery in London – also revealed a general truth. Architectural culture, like the broader society, was fragmenting into different taste cultures. Each one tended to see buildings through its own visual and experiential codes. With Prince Charles and the Classical revivalists joining the debate in 1984, the Style Wars complicated an already contested territory. Now each side of the debate caricatured its two other main opponents; and with Post-Modernism becoming commercially successful, too big, too fast, too clichéd like its parent, Modernism, the debate took off in another direction.

## Slicing the monolith

The fourth stage of Post-Modernism, starting at about 1985, was also concerned with historical meanings in reacting to its own inflationary success. Instead of the huge corporate structure expressed as a single volume, the over-large office was now broken up into 'small blocks' that were expressed in many articulations.

Jane Jacobs had recommended small-block planning in the 1960s, Leon Krier did likewise in the 1970s, and by the late 1980s James Stirling, Hiroshi Hara, Kisho Kurokawa and Antoine Predock (among many others) were looking to historical precedent for breaking up architectural volumes into discrete and grammatical units. Seventeenth- and eighteenth-century cities were consulted, including a study of the perimeter blocks of Naples; and the coherent juxtapositions of small Classical units in ancient Greece were very persuasively demonstrated in the seductive drawings of Leon Krier, who by the late 1980s was very much in the traditionalist camp with Prince Charles and was the main theorist behind the new town of Seaside, Florida. So the past could, once again, suggest precedents that could be transformed.

*The Language of Post-Modern Architecture* (sixth edition, 1991), with Antoine Predock's Fine Arts Center, Arizona State University, Tempe, Arizona (1987–9). Small blocks, in a purple grey concrete sympathetic to the Arizona context, are abstracted transformations of a Classical grammar. The book was translated into 11 languages, and in its several editions became an 'evolvotome', evolving in its message with the movement of Post-Modernism – which continues to change. By the early 1990s many people declared Post-Modernism 'dead', not understanding that as long as Modernism remains the dominant mode there will be a resistant Post-Modernism.

Furthermore, Post-Modernists reacted against the overstated symbolism of such things as Michael Graves's swans at Disneyworld by adopting a more abstract representation, an allusive and enigmatic symbolism. This was evident in Kisho Kurokawa's Hiroshima Museum of Contemporary Art, which alluded to many previous eras of Japanese and Western architecture as well as to the more recent destruction of Hiroshima. In the sense that modern technology and warfare produced the bomb and destroyed Hiroshima, their erasure is the ultimate Modernist attack on time and memory. While Kurokawa's building alludes to this past, it also signifies the future, with veiled hints of a

Kisho Kurokawa, Museum of Contemporary Art, Hiroshima (1988–9). This building marks the fusion of the past (Edo stonework), the recent past (the burned scorch marks are incorporated), the present (white tile), and the future (aluminium space imagery). This fusion, opposed to the usual Post-Modern method of violent juxtaposition, is seamless, harmonious and peaceful. It reflects Buddhist attitudes towards reconciling irreconcilable discourses.

spacecraft and high-tech equipment. His Hiroshima museum manages to tie different periods and cultures together through this understated allusion. In a city that was totally devastated by the ultimate product of Modernism, in a city that has literally suffered urban amnesia, Kurokawa has designed a healing amalgam of time. The cracked stone base alludes to Edo culture and represents the past. The centre of the building, with its white tile, is reminiscent of modern structures, and the aluminium top has many overtones of the future, including space travel. In many more ways the building binds historical periods together and in this sense becomes a clear alternative to the timeless, abstract Modernism that continues today in its 'late' and 'neo' forms. The contrasts are obvious.

In a broad sense, this building could also be seen as part of the Post-Modern tradition that gave birth to several Holocaust museums that started to be built in the early 1990s. Again Post-Modern text and Post-Modern building marched in two-step. Jean-François Lyotard had famously, and polemically, declared that 'Auschwitz ... is a crime opening up postmodernity'. The argument is complex and contentious, depending on the view that the Holocaust was the supreme example of instrumental reason being applied to the mass production of death. Modernism and modernity, as heirs to Enlightenment reason, may have been complicit in this crime or not sufficiently resistant to instrumental reason, the application of pragmatic thinking to the Final Solution. Such were Lyotard's arguments put forward in *The Postmodern Condition: A Report on Knowledge* in 1979 and *The Postmodern Explained to Children* in 1986 (the dates are those of the French publications).

Inevitably, Modernists denied this reproach, and a furious debate started, as one-sided as the style wars that were dividing architects. The issues are much too deep and important to discuss here, but one can follow the reasoning in further books such as Zygmunt Bauman's *Modernity and the Holocaust* (1989). The significant thing for architecture was that buildings, such as Daniel Libeskind's Jewish Museum in Berlin (1989–99) (overleaf), were now dealing with explicit public content in a symbolic way and coming to terms with a part of modern history that had been suppressed. Cultural amnesia was again under attack; and Libeskind has followed with further competition-winning schemes that are, I would argue, one fulfilment of the Post-Modern agenda. They bind past, present and future, if not into a continuum, then into a discussion.

## Complexity in its second incarnation

The fifth stage of Post-Modern architecture, which started in the early 1990s, presents yet other ways of dealing with time and cultural pluralism. One way is through the broad architectural movement I discuss in *The Architecture of the Jumping Universe*, based on complexity theory, which sees time as the master builder.[5] The most convincing example of this is DNA, molecules of memory that have taken more than three billion years to build up organisations complex enough to produce us, among other creatures. Architectural memory and complexity also are the work of long periods of destruction and restructuring. By the 1990s, with the aid of the computer and a new complexity theory coming from Ilya Prigogine and the Santa Fe Institute, the 1960s' ideas of Jane Jacobs and Robert Venturi took on a new twist. Now one could understand emergence, self-organising systems and how complexity arose over time. Secondly, the old standbys of collage and juxtaposition were not the only ways of dealing with pluralism.

One aspect of the new movement is framed under the guise of 'folding' theory, which stems from Gilles Deleuze and his writings on *Le Pli*. Greg Lynn and Jeffrey Kipnis, among many younger architects, and Peter Eisenman and Daniel Libeskind, among a few older ones, have seen a way beyond discordant collage. Finding the oppositional methods of Stirling at Stuttgart and the ironies of Venturi in London too confrontational, they have fashioned a method of folding in difference. Here variety and pluralism are allowed but are subsumed into a supple, continuously changing whole. As Kipnis argues, it is coherent and congruent, yet still inclusive of difference.[6]

**190** | Charles Jencks

Daniel Libeskind, Jewish Museum extension to the Berlin Museum, Berlin (1989–99). Libeskind wrote: 'What I have tried to convey is that the Jewish history of Berlin is not separable from the history of Modernity, from the destiny of this incineration of history; they are bound together … through an absence of meaning of history and an absence of artefacts.' Some of the symbolic forms include the void down the centre, several voided towers, the jagged, wandering line, the drunken walk of a lost civilisation.

The recent work of Frank Gehry epitomises both the folding and complexity theories without explicitly being based on either. Gehry is aware of the writings on both and respects them, but he is led more by his intuitive concerns. Nonetheless, his new Guggenheim Museum in Bilbao characterises the supple, pliant, moving quality of the one and the notions of self-organising systems and the fractal order of the other. For instance, the all-over titanium panels of the museum repeat endlessly as they fold into self-similar, fractal shapes of natural forms: the two most obvious are flower petals and the shimmering water of the Nervion River into which the building springs.

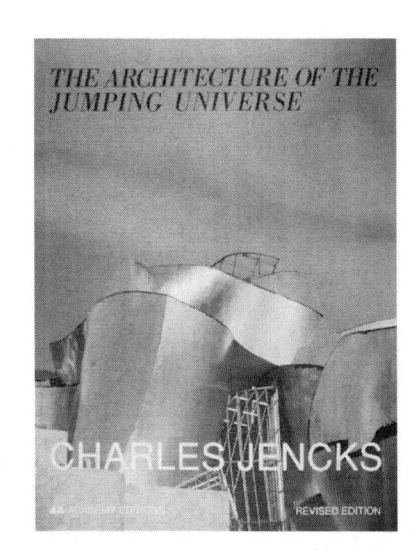

*The Architecture of the Jumping Universe* (second edition, 1997), with Frank Gehry's New Guggenheim, Bilbao (1993–7). The architecture of the new complexity, an extension of Venturi's complexity, partly based on folding theory, fractals and production by computer.

Into these continuously changing curves many types of space are poured – Gehry's pluralism is typological more than semantic. The interior galleries run the gamut through all the types: spaces that are long, thin, white, curved, and high; spaces that are small, squashed, square, coloured and low; and both abstract spaces and art-specific rooms. Furthermore, the hills, streets and river of Bilbao are very much pulled into the museum and celebrated, with both glimpsed views and vast, sixty-foot-high, tilted and warped windows.

The pluralism is most apparent in references to the site. The building slides under an existing highway to one side, and then with its industrial surface acknowledges the trains and the railroad station to the other. Following the fourth stage of Post-Modern architecture, which also reacts against explicit symbolism, these references are understated and oblique, but for those who care to look they are palpable.

**192** | Charles Jencks

When the building opened, the Basques may have found that the art and culture were too American, too bombastic, or too hegemonic, but they soon appreciated the way Gehry implicitly responded to the site and the pre-existing industrial landscape to create a building that resuscitates a dying rust-belt city. Again we should step back to see the bigger picture. If ever Post-Modernisation existed as a quaternary industry replacing modernised manufacturing, it is here. The cultural industry has, through this and other creations, revived Bilbao's economy and thus has created new links across time that would have surprised the Modernists and materialists.

## Time and architectural DNA

For Karl Marx, as for many Modernists, history was an intolerable burden that weighed down on the present; it made creative action impossible. For Henry Ford, the quintessential Modernist, history was 'bunk' and a 'scrap heap' on which to throw obsolescent bodies, outmoded concepts – or old Model Ts. For Isaac Newton, as for the Classicists, history was timeless, eternal – that is, non-historical. Indeed, for many physicists, because equations can be conceived and read in any direction, time does not have a basic reality. For Le Corbusier and Mies van der Rohe, time in the modern period had been irrevocably ruptured from the past: historical consciousness was irreversibly broken, and the 'great tradition' had ended with nineteenth-century eclecticism, or what they considered to be false consciousness. The new city was thus to be a tabula rasa on which one could inscribe totally new and functional ideas.

Rem Koolhaas's manifesto *S,M,L,XL*, produced with the graphic designer Bruce Mau, reiterated these ideas of rupture in a new way in 1995. Partly this extra large tome

Rem Koolhaas, cover (left) and pages (right) from *S,M,L,XL*, a Post-Modern hypertext carrying the thoroughly modern message of tabula rasa and runaway growth. The book, designed by Bruce Mau, transferred the graphic language of magazines, comics and desktop publishing into a new genre that immediately influenced Dutch architecture and the architectural monograph.

**193** | Post-Modernism and the revenge of the book

was a classic Post-Modern hypertext, mixing genres as an ultimate hybrid. As the authors write on the book jacket, not only is it a 'novel', but it 'combines essays, manifestoes, diaries, fairy tales, travelogues, a cycle of meditations on the contemporary city, with work produced by Koolhaas's office'. The piling on of images over 1,345 pages, many double-page spreads of varying graphic techniques, guaranteed it a popular success, especially among the MTV generation and architects persuaded of its message. This was resolutely ultramodern and often explicitly anti-Post-Modern. Describing the tabula rasa of Singapore and (exulting in) such Modernist developments as the huge, soulless Bijlmermeer housing development in Holland, what Koolhaas describes acidly as the 'Las Vegas of the Welfare State', he comes to terms with the forces that are destroying 'what we used to call the city'.

A characteristic essay is 'Bigness', which is part description and part aphoristic manifesto for the new mutation in city proliferation. Its argument by telegraphic assertion is reminiscent of Le Corbusier, and even more apocalyptic in tone:

> Bigness is ultimate architecture ... Such [a big] mass can no longer be controlled by a single architectural gesture ... Issues of composition, scale, proportion, detail are now moot ... The humanist expectation of 'honesty' is doomed: interior and exterior architectures become separate projects ... Bigness is no longer part of any urban tissue. It exists; at most, it coexists. Its subtext is *fuck* context ... Only Bigness can sustain a promiscuous proliferation of events in a single container ... Although Bigness is a blueprint for perpetual intensity, it also offers degrees of serenity and even blandness. It is simply impossible to animate its entire mass with intention ... Bigness is impersonal: the architect is no longer condemned to stardom ... Beyond signature, Bigness means surrender to technologies: to engineers, contractors, manufacturers; to politics; to others ... Bigness, through its very independence of context, is the one architecture that can survive, even exploit, the now-global condition of tabula rasa ... Bigness surrenders the field to after-architecture.[7]

As a description of the urban condition, Bigness has some obvious truths: in many respects the city is out of control, and has nothing whatever to do with architectural merit or value. It is 'after-architecture', and mega-development, as Koolhaas puts it brutally, does '*fuck* context'. The weakness of the argument is that, counter to what the book jacket claims, the issues of economics and politics are not engaged, for these are the engines behind what Koolhaas describes: the 'group of seven' nations that steers the world economy; the 380 corporations that control 75 per cent of world trade production. Or, what leads to fast overdevelopment, the concentration of land ownership and development capital in the hands of the few and its sudden descent onto the urban periphery.

The city, of course, has always been driven by economic forces and in this sense is always out of control – whatever Alan Greenspan and his apologists may hope. As for architects, they have never built more than 5 per cent of a nation's buildings, and usually less than 1 per cent. What Koolhaas brings to attention is not some new condition, but the exaggeration of previous ones. And whereas, for instance, Venturi also identifies the split between inside and outside, and contradictory forces,

Venturi also writes of the 'obligation toward the difficult whole' – the context, and architecture.

Koolhaas's great contribution, however, is to enter areas of fast production – such as the Atlanta suburbs or the Pearl River Delta – and find the opportunities for statistical collage. In writing and filming his experiences in Singapore, he instantly becomes a Walt Whitman of that corporate-nation: both a very funny witness-poet and an amateur sociologist. His projects, because they are radical mixtures of urban functions, are even Post-Modern when they exploit metaphor, symbolism and the radical diversity of function. But his intentions remain ironic and descriptive about amnesia and the tabula rasa; as an ultra-Modernist he looks to exploit, not counter, these forces.

This kind of thinking, although enjoying a vogue today, is at least contested. Even the new Modernists and deconstructionists consciously revive their chosen history and acknowledge that creativity must exist within a socially constructed reality. So the Post-Modern defence of place, and the essential importance of time and history, have become widespread goals. Proof of this, if needed, comes from an unlikely quarter: the work of Richard Rogers, his practice and the Urban Task Force.[8] Lord Rogers, designer of the Pompidou Centre and Lloyd's, has from the beginning of his work in the 1960s been a strong Modernist, both in practice and in word. Yet from the mid-1980s his work has become contextually sensitive and responsive to urban history, and his Urban Task Force, set up under Tony Blair's government, has promoted an agenda that includes many Post-Modern values. Among these are a commitment to building on brownfield sites, the support of local communities and their further empowerment, an emphasis on mixed use, and the major goal of an urban renaissance. All these points, underlined by the example of Barcelona, resist those economic and political forces that Koolhaas shows are eroding the city. Significantly, Rogers is the first major architect since Le Corbusier to effectively change public urban policy, and unlike his forebear Rogers actually loves the city as he finds it. Rogers is, in effect, Jane Jacobs in high-tech garb, proof that even if there is not progress in architecture there is learning. And Rogers too has expounded his ideas in a book: *Cities for a Small Planet* (1997).

Many Post-Modern writers, such as Ed Soja, have shown that the old city has expanded and changed into something else, variously named 'the 100-mile city', 'Edge City' and the 'exopolis'. No doubt the old architectural means for dealing with this amorphous sprawl treat only local concerns, but another Post-Modern conception will, I believe, influence architects in the future. Learning from those sciences of complexity that are the heart of the movement, the authors Michael Batty and Paul Longley have shown in their book, *Fractal Cities,* how to conceive of even the 1,000-mile sprawl.[9]

It is beyond the scope of this article to outline the theory of fractals and explain how it affords an ordering and conceptual system rich enough to cope with the exopolis at the point of its dissolution. But the last word on Bigness has hardly been spoken, and one can be sure that before long it will appear – where else – but in a book.

## Postscript

### 13 propositions of Post-Modern architecture

*General values*

1. Multivalence is preferred to univalence, imagination to fancy.
2. 'Complexity and contradiction' are preferred to over-simplicity and 'Minimalism'.
3. Complexity and chaos theories are considered more basic in explaining nature than linear dynamics; that is, 'more of nature' is non-linear in behaviour than linear.
4. Memory and history are inevitable in DNA, language, style and the city and are positive catalysts for invention.

*Linguistic and aesthetic*

5. All architecture is invented and perceived through codes, hence the languages of architecture and symbolic architecture, hence the double-coding of architecture within the codes of both the professional and the populace.
6. All codes are influenced by a semiotic community and various taste cultures, hence the need in a pluralist culture for a design based on radical eclecticism.
7. Architecture is a public language, hence the need for a Post-Modern Classicism that is partly based on architectural universals and a changing technology.
8. Architecture necessitates ornament (or patterns), which should be symbolic and symphonic, hence the relevance of information theory.
9. Architecture necessitates metaphor and this should relate us to natural and cultural concerns, hence the explosion of zoomorphic imagery, 'face' houses and scientific iconography instead of 'machines for living'.

*Urban, political, ecological*

10. Architecture must form the city, hence contextualism, Collage City, neo-rationalism, small-block planning, and mixed uses and ages of buildings.
11. Architecture must crystallise social reality; in the global city today, the

Heteropolis, that very much means the pluralism of ethnic groups – hence participatory design and ad hoc-ism.
12   Architecture must confront the ecological reality, and that means sustainable development, green architecture and cosmic symbolism.
13   We live in a surprising, creative, self-organising universe that still gets locked into various solutions; hence the need for a cosmogenic architecture that celebrates criticism, process and humour.

**Notes**

1   Jane Jacobs, *The Death and Life of Great American Cities* (New York: Vintage, 1961), pp. 428–32.
2   Robert Venturi, *Complexity and Contradiction in Architecture* (New York: Museum of Modern Art, 1966).
3   Charles Jencks, *The Language of Post-Modern Architecture,* 6th edition (London and New York: Academy Editions, 1991).
4   Robert Venturi, Denise Scott Brown, Steven Izenour, *Learning from Las Vegas* (Cambridge, MA: MIT Press, 1972).
5   Charles Jencks, *The Architecture of the Jumping Universe,* 2nd edition (London and New York: Academy Editions, 1997).
6   Jeffrey Kipnis, 'Towards a New Architecture', *Architectural Design* 63:3/4 (1993), p. 41–9.
7   Rem Koolhaas and Bruce Mau, *S,M,L,XL* (New York: Monacelli Press, 1995), pp. 495–516.
8   Richard Rogers and Urban Task Force, *Towards an Urban Renaissance* (London: Department of the Environment), available from: DETR Free Literature, PO Box 236, Wetherby LS23 7NB, UK.
9   Michael Batty and Paul Longley, *Fractal Cities* (San Diego, CA: Academic Press, 1994).

Chapter 14
## Architectural publishing
An alphabetical guide
**Paul Finch**

**A** is for Alvar Aalto and the Alternative Tradition – two Modernisms rather than one. If we don't see half a dozen new books a year on Aalto, it means it's not his centenary any more. Aalto has the advantage – like Aardvark taxis – of being first in every type of alphabetical architectural listing, and so is a thoroughly reliable publishing candidate. A is also for Advance – what publishers regard as a princely sum with no certainty of delivery; what authors see as a miserly but somehow irresistible pittance to take on another millstone.

**B** is for (Irritable) Bilbao Syndrome, in which a single building transforms the image of a city, encouraging tourism, tourist guides, monographs and, most importantly, tax deductible visits to research the building in question. Best of all is when a US architect works in Europe, thereby perpetuating the Old World/New World cliché.

**C** is for Le Corbusier, about whom there can never be enough written, especially by those who, never having met him, feel more than entitled to refer to him as 'Corb' or 'Corbu'. The publisher's nightmare is to fall foul of the Fondation Corbusier, which protect its rights in the Great Man's work. C thus also stands for Copyright, and don't you forget it. C is also for *Changing Rooms,* an extraordinary UK TV phenomenon in which cameo designers do MDF makeovers of ordinary homes, whose success or failure is then reported in the tabloid press. An architecture media meta-narrative that has reversed the former widely held belief that 'you can't do architecture on TV'.

**D** is for Deconstruction, architecture's answer to bebop. Particularly admired in the book world are those examples of this genre, for example Parc de la Villette, in which deconstructivist buildings appear against a background of wide open space, deconstructed of all buildings except the object in question. Deconstruction was a hugely fashionable term in the 1980s and '90s when complex forms and complex words seemed inexorably linked. It fell from fashion with a dose of Irritable Bilbao Syndrome

– the most complex building shape of the lot but headed straight at the heart of the popular market.

**E** is for Expenses, the curse of the publisher's life. Why cannot authors simply pay these costs out of their advance? Do they really need to visit the buildings they are writing about when they could simply look them up in the library? For some reason authors – some authors, anyway – take a different view. E is also for e. See William Mitchell.

**F** is for Foreword, a genre of the publishing world promoted within the increasingly ubiquitous monograph. Intended to lend gravitas to what are essentially examples of vanity publishing (see V), they are intimately associated with the name Kenneth Frampton.

**G** is for Guides. There are now architectural guides not simply to cities and countries, but to new buildings, old buildings, restaurants, bars, etc. This trend has been accentuated by the mini-format guides promoted by Ellipsis. A publisher's dream, since they need constant updating.

**H** is for Louis Hellman, the world's greatest architectural cartoonist, whose work for the *Architects' Journal* and the *Architectural Review* is now in its fourth decade. Made an MBE, Hellman went to Buckingham Palace to receive his honour from the Queen. After confusion as to whether the medal was for services to agriculture, HM asked him what he did in relation to architecture. 'I satirise it,' came the reply. The Queen moved on.

H is for Hellman ...

**I** is for Image. The iconic image of a building comes from the architectural photograph, that most expensive element in the publisher's cost line. The photographer must be commissioned or, at the very least, paid copyright fees; the architect, who creates the image from which the photographer benefits, receives nothing. Images of buildings published in magazines are often, if not usually, paid for by the architect. The less famous architect therefore subsidises the magazine as a form of self-promotion. The more famous architect can therefore expect the magazines to behave well if they want to publish the next project (see V).

**J** is for Charles Jencks, author of *The Language of Post-Modern Architecture,* claimed to be the biggest-selling architectural book of the post-war years, which made the architectural textbook both readable and affordable and popularised doublecoding, labelling (inventing new 'isms') and the long, self-contained text caption. Since the 1960s Jencks has been the cause of controversy, rage, and grudging recognition. The definition of a Post-Modern building is one that CJ has a slide of.

**K** is for Louis Kahn, who gives encouragement to all who have come to architecture late in life. Any architectural bluffer's guide explains the difference between Kahn's 'served' and 'servant' spaces. People who have never met him refer to him as 'Lou'. K is also for Koolhaas, inventor of new architectural concepts such as 'Big'. Koolhaas's books, especially *S,M,L,XL*, have reinvented the architectural activity of writing and designing books as projects in themselves.

**L** is for Learning – as in *Learning from Las Vegas,* Robert Venturi's architectural blockbuster, which taught us to distinguish the decorated shed from the building-as-duck, and to value the ordinary. Publishers love the apparent gap between his urbane anglophile personality and his role as promoter of Post-Modernism, which made him architecturally incorrect to purist Modernists.

**M** is for Minimalism, and also for Monograph. The former is a popular subject for the latter, since it requires little writing and can result in considerable savings in publishing costs. The retail price is always high. (See V.)

**N** is for Neo-Classicism which, like the poor, is always with us. Post-Modern Classicism is an unpleasant variant that the earlier version has now seen off. The continuing failure of contemporary architecture to produce an equivalent form is as baffling as it is frustrating, implying as it does that the Georgians had the last word in housing architecture. N is also for News Values, a form followed strictly by architectural magazines

– don't even think of trying to approach two competing magazines with your newly completed and beautifully photographed scheme.

**O** is for Oeuvres Complètes, a relatively new publishing phenomenon that panders to the architect's vanity, appeals to the tidy-minded collector and inspires the publisher, who feels that an additional volume (with a big pre-order from the architect) may be just round the corner. Only death can intervene. These volumes do not, of course, include work that now looks embarrassing.

**P** is for Post-Modernism, that architectural style which seemed to take over the world but died within a decade, although Charles Jencks (see J) argues that we are all Post-Modernists now. At its best it provided a sophisticated and dynamic alternative to the excesses of tired International Modernism. At its worst it was execrable. After the completion of EuroDisney outside Paris, it had nowhere else to go except monographs. P is also for People (don't expect to find them in architectural photos), for Photos (usually the only proof needed or accepted for any building outside London) and for Photoshop (a good alternative to actually building buildings). P is also for Parentheses that demonstrate the user's adherence to radical theory, as in Coop Himmelb(l)au (parentheses added in the 1990s). And for Pluralism, which means nobody's sure what type of architecture they're talking about.

**Q** is for Quinlan Terry, apostle of English Classicism and the man who once claimed that Modernism was the work of Satan. Publishing always finds a place for an architect who is part of the God Squad and can stand his ground on the timeless importance of Classical disciplines, especially as they relate to houses for millionaires. Favourite publishing outlet: upmarket estate agents' brochures.

**R** is for Remaindered. This is what frequently happens to the products of vanity publishing (see V).

**S** is for Sex. Curiously, little has been published about the relationship between sex and architecture, though there has been much about sex and architects (Stanford White, Frank Lloyd Wright). A blockbuster cannot be far away. Compare Woody Allen's remark: 'The last time I was in a woman it was the Statue of Liberty.' S is also for Karl Sabbagh, the scientific TV producer who managed to make architecture into acceptable TV viewing by rendering architects as troublesome, quirky, artistic egomaniacs: very inventive.

**T** is for Timing. Publishers (like editors) love an anniversary, a new building opening, an exhibition. Any excuse to give a book a certain (usually bogus) topicality – or a newspaper an excuse to roll out a big general article. Timing in any form of publication is essential and has nothing whatever to do with the architecture it's trying to portray. Don't expect any type of media to be interested in waiting to publish a building till it's actually finished. That'll be too late – anyone could have seen it.

**U** is for U-turn. The only consistent thing about architectural publishing is its inconsistency, in which today's orthodoxy is tomorrow's remainders, with a few honourable exceptions (Alberti, Banister Fletcher, Le Corbusier). Philip Johnson's remark that all architects are whores applies equally to their publishers. Actually there is one form of consistency: the publisher is sure to lose your photographs.

**V** is for Vanity publishing. The deal works like this: practice wants a showpiece of its work, or sometimes all of its work. Publisher sets up deal. Architect does all the picture and drawing research, spends endless hours with author, corrects proofs – and pays the publisher for the privilege. The payment comes in the form of pre-orders, without which the book would not appear. Books like this are hardback practice brochures: don't expect them to contain sharp criticism. Some practice books are not paid for, but how can you tell?

**W** is for Frank Lloyd Wright. This architect is a publisher's dream, especially US publishers. Why? Because every self-respecting US academic needs to have a 'position' on the master, hence the Fallingwater of books about him which appear every year. (Also note desk diaries, repro lampshades and the Frank Lloyd Wright puppet, available from the Robie House gift shop and recommended outlets.) From a publishing point of view he was probably the architect of the twentieth century – probably because so many Americans have houses a bit like this.

**X** is for Xerox. Very little has been written about the mechanisation of architectural reproduction, but it has played a crucial role in the development (or decline) of the relationship between drawing and building. Just compare the number of drawings required for a job today with 75 years ago and you get the picture. This is a medium which specifically spanned the prosaic (*Everyday Details*), the theoretical (photocopy this heavy book, then you won't have to read it) and the avant-garde (David Greene photocopying himself naked in a cupboard at the Architectural Association: architectural suicide; embracing and being embraced by the machine). Anatomical photocopies are a normal part of minor office rebellion. An understudied medium.

**Y** is for Yale. Or rather, that time at Yale, around 1960, when Foster, Rogers and Stern were there, being taught by Scully, Rudolph, Stirling et al. The results were to shape the architecture of the last quarter of the twentieth century – published only in the Yale schools' annals thus far. An opportunity awaits.

**Z** is for Zaha Hadid. The perfect contemporary architect for a publisher to promote. Glamorous, dangerous, working across Europe and America, multicultural, cutting edge – who cares how much of her work actually gets built? Just keep those drawings coming. Z is also for Zumthor, architecture's opposite of Aardvark – another reliable architectural bookend, whose status no alphabet-proud publisher would dare to challenge.

# Part 4
# The construction of theory

To the outsider, architectural theory – the pinnacle of our media definition of 'architecture' – might seem like a very peculiar construct: a whole culture of writing about other writings, whose source was not normally architecture in the first place. Foucault, Benjamin, Deleuze, Barthes, Virilio, Lacan and so on – the absolute key sources for critical theory in books, conferences and lectures – were not architectural writers, and it's probably safe to say that they're not read by the vast majority of architects. But from them, contemporary critical theory of architecture has constructed arguments which it uses to consider the works of the canon of great architects – alongside 'everyday' architecture.

This type of architectural writing has radically expanded what is considered high-code architectural subject matter. Indeed, it often sets out to overturn assumptions about subject matter, breaking down the barriers between 'practices', and attempting to escape from the segmenting culture of conventional architectural thought. But in doing so this type of writing inevitably sets up its own variant of media bias: its own tendencies, its preferred subject matter, its own cultural shading and its own highly elaborate, highly specific, highly self-referential language.

The bulk of recent studies of the relationship between architecture and the media has come from this type of writing. In doing this, and in the sheer volume of publication, it has established an effective monopoly on all ways of describing the relationship of architecture and the media. Critical theory writings are written for a specific and very highly specialised audience, with a highly specific language and a generally academic, discursive purpose.

Despite this, critical theory is the source of much of the best writing and analysis about architecture and the media, and its concerns have pervaded the whole culture of architecture. Many essays throughout this book (and not necessarily those in this part) are more or less of this type. But one aim of this book was to avoid the normal freehold that critical theory seems to have on writing about architectural media, and I have therefore deliberately discriminated to make sure that other types of writing – by historians, journalists, designers – should be equally treated, on the understanding that they are equally valid and indeed essential to an understanding of the subject matter. If this has meant omitting a mass of critical theory concerned with the media, it is widely available elsewhere.

The following chapters describe and discuss what some of these current concerns are. The first is the 1988 essay by Beatriz Colomina that appeared as the introduction to *Architectureproduction,* a book she edited and which directly tackled the subject of architecture and the media (but which is currently out of print). In it she introduces the idea that the definitive characteristic of 'architecture' is interpretation. Colomina, whose writing is central to the best of critical theory, has since written (among other works) the seminal *Privacy and Publicity: Modern Architecture as Mass Media.* Fourteen years on, the questions that she raised about architecture's relationship with its interpretative media are still open.

If critical theory has been a force in repositioning the core of what is considered architectural, so too has the changing world of work practices and the information revolution. Most architects may well do more or less what they always did (though with more computers), but most architects don't get written about. New young firms – the ones who do get written about – design installations, exhibitions, artworks, community events, advertising and publish books. And through their work the architectural canon shifts to include these projects.

The final three contributors put forward the view from the turn of the twenty-first century: a time when advertising, mediation, branding, lifestyle magazines and highly marketed commercial development are fused into the reinterpretation of early twentieth-century Modernism (which was also interested in such things) as the centre of attention. A recurring argument – though expressed differently from different viewpoints – is whether architecture has itself become a medium, a form of branding for environments, a sign language used and read as a means of communication in a global economy – and where this takes – or leaves architecture's real substance.

Chapter 15
# Architectureproduction[1]
Beatriz Colomina

## Ariadne's house

Greek legend insists that Daedalus was the first architect, but this is hardly the case: although he built the Cretan labyrinth, he never understood its structure. He could only escape, in fact, by flying out of its vortex. Instead it may be argued that Ariadne achieved the first work of architecture, since it was she who gave Theseus the ball of thread by means of which he found his way out of the labyrinth after having killed the Minotaur.

Thus while Ariadne did not build the labyrinth, she was the one who interpreted it; and this is architecture in the modern sense of the term. She achieved this feat through representation; that is to say, with the help of a conceptual device, the ball of thread. We can look at this gift as the 'first' transmission of architecture by means other than itself, as architecture's first *re-production*. The thread of Ariadne is not merely a representation (among the infinite ones possible) of the labyrinth. It is a project, a veritable production, a device that has the result of throwing reality into crisis.

The foregoing story implies this: architecture, as distinct from building, is an interpretive, critical act. It has a linguistic condition different from the practical one of building. A building is interpreted when its rhetorical mechanism and principles are revealed. This analysis may be performed in a number of different ways, according to the forms of different types of discourse; among these are theory, criticism, history and manifesto. An act of interpretation is also present in the different modes of representational discourse: drawing, writing, model making and so on. Interpretation is also integral to the act of projecting.

## Reproduction

> For the first time in world history, mechanical reproduction emancipates the work of art from its parasitical dependence on ritual. To an ever greater degree the work of art reproduced becomes the work of art designed for reproducibility. From a photographic negative, for example, one can make any number of prints; to ask for the authentic print makes no sense. But

> the instant the criterion of authenticity ceases to be applicable to artistic production, the total function of art is reversed. Instead of being based on ritual, it begins to be based on another practice – politics.[2]

The word reproduction in the title of this publication [the original *Architecture-production*] is undoubtedly ambiguous, and it is not by chance that today its role in the social division of labour is being discussed. *The Pocket Oxford Dictionary* offers the following:

> reproduce v.t. & i. (~cible). Produce copy or representation of; cause to be seen, heard etc., again; produce offspring of (oneself, itself); produce further members of the same species by natural means; ~duction n., reproducing of copy of painting, etc. (attrib. of furniture, etc.) made in imitation of earlier style.[3]

This definition immediately manifests a tension between organic and manual (or mechanical) reproduction, between Nature and Culture, between the biological and the historical reproduction of society. An obvious example of such a division between Nature and Culture is agriculture. The peasant (the producer) plants the seed, and the task of nature is its reproduction.

A closer reading reveals that this definition corresponds to a still precapitalist, preindustrial view of the world. It ignores technical reproduction, not so much in not referring to it explicitly (photographic reproduction, for instance, is not mentioned), but in depicting a condition in which production and reproduction, original and copy, stand apart. 'Produce a copy or representation of', 'cause to be seen, heard again' suggest the previous existence of a legitimate, original, authentic act against which any 'reproduction' is at best a replica and at worst a forgery. Today, in a stage of late capitalism, production and reproduction stand as two terms within a continuous cycle, their roles overlapping.

The craftsman, the storyteller, is the subject implicit in this dictionary definition of reproduction. The craftsman's universe is that of the identification of the object with the world. The object carries the traces of its maker: the clay vessel betrays the fingerprints of the potter, just as the story reveals traces of the narrator. This continuity between man and object belongs to a classical notion of the artefact. With industry, mass production, and reproduction, this relationship is reversed. The product (the 'original') and its reproduction (the 'copy') are confused with each other. The relations between maker and object, object and user (or viewer), are now those of producer, product and consumer (or audience), determined by their respective position in the continuous process of production. The importance of the process increases at the expense of the individual product and its 'authority as thing' (once the repository of all communicative value), and of the author as transcendent self and bearer of meaning.

The crisis of the classical art object that occurs with its insertion into the cycle of everyday life, with its mass reproduction, was at the centre of the investigations of the historical avant-gardes, and it is not by chance that four articles in this publication [the original publication *Architectureproduction*] were devoted to experiences that fall within this trajectory (Meyer and Hilbersheimer, Mies van der Rohe, Melnikov and Le Corbusier). These contributions tend less to be 'historical' in the academic sense of the term, even if they were grounded in historical and philological research, than to be reconsiderations of the methods of architectural history. More precisely, they attempt to revise the understanding of 'Modernism' that has come down to us by way of the masters of modern art criticism and the operative critics of architecture. I shall come back to this subject.

'The enormous changes which printing, the mechanical reproduction of writing, has brought about in literature are a familiar story,' writes Walter Benjamin.[4] We can hardly make a parallel claim concerning the introduction of reproduction into the processes of architecture and the crisis resulting from it. While many pages have been devoted to the impact of the new production materials and techniques upon architecture, and a few studies have been done on the history of specific architectural magazines, these accounts tend to overlook the transformations in the relationship between producer, product and audience which are at the base of the new condition.

Until the advent of photography, and earlier of lithography, the audience of architecture was the user. With photography, the illustrated magazine and tourism, architecture's reception began to occur also through an additional social form: consumption. With the enormous amplification of the audience, the relation to the building changed radically. The audience (the tourist in front of a building, the reader of a journal, the viewer of an exhibition or a newspaper advertisement, and even the client who is often all of the above) increasingly became the user, the one who gave meaning to the work. In turn, the work itself is changed.

## Reinterpreting Modernism

> The reality of production and technology in which we find ourselves has not left behind the great problems relating to the 'technical reproducibility' of the work of art, to the crisis of the object and to the 'fall of the aura'. What is new is the awareness of the links between instruments of communication and collective behaviors that has come into being with the sophistication, rapid renewal and extension of the mass-media.[5]

The concepts of production and reproduction to which we refer in this issue are initially indebted to those put forward by Walter Benjamin in his famous studies 'The Author as Producer' (delivered as a lecture in 1934) and 'The Work of Art in the Age of Mechanical Reproduction' (published in 1936). For pointing to the recuperation of Benjamin's analyses for a critical study of architecture as an institution, we are indebted to Manfredo Tafuri.

By 'architecture as an institution' Tafuri understands 'what architecture has meant up to now, first in the anticipation of ideologies, then as a process directly involved in modern production processes and the development of the capitalist society'.[6] Referring explicitly to Benjamin, he writes:

> To ignore either the limitations of the possibilities of communication or the new horizons opened by the means available to architecture clearly leads to an evasive attitude. Walter Benjamin's analyses of the semantic, operative, mental and behaviorist consequences of modern technology remain an isolated case in the history of contemporary criticism (and we suspect that it is not by chance). The misunderstandings that have dominated architectural culture from 1945 onward derive in great part from the interruption of Benjamin's analyses: *structural* analyses, we must stress, beyond any evasive or fashionable meaning of the term or the concept.[7]

Thus as early as 1969, and in the very field of architecture history, we encounter the call for a reconsideration of critical methods, and more specifically for a reinterpretation of Modernism as it had evolved in the years following 1945 in the accounts of such writers as Theodor Adorno, Clement Greenberg and their followers. That is, we find a problematic parallel to that at the centre of the more recent discourse which has developed in art and literary criticism, typified by contributions such as Victor Burgin's 'Modernism in the Work of Art', Mary Kelly's 'Reviewing Modernist Criticism', Thomas Crow's 'Modernism and Mass Culture in the Visual Arts', Fredric Jameson's 'Reification and Utopia in Mass Culture' and Andreas Huyssen's 'Mapping the Postmodern'. This is to name only a few of those who, despite all their differences, have helped in recent years to dismantle the structure of the discursive edifice of 'Modernism'.

By 'Modernism', it may be worth emphasising, rather than the actual art practices originating around the mid-nineteenth century, these authors understand their (re)construction in the critical discourse produced in America in the years following 1945. The codification of Modernism took place in the years preceding and during the Cold War. As Andreas Huyssen has noted:

> Aesthetic categories such as those of Greenberg and Adorno cannot be totally divorced from the pressures of that era .... It is a specific image of modernism that has become the bone of

contention for the postmoderns, and that image has to be reconstructed if we want to understand postmodernism's problematic relationship to the modernist tradition and its claims to difference.[8]

It also should be noted that critical terms such as *modernism*, *modernity*, the *avant-garde*, and *postmodernism* are used differently in different cultural milieus, and also on opposite sides of the Atlantic. 'Modernity,' as Alice Jardine has written, 'traditionally refers in English to the classically defined 'modern period'; while in French, *la modernité* refers to a radical conceptual process which, while limited to no particular chronology, most often refers to certain kinds of texts written since the late nineteenth century. It is increasingly used in France as synonymous with the American 'postmodern'.[9] Moreover, while postmodernism in architecture is generally understood in aesthetic and stylistic terms, as the crisis of confidence in modernist aesthetics, in cultural theory the product of postmodernism, as Victor Burgin writes, 'has involved dismantling the philosophical apparatus which supports the terms in which art is conceived in society'.[10]

Modernist criticism – and to the names of Adorno and Greenberg for music and the visual arts we should perhaps add Colin Rowe and Robert Slutzky for architecture on this side of the Atlantic[11] – has focused on the internal life of the autonomous, self-referential object. What recent critical discourse has in common (from Tafuri to Hays, from Kelly to Burgin, from Huyssen to Bürger), and despite its differences, is its attention to art and architecture as institutions, rather than as a series of individual protagonists or monuments. As Burgin has written:

> The question of the 'political' effect of art is a complex one, not confined to crude cases of simple instrumentality in the service of a pre-formed 'message.' Consideration must be given not only to the internal attributes of a work but also to its production and dissemination in and across the institutions within which its meaning is produced.[12]

To the recent discourse on Modernism belongs Peter Bürger's polemical *Theory of the Avant-garde*, a book frequently referred to in this publication [*Architectureproduction*]. Bürger has taken as his task the conceptual distinction between modernism and the historical European avant-garde. He argues that unlike modernism the goal of the avant-garde (and he limits himself here to Dada, early Surrealism and the post-revolutionary Russian avant-garde) was primarily an attack on the bourgeois 'institution art' and its ideology of autonomy rather than merely a change in artistic or literary modes of representation. By 'institution art' Bürger means to refer to the ways in which art's role in society is perceived and defined; to use his own words, 'to the productive and distributive apparatus and also to the ideas about art that prevail at a given time and that determine the reception of works'.[13] The avant-garde, Bürger concludes, was an attack on the highness of high art and on the separateness of art from everyday life that had evolved in nineteenth-century aestheticism.

Bürger's account of the avant-garde is historically and theoretically more precise than Renato Poggiolo's earlier book of almost identical title, *The Theory of the Avant-Garde* (1968), where he equates the avant-garde with modernism over a historical span going back as far as the late eighteenth century and paralleling the development of bourgeois capitalist society. Poggiolo's theory is at best a theory of modernity and as such insufficient to characterise the historical avant-gardes, as Schulte-Sasse notes in his introduction to Bürger's book.[14]

But there are also certain limits to Bürger's critical categories. The conventional understanding of Modernism carries connotations of an autonomous, inward, self-referential and self-critical artistic practice, and Bürger remains somewhat locked in this Adornian concept. The same conception also assumes the relationship between modernist art and mass culture to be one of continuous refusal. A few studies have recently shown, on the other hand, the continuous involvement between modernist art and the materials of low culture. Most notable among these is Crow's 'Modernism and Mass Culture in the Visual Arts', where he writes, 'Modernism repeatedly makes subversive equations between high and low which dislocate the apparently fixed terms of that hierarchy into new and persuasive configurations, thus calling it into question from within.'[15] Some of the studies here published [in *Architectureproduction*] – Michael Hays on Hannes Meyer and Hilberseimer, Jean-Louis Cohen on Melnikov, and my own on Le Corbusier – elaborate on this theme of the relations between modernism and mass culture.

Indeed, dichotomies such as modernism/avant-garde, high art/mass culture, art/life become highly problematic when we turn our attention to the specific conditions of architecture's production. What does an 'avant-gardist' position mean in the domain of architecture? This is a problem clearly distinct from that posed by the visual arts.

The most radical architect of this century [the twentieth century], Adolf Loos, devoted his life to demonstrating that between art and life there was no possible bridge. Life was necessarily 'the Other' (*das Andere*) of art. But for Loos architecture, like everything else which serves a purpose, did not belong to the realm of art; the only exceptions were the tomb and the monument, that is to say those programmes from which life is necessarily excluded. Can Loos therefore be said to be an avant-gardist *avant la lettre*?

When Loos undertook to publish *Das Andere*, a 'Journal for the Introduction of Western Culture into Austria', of which only two issues appeared, in 1902–3, he did not use its pages to represent (his own or others') architecture. He delights us instead

**213** | Architectureproduction

with stories drawn from his personal experience and in particular from his mythical trip to America. 'My uncle is a watchmaker in Philadelphia …' are the opening words of a journal where Loos tells us all about salt spoons and table manners, men's and women's fashion, toilet paper, furniture, cooking, upholstery and above all (underlying all this) the American way of life. No photographs are published in this journal; it is illustrated with advertisements for the work of Viennese craftsmen (with the exception of the front of a butcher shop with the corpse of a cow in the foreground, for which no clue is offered in the text).

The profession of architecture, in Loos's view, had little to do with the 'institution art', with the high art world of museums, exhibitions and publications. Loos was reacting against precisely such transformation of architecture into artistry in the Vienna of his time (Hoffman and the architects of the Werkbund being his main target). For Loos, architecture was produced to meet a need and existed in a different context from art (namely the construction site). Further, architecture was culturally disseminated through publications, a phenomenon, as Loos was early to realise, that in turn affected the design of architecture. His critique was directed to that confusion of architecture with its image that was infecting architects infatuated with the magazines.

The artistic avant-gardes of the first decades of the twentieth century, on the other hand, saw in publishing, exhibitions and public events another context of production. Their work in these media often preceded the artistic product itself. The Futurist manifesto published on the front page of as wide-reaching a newspaper as Le Figaro, before there was anything that had materialised as Futurist art, is only one of the most obvious examples. As Caroline Tisdall and Angelo Bozzolla have written, 'The birth of Futurism was in itself a stroke of advertising genius.'[16]

Le Corbusier, conventionally read as the epitome of 'modernism', was perhaps the first architect fully to grasp the nature of the media. He understood the press, the printed media, not only as a medium for the cultural diffusion of something previously existing but, like some of his contemporaries in the visual arts, a new context of production, existing in parallel with the construction site. Le Corbusier is the architect of his own *Oeuvre Complète,* the spectacle of the succession of his works, carefully constructed on each page and, taken as a whole, more significant than any reproduction could ever be, as von Moos points out.[17] As in Lacan's famous analyses of the 'mirror stage' of psychological development, the printed media provide for Le Corbusier both a turning point and a moment of constitution of his architectural 'self'.

Lacan's text, 'The Mirror Stage as Formative of the Function of the I as Revealed in Psychoanalytical Experience',[18] is about the formation of an I, of an identity, as we experience it in psychoanalysis – an experience, Lacan goes on to say, that leads us to oppose any philosophy directly issuing from the *cogito.* The classical conception of the mirror (and of photography for that matter) is that it reflects a self, that it produces a secondary, more or less faithful, likeness, an imitation, a translation of an already constituted original self. But Lacan posits that the mirror *constructs* the self, that the self as organised entity is actually an imitation of the cohesiveness of the mirror image. In Jane Gallop's words:

> In the mirror stage, the infant who has not yet mastered the upright posture and who is supported by either another person or some prosthetic device will, upon seeing herself in the mirror, 'jubilantly assume' the upright position. She thus finds in the mirror image, 'already there,' a mastery that she will actually learn only later … . The mirror stage is a turning point. After it, the subject's relation to himself is always mediated through a totalizing image that has come from the outside.[19]

Actually, anybody actively involved with publishing is familiar with this experience. The printed media are the mirror wherein the bits and pieces of one's writings and work (often unrealised) return miraculously to their author in a 'complete' image. The exhilarating effect on one of the press is not unlike the jubilation of a six-month-old baby in front of a mirror. The question is how to proceed from this vision, this 'mirage', through the anxiety that necessarily follows it, to the acceptance of castration. In other words, rather than remain narcissistically enamoured of it, how does one establish with the mirror image a productive rather than a reflective relationship?

## What is criticism?

> Critical texts have focused either on the analysis of the individual tableau (sometimes an individual artist's *oeuvre*) or on the construction of general cultural categories and typologies of art … . Interpretation is not simply a matter of what can be discovered at the interior of a composition. A reconsideration of critical methods is required if one takes account of the specific conditions which determine the organization of the artistic texts and their readings at the present time; that is, the temporary exhibition and its associated field of publications – the catalogue, the art book and the magazine. From this point of view, 'art' is never given in the form of individual works but is constructed as a category in relation to a complex configuration of texts.[20]

While the gallery system has been a basic institution in the art world bringing together and mediating the relationship between producers and consumers, artists and audiences, the same does not hold true for architecture. The phenomenon of the museum of architecture, of architecture's exhibition in a gallery, is something so recent we have hardly managed to grasp its meaning.

The traditional channel for the cultural diffusion of architecture has been, and still will be for a while, the professional journals, which, unlike the art magazines, have no connection with the gallery system. As architecture enters the world of the art market, of shows and sales and published criticism, those involved in its production, publicisation and diffusion must critically address its changed cultural meaning.

The fundamental question posed by Walter Benjamin in 'The Author as Producer' becomes relevant: what is the position of the work within the relations of production of its time? This question applies not only to the relations of production involved in the construction of the material object, the building, but also to those of its distribution and consumption through the channels of the culture industry: newspapers, periodical publications, professional magazines, exhibitions and their accompanying catalogues, radio and television, advertising. In other words the way in which architecture is produced, marketed, distributed and consumed is part of the 'institution architecture' – that is, of the way in which architecture's role in society is perceived and defined in the age of mass (re)production and the culture industry. The question criticism itself must pose to architecture is the same one that it must pose to itself: as Tafuri writes in 'The Historical Project', in what ways does criticism enter the production processes?[21]

The essays in this publication [*Architectureproduction*] are inscribed in this problematic. Critical methods and the focus of analysis differ, sometimes radically. An immediate distinction is between those authors who have occupied themselves with technical reproduction as it concerns itself with the material production of the architectural object (most notably Hays in his article on Meyer and Hilberseimer) and those who have attended to the circulation and diffusion of architecture on the printed page. Both approaches are encompassed in Benjamin's analyses of the transformation of the work of art in the age of its technical reproduction. In [K. Michael] Hays' study,[22] the classical (formalist) critical attention to the object is shifted to the mechanism of its production. To quote Hays with reference to Hannes Meyer, 'the work is only a trace or direct registration of those materials and procedures of reproduction from which it is constructed'. In other words, it is the technique of reproduction itself, rather than the single object produced through it, that for Hays (as for Benjamin) becomes significant. Hays' text thus opened discussion of the ideological assumptions underlying the thesis and methods of Modernist criticism.

A few contributors in this publication [*Architectureproduction*] are about (or written from within) specific architectural journals – those on the *Revue Générale de l'Architecture, L'Esprit Nouveau, Oppositions* and *Casabella*. Two contributions are about ephemeral constructions: Mies van der Rohe's German Pavilion at the Barcelona International Exhibition of 1929 and Konstantin Melnikov's Soviet Pavilion at the Paris Exposition Internationale des Arts Décoratifs of 1925. However, the relationship

**216** | Beatriz Colomina

between these texts was not so clear cut to allow for an easy taxonomy. The theme of reproduction takes on different dimensions with each contribution. I will comment on a few aspects that generated discussion among the [*Architectureproduction*] editorial group but have not been addressed in the responses found in the second part of this volume.

Jose Quetglas's essay on the German Pavilion at the 1929 Barcelona International Exhibition, a work commissioned by the German government of Mies van der Rohe and Lilly Reich, may require contextualisation for many readers. It is hardly known that, owing to its limited temporal existence (and the fact that 1929 was not exactly a year for leisure travel), the German Pavilion was seen by 'nobody', with a few exceptions such as Peter Behrens and, of course, local architects and the public. Despite this, the pavilion was soon recognised as a masterpiece of modern architecture, and its drawings and photographs widely reproduced. The rebuilding of the pavilion in Barcelona was the event that provided the political occasion for Quetglas's essay. His reading of the Mies pavilion is a metareading, of both the local reaction, represented in the local newspapers of the time, and the photographs and texts circulated by way of the canonising volumes. For Quetglas, the pavilion exists in these printed pages and photographs, which constitute our memory of it. But not only is the pavilion known to us by its 'reproduction'. As Quetglas showed, it in itself comprises a set of reproductions of preceding works and projects by Mies himself, by Bruno Taut, and by Peter Behrens. It also operates in much the same way as a theatrical re-presentation, as, in his opinion, do other projects by Mies, for instance the monument to Rosa Luxemburg and the Seagram Building. Quetglas's rhetorical artifice of taking the 1929 visitor through the building returns us to a problem I raised earlier: the transformations in relations between architect, work and audience. Quetglas's analysis of Mies's pavilion explores the way in which the observer (the viewer), who has replaced the user in the role of giving meaning to the work, is caught in an ambiguous position, at once inside and outside the architectural work. No longer is critical detachment between the viewer and object possible.

Hélène Lipstadt has focused on César Daly and the journal that he edited, the *Revue Générale de l'Architecture,* to contribute a historical analysis of the transformations of the institution of architecture at the inception of the existence of the professional journals. The legitimation apparatus ceases at this point to emanate only from the traditional sanctuaries of the institution – the academy, the *Grand Prix* and so forth – to enter the space of the press. Minor architects make their appearance in the pages of the *Revue* under the same title as those legitimised by the traditional channels. Lipstadt points out the ways the work of architecture was socially transformed through the agency of the press; what was once essentially a professional service rendered to a client (who thereafter possessed the building) now began to become an art object. As she writes, 'The architect regains control over the tool of his own emancipation thanks to the French laws of artistic property, which granted to the architect possession of the image of his creation.'[23]

Conventional historical analyses of the *Revue* have viewed it as either a personal creation of the editor or as a mirror of contemporary production. Both approaches, Lipstadt argues, assume that the magazine reflects a reality external to itself: Daly's theory of architecture or the architecture of its time. Lipstadt instead reads the *Revue* as a 'production place' in and of itself. She describes how the press was free to invent the architectural present, making architectural news almost entirely a creation of the magazines. Lipstadt's study of one of the first and most relevant architectural journals remains an isolated case in a field of much needed historical research, and we suspect that there are more than technical reasons for this lack. (Lipstadt herself points out some of the difficulties and obstacles involved in such studies.)

Turning from the oldest magazine represented here [in *Architectureproduction*] to one that is very much ongoing, Pierre-Alain Croset, an editor of the *Casabella* of Vittorio Gregotti, posing for himself a problem that is his everyday concern: how to publish built architecture today? As Croset writes, the photograph cannot reproduce the temporal experience of a building. But the magazine, he argues, should evoke this dimension using as a critical tool *narration*.

*Casabella* under Gregotti has never seen itself as an avant-garde magazine (in the historical sense of the term) or, on the other hand, a 'trade journal' for professional reference such as exists in the Anglo-Saxon tradition. It is rather a magazine of *tendenza,* highly selective in its choice of work as well as in its collaborators. Gregotti has been concerned with the problem of publishing 'meaningful' contemporary built architecture, a programme akin to Kenneth Frampton's project of 'critical regionalism'; that is, he has focused on those architects concerned with rooting their work in traditional culture. The dilemma of this project, which Croset implicitly addresses in his essay, lies in how to use an instrument of universal civilisation that cancels out local traditions, namely the printed page and image, to recover these experiences that have as their programmatic end a resistance to commodification. Croset proposes 'narration' as a critical instrument to salvage 'real' architecture from the ravages of consumption.

Croset's proposal is inspired by Walter Benjamin's essay 'The Storyteller'.[24] The critic is to take on the function of the storyteller of ancient times, of those times prior to mechanical reproduction when, to say it in the words of Loos, 'the work of the old masters was quickly known in the most out-of-the-way places of the earth, despite, or more exactly, precisely because, there was no post, no telephone, no periodical'.[25]

Croset, however, overlays on this Benjaminian analysis a Barthesian idea, arguing that the narration of a building should above all stimulate the reader's *desire* to produce architecture. The question presents itself of how much these two notions – Benjaminian narration and Barthesian desire – are compatible, and further, whether Croset should not replace desire with 'resistance'. For what Croset is arguing, and this is his most forceful argument, is for the sensual experience of the architectural object in its original place and time, that is, for all that the printed media eliminate of architecture, and that narration could restore to us by being embedded in the life of the critic who was there and touched it (as opposed to the critic who writes by relying on photographs or who writes about an architecture that does not demand touching).

The theme of desire and architecture has also been addressed – but in a very different way – by Bernard Tschumi. In his *Architectural Manifestoes,* an exhibition held at Artists Space gallery in New York in 1978, Tschumi wrote, concerning his 'Advertisements for Architecture' of 1976:

> The paper representation of architecture will have the sole purpose of triggering desire for architecture. The somehow ironical images of these advertisements were all prepared in the context of magazine articles which could not be illustrated in the conventional way. After all, architectural drawings and photographs are just paper spaces – there is no way to 'perform' real architecture in a magazine and through a drawing. The only way is to make believe. So, just as ads for architectural products (or cigarettes and whiskey) are made to trigger desire for something beyond the glossy illustration, these ads have the same purpose: to trigger desire for architecture.[26]

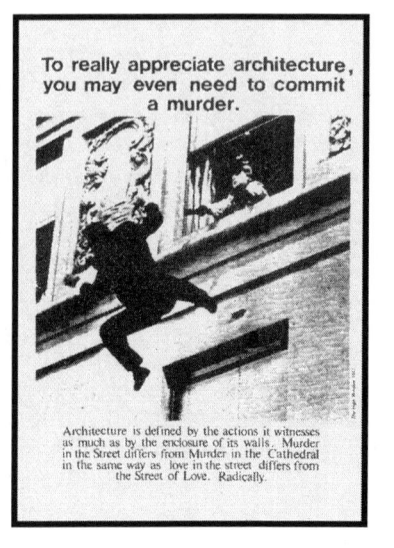

Advertisements versus narration: *Ceci tuera cela*. Narration implies an object, a truth existing previous to its discursive formation, an object that the narration will represent in the most faithful manner. In the advertisement there is a void in place of the object. It triggers desire in the society of consumption. Mary Kelly has written:

> The field of vision is ordered by the function of images ... Since the fascination in looking is founded on separation from what is seen, the field of vision is also, and most appropriately, the field of desire.[27]

Tschumi used the exhibition space and the printed page to reflect on the status of the architectural object in the society of media and advertising. The space from which he was speaking, the gallery, was already a manifestation of a new (postmodern) condition. In the last ten years, architecture entered the space of the museum and the gallery, traditional spaces of the institution of art. These spaces combine with the printed media, traditional place for the diffusion of architecture, in creating a cultural phenomenon and artistic product. Critical attention has to be directed to this area too.

The history of the architectural media is much more than a footnote to the history of architecture. The journals and now the galleries help to determine that history. They invent 'movements', create 'tendencies' and launch international figures, promoting architects from the limbo of the unknown, of building, to the rank of

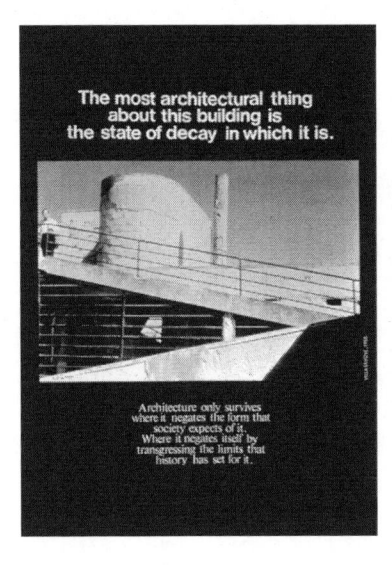

**The most architectural thing about this building is the state of decay in which it is.**

Architecture only survives where it negates the form that society expects of it. Where it negates itself by transgressing the limits that history has set for it.

The game of architecture is an intricate play with rules that you may break or accept. These rules, like so many knots that cannot be untied, have the erotic significance of bondage: the more numerous and sophisticated the restraints, the greater the pleasure.

**ropes and rules**

historical events, to the canon of history. And later they may kill off these same figures. As Victor Burgin has written:

> The canon is what gets written about, collected, and taught; it is self-perpetuating, self-justifying and arbitrary; it is the gold standard against which the values of the new aesthetic currencies are measured. The canon is the discourse made flesh; the discourse is the spirit of the canon. To refuse the discourse, the words of communion with the canon, in speaking of art or in making it, is to court the benign violence of institutional excommunication.[28]

Despite differences among the authors involved in this publication [*Architectureproduction*], we had in common something that is well expressed in Roland Barthes' words:

> All criticism must include in its discourse an implicit reflection on itself; every criticism is a criticism of the work and a criticism of itself. In other words, criticism is not at all a table of results or a body of judgments, it is essentially an activity .... Can an activity be 'true'? It answers quite different requirements.[29]

## Notes

1. First published as 'Introduction: On Architecture, Production and Reproduction', in *Architectureproduction,* 2nd vol. in the series *Revisions: Papers on Architectural Theory and Criticism,* guest ed. Beatriz Colomina (New York: Princeton Architectural Press, 1988), pp. 6–23. I am indebted to Beatriz Colomina for suggesting this reprinting. KR
2. Walter Benjamin, 'The Work of Art in the Age of Mechanical Reproduction', in *Illuminations* (New York: Schocken Books, 1969).
3. *The Pocket Oxford Dictionary,* 6th edition (1978).
4. Benjamin, *The Work of Art in the Age of Mechanical Reproduction.*
5. Manfredo Tafuri, *Theories and History of Architecture* (New York: Harper & Row, 1976), p. 232.
6. Manfredo Tafuri, 'Note to the Second (Italian) Edition', in *Theories and History of Architecture.*
7. Tafuri, *Theories and History of Architecture*, p. 232.
8. Andreas Huyssen, 'Mapping the Postmodern', *New German Critique* 33 (Fall 1984). Reprinted in *After the Great Divide: Modernism, Mass Culture, Postmodernism* (Bloomington and Indianapolis: Indiana University Press, 1986).
9. Alice Jardine, 'At the Threshold, Feminists and Modernity', *Wedge* 6 (1984), p. 15.
10. Victor Burgin, *The End of Art Theory: Criticism and Postmodernity* (Atlantic Highlands, NY: Humanities Press International, 1986).
11. Clement Greenberg, 'Avant-Garde and Kitsch,' *Partisan Review* 6 (1939), and 'Towards a Newer Laöcoon', *Partisan Review* 7 (1940). See also T.J. Clark, 'More on

the Differences between Comrade Greenberg and Ourselves', in *Modernism and Modernity,* ed. Benjamin H.D. Buchloh (Halifax: Press of NSCAD, 1983); Theodor Adorno, 'On the Fetish Character of Music and the Regression of Listening' (1938), in Andrew Arato and Eike Gebhardt, *The Essential Frankfurt School Reader* (New York, 1978). See also Andreas Huyssen, 'Adorno in Reverse', in *After the Great Divide;* Thomas Crow, 'Modernism and Mass Culture in the Visual Arts', in *Modernism and Modernity,* esp. note 45; Colin Rowe and Robert Slutzky, 'Transparency, Literal and Phenomenal' (1955-6), in *The Mathematics of the Ideal Villa and Other Essays* (Cambridge, MA: MIT Press, 1976). For a discussion, see Michael Hays, 'Reproduction and Negation: The Cognitive Project of the Avant-Garde', and Christian Hubert, 'Response to Michael Hays', both in this publication [*Architectureproduction*].

12    Victor Burgin, 'Modernism in the Work of Art', *20th Century Studies* 15-16 (December 1976), reprinted in *End of Art Theory,* p. 24.
13    Peter Bürger, *Theory of the Avant-Garde* (Minneapolis: University of Minnesota Press, 1984), p. 22.
14    Jochen Schulte-Sasse, 'Foreword: Theory of Modernism versus Theory of the Avant-Garde', in Bürger, *Theory of the Avant-Garde,* p. x.
15    Crow, 'Modernism and Mass Culture in the Visual Arts'.
16    Tisdall and Bozzolla, *Futurism* (London: Thames & Hudson, 1977), p. 9.
17    Stanislaus von Moos, *Le Corbusier: Elements of a Synthesis* (Cambridge, MA: MIT Press, 1979), p. 302.
18    Jacques Lacan, *Ecrits: A Selection* (London: Tavistock, 1977), pp. 1-7.
19    Jane Gallop, *Reading Lacan* (Ithaca, NY: Cornell University Press, 1985), pp. 78-9.
20    Mary Kelly, 'Reviewing Modernist Criticism', *Screen* 22:3 (Autumn 1981).
21    Manfredo Tafuri, 'The Historical Project', in *The Sphere and the Labyrinth* (Cambridge, MA: MIT Press, 1987), pp. 2 ff.
22    K. Michael Hays, 'Reproduction and Negation: The Cognitive Project of the Avant-Garde', in *Architectureproduction,* pp. 152-79.
23    Hélène Lipstadt, 'The Building and the Book in César Daly's *Revue Générale de l'Architecture*', in *Architectureproduction,* pp. 56-99.
24    Walter Benjamin, 'The Storyteller. Reflections on the Works of Nikolai Leskov', in *Illuminations.*
25    Adolf Loos, 'Architektur' (1910), in *Trotzdem* (Innsbuck: Brenner, 1931), pp. 101-2.
26    Bernard Tschumi, *Architectural Manifestoes,* exhibition catalog (New York, 1978).
27    Mary Kelly, 'Desiring Images Imaging Desire,' *Wedge* 6 (1984).
28    Victor Burgin, 'The End of Art Theory', in *The End of Art Theory,* p. 159.
29    Roland Barthes, 'What is Criticism?' in *Critical Essays* (Evanston: Northwestern University Press, 1972).

Chapter 16
# From dematerialisation to depoliticisation in architecture
Clare Melhuish

From the printing press to the Internet, the impact and influence of the media have been determined and defined by advances in technology. In the same way, the history of architecture has been indissolubly linked to the discovery of new materials and the development of engineering science, generating continuous innovation in construction techniques. As society moves out of the mechanical and into the electronic engineering era, questions surrounding the meaning of the material object and its life cycle, and of the way that individual human identity is manifested through the production and use of physical objects, are equally significant in debates about the media and about architecture.

Technology is fundamental to the making of things; yet now it is seen as offering a remarkable potential for dematerialisation of the physical environment – or at least a takeover of the physical domain by endlessly replicated computer terminals. In the 1990s the architectural discipline hastened to embrace and apply the implications of the information revolution to its own field of enquiry, driven by its inexorable history of tension between the technological and aesthetic-symbolic sources of architectural production.

The Modern Movement had asserted the predominance of the technological imperative in defining and predicting the aesthetic form of architecture, and its place within the culture of its time. Its leading figures acknowledged the implications of industrialised mass production as inevitable and set out to explore the formal and spatial possibilities offered by the new technologies in a spirit of enthusiasm and determination. Negotiating a period of global crisis and destruction, they clung to the hope that the new avenues of exploration could realise idealistic social programmes providing everyone with higher expectations of life. Yet their unswerving commitment to new technology can now be seen as having paved the way for a dematerialisation of architecture that was to be justified by an increasing dependency on media theory in the late twentieth century, even though its implications for an erosion of social programme and political idealism now seem clearly arguable.

One of the most significant impacts of industrialised construction technology was in its potential for the reduction of building mass. As load-bearing walls were replaced by concrete and steel-frame structures, with infill panels or suspended curtain-walling, the concept of the building envelope as a thin, insulated membrane held rigid by precisely manufactured, pared-down structural components began to take over from the idea of the building as a dense, solid mass, in which sheer quantity and weight of materials was an essential prerequisite for structural stability and internal environmental comfort. In a sense then, the process of technological development in the construction industry can be seen as a force leading towards a gradual dematerialisation of architecture in the urbanised Western world, even at that time.

A common reason given for dislike of modern architecture is its appearance of flimsiness, insubstantiality or impermanence, yet the gradual evolution of new materials and construction technologies up to the present day has made it possible to dispense with sheer building mass to an even greater degree. From an environmental point of view, this opens up possibilities of building more lightly on the earth, which is not only essential to the future of the human race on the planet, but is also in tune with the building techniques and technologies of many traditional societies, such as the nomadic peoples of Aboriginal Australia, the Mongolian steppes or Moroccan High Atlas. But, unlike these traditional vernacular architectural forms, contemporary Western industrialised building often matches its lack of material substance with an inability

Dom-Ino – prototype of concrete building principle, 1914, from Le Corbusier's *Oeuvre Complète*
Fondation Le Corbusier/ADAGP, Paris and DACS, London 2001

to perform the role of cultural representation, or only at a manufactured, superficial level, which is one of the key functions of architecture in society.

Hence it becomes possible to identify 'the problem' of contemporary Western architecture as lying in a loss of cultural substance, which has accompanied a reduction in material substance generated by technological development and sophistication. This reduction in material substance should be read in conjunction with a rise in the use of new materials, with the capacity to respond to varying environmental stimuli through the operation of sensors and computer programming, and even the possibility of using biotechnological processes to 'grow' all-natural building materials in the foreseeable future. The result is a thoroughgoing destabilisation of physical form and structure, and the creation of an architecture of mutability which undermines conventional social and cultural expectations of architecture's role in providing and constituting a framework of ontological security.

If these conditions of destabilisation and mutability in architecture, resulting from technological advances, are accepted as characteristics of the contemporary Western urban environment, it seems reasonable to argue that they reflect, or make manifest, conditions of economic and cultural globalisation accelerated through the expansion of Western capital and the operation of information and media technology, particularly television and the Internet, at a global scale.

Globalisation can be read both as a force for cultural homogenisation and, paradoxically, as a force for fragmentation and exaggerated cultural differentiation. On

Central Asian yurt, in Archala autumn pasture (*Kyrgyz boz uy*)

the one hand, as Christopher Tilley argues, place or space becomes a commodity[1] under capitalism like any other, and in that sense it is the same anywhere. The more homogeneous that global conditions are, the more congenial they become to the operation of the capitalist market. As Nigel Harris has shown, cities across the world, from Mexico and Colombia to Cyprus, the Philippines and elsewhere, have made strenuous efforts to reinvent themselves in the image of their Western European and American counterparts in order to attract inward investment – for 'the condition of the city is essential to profits'.

Yet at the same time the myriad burgeoning movements for regional and ethnic differentiation and autonomy throughout the world have thrown the politics of the nation state into a turmoil of fragmentation and have subjected communities everywhere to the sufferings of terrorist campaigns and vicious civil warfare. Saskia Sassens argues that the Internet, which on the one hand has provided such a powerful tool for global unification, has perhaps had an even more significant impact by empowering and giving a voice to peripheral minority groups in a world where globality should be understood not so much as an overarching condition but rather as a 'multitude of localities' involved in global projects.[2]

In a society where the polar forces of homogenisation and fragmentation are embodied in the physical flows and juxtapositions of peoples and an excess of information and images circulating around the globe, the possibility of any clear and direct form of cultural representation becomes increasingly elusive. In the big cosmopolitan, postcolonial metropolises of the West, cultural value systems and religious beliefs are mediated by the prevailing official creed of relativism and tolerance and become subject to the same forces of consumer choice as any other commodity. Thus the material condition of a physically destabilised and increasingly mutable architecture is paralleled by neutrality, abstraction, fundamentalism or simple incoherence in terms of its articulation of cultural ideas.

For the intellectual elite in architecture, contextualism increasingly means abstraction, for it is a contextualism which responds to the conditions of an international culture sustained by a global circuit of key cultural institutions, the technology of swift air travel and a sophisticated media network. It takes the universal ideal of Modernism a logical step further, creating a series of contemporary 'wonders of the world' – such as Bilbao's Guggenheim or Helsinki's Kiasma – which are understood by local populations for what they are: powerful media images designed to transcend local conditions, to speak to and draw in a global audience. For the populist, downmarket end of architecture (or, shall we say, basic construction), contextualism means a response to ideas of the traditional, involving the mass-produced, superficial reproduction of familiar images, also circulated by the media, which represent readily recognisable ways of life and patterns of aspiration: brand recognition.

At both ends of the spectrum, architecture seems to have been absorbed into the operation of the media: a dematerialised production of image or text for visual or intellectual consumption which effectively displaces and negates the need to experience embodied architecture. Viewed from one angle, this is the logical result of the emphasis on structuralist theory in Post-Modernist architectural discourse during the 1980s. Viewed from another, it is simply part and parcel of the flooding of the senses by images in the global information culture.

As Juhani Pallasmaa has written, in support of his plea for a phenomenological understanding of architecture:

> The architecture of our time is turning into the retinal art of the eye ... Instead of experiencing our being in the world, we behold it from outside as spectators of images projected on the surface of the retina. As buildings lose their plasticity and their connection with the language and wisdom of the body, they become isolated in the cool and distant realm of vision.[3]

This, he suggests, is a problem of 'our culture at large', which 'seems to drift towards a distancing, a kind of chilling, de-sensualisation and de-eroticisation of the human relation to reality'.

The structuralist debate successfully challenged and undermined the idea that any form of consensus of understanding or interpretation was possible. In a society of multiple voices, all cultural phenomena, understood as texts or sign systems, were open to multiple interpretation, depending on which discourse they were located in. Thomas Csordas argues that as a result of this theoretical emphasis on text, sign and signifier, 'the notion of "experience" virtually dropped out of theorising about culture' during this period: 'The text metaphor has virtually ... gobbled up the body itself.'[4] But the implied distrust, or disavowal, of physical experience, and the operation of the senses, or sensorium, in this line of thinking can also be traced back throughout the whole Western philosophical tradition, from Aristotle to Descartes, Kant and on to the present day.

The Aristotelian concept of the human intellect laid the basis for a separation of human mind and body that fundamentally informed the Christian dogma of the transcendence of spirit and the whole philosophical foundation of rationalist thought which flowered during the Enlightenment and brought the modern industrial age into being. According to Victor Buchli, the Modern Movement aesthetic of dematerialisation can be seen as little more than a reassertion of an ascetic, de-corporealising tendency in Western religious and philosophical ideas which had their roots in ancient Classical civilisation, and pointed humankind towards the goal of transcending the earthy, physical and sensuous aspects of creaturely existence.

From this point of view, the impact of contemporary media on human perception of the physical environment, and attitudes towards embodiment, can be understood as simply the latest development in a long tradition of denial of the body and of the primacy of a bodily relationship with objects. The notion of the 'aesthetic' has been emptied of its original meaning of perception through the corporeal sensorium and needs to be replaced by an alternative term – synaesthetic, or corpothetic – capable of indicating a full experience of bodily and affective engagement involving all the senses and emotions.

All these factors have militated against the intellectual credibility of an architectural discourse around the validity of physical experience and material substance in architecture. By contrast, they have placed a strong emphasis on the significance and import of developments in media technology for the future of architecture, in particular the possibility of its physical dissolution. For instance, the phenomenological paradigm in architecture has scarcely touched the fashionable 'cutting edge' of architectural theory and practice – architects such as the Finn Juhani Pallasmaa and even the more publicity-conscious Steven Holl receiving far less press than those with deconstructivist leanings, such as Eisenman, Tschumi or Gehry. The former, producing work which might almost be described as 'quietist' when compared with the visual busyness and dislocation of the latter, are distrusted, perhaps, for a seemingly imprecise, even nostalgic, yearning for spiritual 'essences' regarded by many as irrevocably lost in an age now generally taken to be intensely materialistic – and far more difficult to convey through the medium of the two-dimensional image.

Yet there is strong and increasing resistance from many quarters to ideas of the supremacy of the media imperative. Enzio Manzini states:

> The diffusion of the media is modifying the general perception of the world, and of architecture as a material fact in particular ... The world dominated by the media is a physical environment that is biased towards the throwaway, and it is a semiotic environment profoundly contaminated by a hypertrophy of signs. In its confrontation with this world, architecture in my opinion has to constitute a factor of stabilisation and decontamination.[5]

Manzini's comments warn against acceptance of a condition in which the power of word and image are threatening the viability of physical place as the 'space' of contemporary cultural experience and identity, and so open the way to a degradation and devaluation of physical place that many would claim is already well underway. His position is echoed by Marc Augé, who differentiates between 'non-places',[6] where the link between individuals and their surroundings in space is established through the mediation of words and texts which generate particular images (much the environment that is celebrated in Venturi and Scott Brown's *Learning from Las Vegas*), and 'anthropological places', or places of identity, human relations and history, invested with meaning through reiterated actions or cultural practices. It would be wrong to dismiss such arguments as simply an expression of regret for the passing of previous eras, for to do so would be to ignore the powerful political dimensions of physical place and space. This is hinted at, though not explored in depth, by Augé when he writes: 'as anthropological places create the organically social, so non-places create solitary contractuality'.

As Foucault demonstrated, the hierarchical structures of social and political power and knowledge are embedded in the physical reality of place and architecture, and the ways in which spatial parameters are drawn and identities created represent a crucial political tool in the hands of those in positions of power. An increasing body of research by anthropologists such as Barbara Bender, Felicity Edholm and James Holston shows how complex social relations are inscribed in and fought over in physical structure. For example, Bender[7] has shown how the creation and evolution of Stonehenge reflects a continuous process of shifts in power and influence between different groups over time, right up to the battle in 1985 between 'free festivallers' wishing to celebrate the summer solstice at the site and the police, drafted in to enforce the authority of English Heritage. Similarly, Edholm[8] describes how the Haussmannisation of nineteenth-century Paris effectively disenfranchised working-class women from the freedom of the streets, by creating a new world of high visibility and display on the new boulevards and promenades in which they could have no place – so forcing them into a realm of backstreets and hidden spaces. Such spaces as these are aptly described, within a more contemporary context, by James Holston as 'spaces of insurgent citizenship', which the utopian Modernist masterplan attempted to eliminate from the city altogether, but which must now be recognised as constituting 'new metropolitan forms of the social' and, as such, 'possible alternative futures'.[9]

The deliberate deployment of strategies of physical disorientation, alienation and disconnection against human communities rooted in particular places have been used time and again by those in power to disengage and destroy social entities and identities for political and economic ends. To underestimate the power and significance of physical place is to open the door to such strategies of imposition and manipulation. Christopher Tilley writes:

> Once stripped of sedimented human meanings considered to be purely epiphenomenal and irrelevant, the landscape becomes a surface or volume like any other, open for exploitation and everywhere homogenous in its potential exchange value for any particular project. It becomes desanctified, set apart from people, myth and history, something to be controlled and used.[10]

Human attachment to place is not something that is forged purely through the operation of visual images or textual meanings, in the manner of advertising campaigns, but is a relationship that develops out of routinely repeated physical actions over time and a perception of the environment which is channelled through all the senses and emotions. Architecture then, representing one of the processes through which humans physically shape their environment, has a fundamental role to play in that development and consolidation of identification and attachment lying beyond the surface of the visual.

Paul Virilio has been particularly outspoken in his criticism of the influence of the media on architecture, the ocularcentrism on which it is founded and the implicit political dimensions of this relationship. His recent work on cybertechnology continues a line of enquiry into the relationship between technology and culture, which had previously explored the impact of the car, concrete and cinema on the way that humans relate to the physical world in terms of its spatial and temporal parameters.[11]

According to Virilio, 'cybertechnology threatens the spatial relations fundamental to intimacy and democracy' – that is, the foundations of both private and public life – by its erosion of physical dimensions and distances. He suggests that it condemns humans to a life of inertia, without physical movement, by eliminating the need for travel, and dissolves any notion of the public, because the real-time public image now prevails over public space. 'The crisis in the notion of physical dimensions thus hits politics and the administration of public services', and 'the old public services are in danger of being replaced by domestic enslavement ... intensifying the insularity that has always threatened the town.'

The implications for architecture are fundamental, for with the potential loss of basic notions of inside and outside, high and low, and even of a recognition of natural light, 'all the conceptual bases of architectonics are literally collapsing'. Furthermore, he suggests, 'the acceleration of representations' may 'cause us to lose their depth of field and so impoverish our sight', and he urges 'a revolt against the obsessive emphasis on the visual', a 'right to blindness', or 'an ecology of images'.

Virilio's language carries a certain oratorical edge, yet the concerns he voices for architecture are already borne out, and have been for some time, in the production of buildings. The loss of 'depth of field' is characteristic of a dematerialised architecture lacking cultural substance. Such an architecture, designed to satisfy primarily the criteria of the two-dimensional visual image carried in brochures, in magazines and on television, rather than the physical experience of embodiment, operates within the context of the media more effectively than that of the physical environment of daily routines.

Ada Louise Huxtable describes this form of architectural production with some eloquence in her account of the 'Unreal America',[12] an America where the accelerating construction of theme parks and shopping malls and reproduced historic façades constitutes what she describes as a highly selective reconstruction of 'place as story' to serve political motives. It is a prevalent culture of fakery and illusion that has its roots in cultural entertainment phenomena such as Coney Island and the world fairs, but has also, more insidiously, flourished through the historical conservation movement of the 1970s, reaching its apogee in the ambitious construction ventures of the Disney Corporation.

Huxtable reveals that in the brochure for its new town of Celebration, in Florida, Disney promises those who will buy into its dream 'a whole kind of lifestyle that's not new at all, just lost for a while. That fellow who said you can't go home again, he was wrong. Now you can come home. To Celebration. Your new hometown.' While this may be an extreme example, it typifies the approach taken by commercial developers throughout the world, who know that if they can construct the right image, at however superficial and dysfunctional a level, they will manage to seduce enough buyers into accepting a product which wilfully distorts and misrepresents the realities of social existence and removes any impetus for political action and social change.

## Notes

1. Christopher Tilley, *The Phenomenology of Landscape* (Oxford: Berg 1994).
2. Saskia Sassens, first BJS Millennial Lecture (London School of Economics, January 25th 2000).
3. Juhani Pallasmaa, 'An Architecture of the Seven Senses', in A&U Special Issue, *Questions of Perception: Phenomenology of Architecture* (July 1994), p. 27.
4. Thomas Csordas, 'Embodiment and Cultural Phenomenology', in *Perspectives on Embodiment: the Intersections of Nature and Culture*, Gail Weiss (ed.) (London: Routledge 1999), p. 146.
5. Enzio Manzini, 'Changes in Perception', in *Lotus* 1993, No 75.
6. Marc Augé, *Non-places: Introduction to an Anthropology of Super-Modernity* (London/New York: Verso 1995).
7. Barbara Bender, 'Theorising Landscapes, and the Prehistoric Landscapes of Stonehenge', in *Man* 27: 735–55.
8. Felicity Edholm, 'The View from Below: Paris in the 1880s', in *Landscape: Politics and Perspectives*, B. Bender (ed.) (Oxford: Berg 1993).
9. James Holston, 'Spaces of Insurgent Citizenship', in *Architecture and Anthropology*, Clare Melhuish (ed.), AD Profile 124 (Academy Editions 1996), p. 154.
10. Christopher Tilley, *The Phenomenology of Landscape* (Berg 1994), p. 21.
11. Paul Virilio, *Open Sky* (London/New York: Verso 1995).
12. Ada Louise Huxtable, *The Unreal America: Architecture and Illusion* (New York: The New Press 1997).

Chapter 17
## *Wallpaper* * **person**
Notes on the behaviour of a new species
**Neil Leach**

> Fashion, like architecture, inheres in the darkness of the lived moment, belongs to the dream consciousness of the collective. The latter awakes, for example, in advertising.[1]
> **Walter Benjamin**

In 1903 the German sociologist Georg Simmel published one of the seminal accounts of the subjectivity of the modern metropolitan individual in his essay, 'The Metropolis and Mental Life'. Here Simmel developed the notion of the blasé individual, whose nerve endings, bombarded by the continual stimulation of modern metropolitan existence, had become so frayed that they had learnt to renounce all forms of response. He wrote:

> The psychological foundation, upon which the metropolitan individuality is erected, is the intensification of emotional life due to the swift and continuous shift of external and internal stimuli .... Thus the metropolitan type – which naturally takes on a thousand individual modifications – creates a protective organ for itself against the profound disruption with which the fluctuations and discontinuities of the external milieu threaten it. Instead of reacting emotionally, the metropolitan type reacts primarily in a rational manner, thus creating a mental predominance through the intensification of consciousness, which in turn is caused by it.[2]

To become blasé was a product of – and a defence against – the hectic pace of the modern city, its intoxicating impulses and kaleidoscopic sensations. Moreover, this intellectualised mode of existence could be compared to the objective matter-of-factness of the money economy. For, according to Simmel, 'the money economy and the domination of the intellect stand in the closest relationship to one another'.[3] As a result the modern metropolitan type – the blasé individual – began to adopt a disinterested way of navigating the city, the city of capital, its intellectualised movements echoing the alienated movements of capital itself: 'This psychological intellectualistic attitude and the money economy are in such close integration that no one is able to say whether it was the former that effected the latter or *vice versa*.'⁴ What Simmel offers, then, is a model in which the predominant aesthetic reflex of the modern metropolitan type is related to the structure of the economic system.

One century later it is worth reconsidering Simmel's thesis. What has become of the blasé individual? How might we characterise the Post-Modern metropolitan type? Has the contemporary metropolitan type developed a more effective form of 'protective organ'? As the mechanised rationality of Modernity gives way to the ephemeral dream-world of Post-Modernity – as capitalism itself has mutated into invisible, gaseous forms, such as credit – how might we rework Simmel's connection between a predominant aesthetic sensibility and the money economy for today's society?

I want to propose that there is a new predominant sensibility at large, an individual that I shall call *Wallpaper\** person.⁵ Born to an age that is thoroughly narcissistic, in Christopher Lasch's terms, thoroughly aestheticised, and hence, in my own terms, anaesthetised, an age that is, in Andreas Huyssen's terms, gripped by a form of amnesia, this creature might best be described as the pleasure-seeking amnesiac of today, in constant search of gratification of the most ephemeral kind, and blinkered by its own aestheticised outlook to the social inequalities of the world outside.⁶

*Wallpaper\** person constitutes a still evolving, yet increasingly significant sensibility. For *Wallpaper\** culture presents, if not the dominant paradigm in Europe today, then one to which not just Blairite Britain ('Cool Britannia'), but also much of the rest of Western culture – and especially, I might add, Western architectural culture – aspires. What marks out *Wallpaper\** as a topic of interest from our perspective is not so much the fact that within its logic architecture is reduced to an aspect of life-styling, alongside fashion, dining out, exotic holidays and the like, but rather its very orientation towards the fictive and the imaginary. 'Who will you be in the next twenty four hours?' asks one advertisement.

*Wallpaper\** culture could be described as a form of escapist dream-world that has evolved under conditions of extreme opulence afforded by advanced capitalism. The journal itself has proved extraordinarily successful. Full of virtually captionless advertisements of dreamy models striking often vacant poses, the journal revels in its superficiality – albeit with a subtle sense of irony. Full too of articles of escapist dreaming, the journal offers a snapshot of the carefully manicured, indulgent life of the jet-setting, highly paid executive of today, a dream-life to which many people aspire.

Yet although *Wallpaper\** person is a turn-of-the-millennium creature, born of the extreme affluence of advanced capitalism, its characteristics can be traced back to an earlier model, contemporaries of Simmel's 'blasé individual': the Surrealists. But the Surrealists should be distinguished from the blasé individual. Whereas the blasé individual adopted an essentially negative stance towards the Modernist metropolis, as a form of defence, the Surrealists took a more positive approach towards it. They surrendered themselves to its enticements, its intoxicating impulses and kaleidoscopic sensations. The Surrealists' approach was a self-consciously aestheticising approach, and they exploited the narcotic-like potential of the visual image as a source of intoxication. *Wallpaper\** person has developed a mechanism for 'enjoying' the city. And like the Surrealists, *Wallpaper\** person resorts to the realms of dream and fantasy. The contemporary, neo-surrealist world of *Wallpaper\** culture is, I wish to argue, an enchanted dreamscape, an aestheticised and mythologised dreamscape.

The other model I wish to draw upon is Narcissus, the quintessential model for aesthetic contemplation.[7] Christopher Lasch has described our contemporary culture as a 'culture of narcissism'.[8] Life is dominated nowadays by a form of introversion and self-absorption, prompting an erosion of any awareness of others, and a culture of untrammelled individualism. The mobile phone is a symptom of this narcissistic condition, as users spin themselves bubbles, oblivious to all that is around them. On the train, in the street and in the countryside, strange one-way conversations take place with an invisible, silent 'other'. Meanwhile dating takes place less and less within traditional places of social interaction – the pub, workplace, corner shop or club – and increasingly through abstracted telephone dating systems and zones of cybercommunication. Computer screens further exacerbate this condition. Locked into their interior worlds, computer users grow increasingly divorced from their immediate surroundings. They communicate not with their neighbours but with fellow computer users, floating within some nebulous realm of cyberspace. All this helps to promote a culture that is becoming increasingly individualised and solipsistic, and divorced from its immediate surroundings. In this introverted and self-absorbed domain, individuals are increasingly isolated, cocooned from everything around, like commuters crammed into rush-hour underground trains, studiously ignoring those right in front of their noses.

What we find here is that the contemporary narcissist is cocooned not only in a material way – by the high-tech comfort zones of contemporary existence – but also in a psychological way. This cocoon, an adaptation of the 'protective organ' of Simmel's blasé individual, serves not only as a mechanism of defence, but also as a source of gratification. The term that I want to use to describe this psychological bubble in which the contemporary narcissist exists is 'the aesthetic cocoon', which might be described as a three-dimensional version of the reflective pool in the original myth of Narcissus.[9]

What this amounts to is the ability to recognise oneself in the objects around one, in the reflection of one's own aesthetic aspirations. This recognition constitutes a form of confirmation of those aspirations, which in turn leads to a sense of gratification that may be understood within the framework of Freud's notion of the death instinct – as a form of transcendence of death and return to the unalienated existence of the nirvana of the womb. What this tends to generate is a cocoon-like existence, predicated on aesthetic gratification. The nirvana of the aesthetic cocoon replicates the memory of the nirvana of the womb.[10] And it is this cocoon, this isolated state of being cosseted from reality and locked into some dream-world, that can be expanded and developed to offer a model for much contemporary life.

Yet what is at risk in this process of aestheticisation is that everything becomes aestheticised and thereby anaesthetised. In *The Anaesthetics of Architecture* I have attempted to describe this mechanism:

> The raising of one's consciousness of sensory matters – smell, taste, touch, sound and appearance – allows a corresponding drowsiness to descend like a blanket over all else. The process generates its own womb-like sensory cocoon around the individual, a semi-permeable membrane which offers a state of constant gratification while filtering out all that is undesirable. To aestheticise is therefore to sink blissfully into an intoxicating stupor, which serves to cushion the individual from the world outside like some alcoholic haze ...[11]

Moreover, the real problem of aestheticisation is that it suppresses the political and the social.[12]

The logic of aestheticisation constitutes a distorted, rose-tinted way of looking at the world that inverts that world, robbing it of its deeper political and social concerns, and even converting the sublime – in the sense of the horrific, excessive, the ugly and the brutal – into the beautiful.[13] And in this process of appropriating even the ugly, the brutal and the industrial, and converting it into the 'trendy', there is a disturbing inversion. We enter a topsy-turvy, 'Alice in Wonderland' realm of myth and fantasy, in which nothing is quite what it seems.

What needs to be brought into the frame, then, is the sense of fantasy that underpins many forms of contemporary life. For the narcissist depends not only on the actual admiring glances of others, but also on a certain measure of delusion and escapist fantasy. The original myth of Narcissus can therefore open up a further dimension to this contemporary narcissist – the dimension of escapist dreaming. The point here is that Nemesis punishes Narcissus for scorning the advances of Echo and others by making him fall in love with his own image. She makes him deluded. It is this sense of delusion that needs to be re-inscribed within our understanding of the contemporary narcissist. The narcissist fails to recognise the reflection of the self as the self, and reads it as an alternative 'other' with whom he or she has fallen in love. Recognition is often a form of misrecognition.

But equally this mechanism may work the other way. The contemporary narcissist may 'read' him or herself into a particular situation and 'identify' with a character in that situation. This is the projective side of narcissism that encourages a culture of fantasy identification. Indeed, contemporary conditions foster a culture of role-playing and lifestyle adoption in which media personalities act as role models to be emulated and admired. As Laura Mulvey has observed, the formation of the ego ideal at the mirror stage sets the scene for identification with the ideal egos of the media industry in later life.[14] Mulvey refers to this process as a form of 'narcissistic identification'. In an age of hyper-alienation this urge is exacerbated. It has the effect of turning people into animated mannequins, acting out their lives according to the well-rehearsed steps of some Hollywood role model. And just as role models are reduced to fictive characters, so too architecture is reduced to 'stage sets' – the ephemeral settings in which one might lead out one's fantasy existence.[15] The contemporary world of this modern-day Narcissus, this neo-surrealist, constitutes a form of dream-world.

The signs are already there. We need only look to the titles emerging at the turn of the new millennium – from Slavoj Zizek's *A Plague of Fantasies* to Marc Augé's *A War of Dreams* – to realise that some of the key cultural commentators have detected a new phase in human consciousness, in which dream and fantasy are emerging as dominant themes.[16] Whether we consider how the virtualisation of reality has exposed the imposture of reality itself, as Zizek suggests, or how the increasing preponderance of simulation in our media culture has led to an effacement of the distinction between real and actual, so that life itself takes on the semblance of a soap opera, as Augé suggests, the hegemony of the real is under question. Virtuality, simulation and fantasy are playing an increasing part in the way we live our lives today. Increasingly, contemporary life has become a fantasy domain of role-playing and lifestyle adoption.

But what I want to explore here is how capitalism itself has helped to promote this sense of fantasy. For just as the very movement of capital in the modern metropolis conditioned, for Simmel, the response of the blasé individual, so too the very sense of fantasy propagated by advanced capitalism has fuelled, I wish to argue, a new sensibility.

Advanced capitalism can be understood as a form of mythologised dream-world, wherein the increasing rationalisation of our technological world only spawns its opposite, in terms of the dialectic of the enlightenment: myth. The very abstraction and refinement of our technological world, where technology seeks to hide itself in ever more sophistication, burying itself deep within our subconscious with its streamlined, minimalist, low profiles, such that we have lost any sense of its hegemony, presupposes, in dialectical fashion, an invitation to even greater mythologisation. Like the conjurer's trick, where the magician conceals the true devices at work, so as to fool the audience into attributing them to magic, so technology, in effacing itself, invites us to believe in its magical potential. Just as rationality spawns myth, so hyperrationality spawns hypermyth. The more rational our society becomes – the more sophisticated its technology – the more it encourages the mythic.

'Capitalism,' wrote Walter Benjamin, 'was a natural phenomenon with which a new dream-filled sleep came over Europe, and, through it, a reactivation of mythic forces.'[17] The model of the goods on a supermarket shelf, whose methods of procurement and distribution remain largely hidden such that the goods appear to have been 'conjured up' as if by magic, is one that can be extended to all facets of contemporary life. The supermarket represents the extreme state of our hyperreal dream-world, an utter fantasy land of abundance, where capitalism has so succeeded in concealing itself that even the price tags – painful reminders of the cost to be paid for goods – have been removed and replaced by barcodes. Nor need any physical money change hands, as everything can be accounted for seamlessly by computerised, invisible fluxes of credit. Contemporary life holds out the promise of a consumerist heaven, a promise that is reinforced by these 'magical' methods of procurement.

The supermarket has turned into an enchanted dreamscape, a cathedral of consumption, while the goods themselves have become 'objects of devotion' to be worshipped and adored by customers – 'heavenly' cream cakes, 'divine' chocolate. The credit card, furthermore, the dominant form of payment, enhances this condition. Not only may payment be deferred indefinitely, but the goods purchased appear as objects of wish fulfilment. For the plastic card operates within the realm of the future conditional – 'you too could have this product' – and what is the future conditional other than the potential realm of wish fulfilment?

Here we might reflect upon Walter Benjamin's understanding of the wish-image within the dream-world of modernity. The artefacts of the contemporary metropolis were, for Benjamin, the very embodiment of a collective dreaming. As Graeme Gilloch comments, 'Just as the desires and wishes of the individual are frustrated and repressed in waking life only to reappear in disguised form in dreams during sleep, so the cityscape and the artefacts found therein are dream-like creations of the dormant collectivity.'[18] That dreaming, moreover, is based on utopian wish-images: 'For Benjamin, the edifices and the objects of the metropolis are utopian wish-images, frozen representations or objectifications of genuine wants and aspirations that remain unfulfilled or thwarted.'[19]

Within a Post-Modern context the far-sightedness of Benjamin's comments begins to emerge. Contemporary lifestyle magazines, such as *Hello!* or *OK!*, are precisely catalogues of these wish-images. They contain models of success to which the rest of the population might aspire. For features on the rich and famous, and the environment in which they live, function less as detective narratives, revealing the previously hidden, and more as wish-images for which less fortunate mortals need only dream. And yet through that dream – that sense of fantasy and creative identification with the characters portrayed – readers are 'invited' to imagine themselves in such a situation, to 'dream themselves' into the pages of the magazine.

The utopian wish-image need not be conditioned by the metropolis itself, so much as by the commodities for sale there. It is these commodities that form the wish-images of the 'dream-filled sleep' that has now spread beyond the confines of Europe to all those First World countries saturated by the extreme opulence of advanced capitalism. But in the context of fantasising over commodities this dreaming might more properly be called 'daydreaming'. There is a crucial difference here. Daydreams are dreams in the present which may contain elements of the past but which 'fantasise' about the future. They are quite intentional and unambiguous stories of wish-fulfilment, as Rachel Bowlby comments:

> Unlike the dreams of sleep, daydreams in this instance are said to show their meaning on the surface: there is no subterranean layer to be plumbed. As such, they can provide the varnish on a dream, appearing as a gloss for the unpresentable materials underneath. In themselves, they are what they seem: straightforward – unified and unidirectional – stories of wish-fulfilment.[20]

The credit card fosters this realm of daydreaming by making that dream potentially realisable. The credit card, then, will fulfil the promise of the unfulfilled. And in helping to realise those dreams, it will function as a catalyst for collective dreaming. Advanced capitalism, then – credit culture – in its very nature is grounded in the structure of dreaming and myth, and this is only fuelled by the culture of the credit card.

Advertising reinforces this sense of desire, this materialist sense of dreaming. Rather than constitute an awakening, as Benjamin might have supposed, advertisements seem to lay the foundations for dreams. More than anything else, they are collections of wish images, catalogues of material goods that are proffered up for potential ownership. But advertisements are no innocent catalogues. The fetishisation of the commodity, which Karl Marx had observed, has reached new heights in contemporary advertising culture. Goods have been fetishised and tinged with a halo of sexual allure. The commodity has been sexualised, as Benjamin observed, no less than sex has been commodified.[21] And yet the scope of advertising – its sophistication and its powers of seduction – has transcended whatever Benjamin might have imagined. Nor should we dismiss advertising as an incidental and irrelevant aspect of contemporary life. For advertising has so colonised our symbolic horizons that it is all but co-extensive with the way in which we see the world these days.[22]

Moreover, advertising constitutes an ecstatic form of escapism that masks the world of the actual, and conjures up instead a fantasy dream-world. What advertising agents seek to appeal to above all is this sense of fantasy that dominates contemporary life. Advertisements are, in effect, repositories of dreams. They are intended to conjure up in a Proustian manner a whole dream-world of life-styling and commodity consumption. Viewers are invited to imagine themselves into the scenario depicted, transported there as though on some magic carpet.

A recent advertisement for the Peugeot 206 shows a young man in a cinema watching a movie of a young girl driving the car. The girl winks at him. The young man closes his eyes and suddenly finds himself in the car alongside her. Significantly, the car is being driven through a desert landscape. This particular advertisement therefore partakes in two forms of fantasy – the fantasy of romantic engagement and the fantasy of driving through an exotic landscape – while also revealing the eroticism that lies behind commodity fetishism. The point about this advertisement is that it not only reveals the techniques of romanticisation that underpin advertising culture, it also presupposes a capacity for dreaming in everyday life that extends beyond the space of the advertisement. Indeed, one can only assume that, were the young man to buy such a car, he would drive it around, living out some fantasy of crossing the desert, accompanied by the young lady in the advertisement. Another advertisement exposes the potential of the television to act as some Alice in Wonderland-like looking glass, that would transport you somewhere else as though on some magic carpet. 'You don't have to take the train to escape to the Peak District' reads one advertisement near St Pancras railway station for *Peak Practice,* a television series.

The television, then, the computer screen and the cinema screen serve as a form of interface between our 'real' world and the imaginary world beyond. And yet this interface is somewhat of a Janus: it serves as a two-way valve. Just as we are encouraged to transport ourselves into the space of the imaginary, so too we bring associations of that imaginary dream-world into our actual lives. Everyday life is colonised by the mythic. It is dominated by fantasy and dreaming.

The creature, then, that emerges at the beginning of this new century is one whose capacity for dreaming and escapism has become fully developed, an amnesiac creature, insular, narcissistic, myopic, continually aestheticising and romanticising the present, forever escaping the actual into a dream-world of the 'as-if'. It is, moreover, a creature that has developed a new aesthetic response to new conditions. Just as for Simmel the anonymous circulation of capital at the beginning of the twentieth century was reflected in the disinterested patterns of movement of the blasé individual, so too the dreamlike quality of the credit world of advanced capitalism has helped to engender a new sensibility. The blasé individual has mutated into the neo-surrealist, narcissistic dreamer: *Wallpaper\** person. Above all, *Wallpaper\** person exists within his or her own aesthetic cocoon, a distorted rose-tinted cocoon, removed, cosseted, protected from harsh reality, as much by choice of habitat, as by the dominant escapist mentality. But where does this creature hang out? What architectural environments constitute its habitat?

To some extent the habitat of the *Wallpaper\** person is merely an extension of that very individual, or perhaps rather an inverted mould, as it were, perfectly formed to accommodate his or her every need. The habitat becomes an articulation of that 'aesthetic cocoon' – a heavily serviced, high-tech space of comfort and sensory gratification. And this very sense of cocooning brings with it a corresponding indifference to the world outside. The narcissist knows only his or her pleasures. All else is ignored. Paradise today is a paradise of creature comforts where everything noisome or irksome – mosquitoes, disease, filth, etc. – must be edited out with Disney-like efficiency.

But it is not merely the tedious tasks that must be edited out in our age of pre-packed, microwaveable meals and non-iron shirts, but so too those individuals who do not belong to this Club Med existence. For *Wallpaper\** culture is an exclusive culture, accessible only to the 'haves' and not to the 'have nots'. What emerges is a fortress culture of inclusion and exclusion based largely on economic grounds. It is easy to see, then, how the model of the cocoon extended to the heavily serviced high-tech apartment might be further developed to offer an insular 'fortress LA' model for society as a whole. For the whole principle of this aestheticising thrust is to rinse the world of social and political concerns, while the narcissistic dimension to this *Wallpaper\** existence denies any true engagement with the 'other'. And with this overall shift we may recognise too the potential demise of the public realm itself.

What emerge, then, are 'bubbles of immanence', as Marc Augé has described them, supposedly fictionalised worlds, for which Disneyland is the archetype:

> Theme parks, holiday clubs, leisure parks and residential ones like Center Parcs, but also the private towns which are seeing the light of day in America, and even the fortified and security-patrolled residences which are springing up in the cities of the Third World, like so many fortresses, form what one might call bubbles of immanence.[23]

These 'bubbles of immanence' extend to international chains of stores, hotels and restaurants, which adopt the same decor everywhere in the world. They are instantly recognisable, private, fictionalised cosmologies within a broader world, 'parentheses to be opened and closed at discretion, with the use of finance and the knowledge of a few basic codes'.[24]

Intriguingly, this is precisely the form of 'dream habitat' suggested by *Wallpaper\** magazine, albeit with its tongue in cheek, but nonetheless a revealing description of a proposed 'capsular enclave' ('compound') for *Wallpaper\** people:

> Location, location, location. Exhaustive sun studies will see the first *Wallpaper\** compounds go up in Bondi, Tunis, Beirut, Lisbon, Beverly Hills, Palm Springs and Santa Barbara.
> 
> There will be plenty of space for pooling around on the rooftop lido deck. Liveried cabana boys in terry-cloth jump-suits will see to your every need while you do your lengths in the glass-bottomed pool.

Abstract balcony screens keep the paparazzi guessing while you rinse off in your outdoor shower.

Secure parking spaces for bicycles and scooters. To make more room for subterranean services (kitchens, dry-cleaning facilities), the architects have done away with underground parking. Residents have the use of five stretch Saabs, complete with drivers.

No time to cook? E-mail your concierge from the air and a Balinese buffet will be waiting for you when you walk through the door.

Every hour is happy hour in the lobby lounge. A round-the-clock bar and serious snack service turns the courtyard into a hub for hanging. Remember, you helped to vet your fellow residents, so you actually like the people you live with.

A team of concierges look after your life, whether you're cross-town, or across the planet.

Security is not an issue, as those cabana boys also do night duty ...

Located in Sudan, Beirut, Seville or any other sun-trap you care to mention, this block is soundproof and safe. Stretching to four floors, it consists of 24 apartments of 100 square metres each. An egalitarian enclave, there are no plush penthouses. Thick, concrete slabs between each unit block out noisy neighbours; none of the residents share party walls; and when it comes to security, this block is harder to crack than Quantico. Discreet alarms and video cameras cover all the hidden corners, while clued up concierges check the mail and quiz couriers ...

You're not at home very often, but when you are, you want a wipe-clean and sweep-easy life. You live in a service sector, after all, and who is to say it should stop at the front door? Concierges are on hand 24 hours a day to take care of the laundry and the domestic chores, and they'll fix you up a lunch-box to take in to work. Filled with your favourite snacks (aubergine spring rolls, club sandwich, pumpkin pie), this tailor-made tiffin will see you through the day ...[25]

*Wallpaper** completes the article with an appeal to any would-be developers interested in such a proposal: 'Developers interested in erecting the *Wallpaper** compound should e-mail wallpaper_magazine@time.inc-com.'

The picture is complete. The fictionalised 'dream' compound presented by *Wallpaper** for the would-be 'dream' occupant of this ethereal world is offered up to would-be 'dream' developers of such a world. The point is that these 'compounds' need not be built. They are merely conjured up as idealised dream-worlds. As such, they belong to an emerging tradition of architectural dream-worlds. Beginning with *Paris Match,* and extending into a second generation of celebrity lifestyle magazines such as *Hello!,* the houses of the famous have been illustrated as dream interiors to which the rest of society might aspire. Now *Wallpaper** has developed the virtual interior, employing architects to design buildings that are never intended to be built – virtual, dream interiors. The 'compound' is the latest development of this trend.

Contemporary cultural commentators, such as Fredric Jameson and Jean Baudrillard, describe our present condition in terms of images. Under 'late capitalism', according to Jameson, everything has been co-opted into commodities and images. Yet this vision presents a rather straitened understanding of contemporary life. There is no space in their accounts for the role of myth – for fantasy, magic or even dreaming. And yet advanced capitalism, I would maintain, has turned the world into a mythologised dream-world, based on fantasy and escapism.

Baudrillard describes our contemporary hyperreal culture as a world of images that has lost touch with its referents in the 'real' world, such that the image constitutes our new 'reality'. Perhaps we need to revise this notion. Instead of a hyperreal world of images we have a *Wallpaper\** culture in which the image has mutated into the 'wish-image'. *Wallpaper\** culture, then, is a dream-world not of images but of wish-images, fuelled by a culture of credit and advertising, a dream-world that has itself become our new reality.

And if, as Benjamin claimed, the fantasies of an epoch remain sedimented in the buildings it spawns, maybe the fantasies of our 'dream epoch' reside in the 'dream buildings' it spawns.[26]

## Notes

1. Walter Benjamin, *The Arcades Project* (Cambridge, MA: Harvard University Press, 1999), p. 393.
2. Georg Simmel, 'The Metropolis and Mental Life', in Neil Leach (ed.), *Rethinking Architecture* (London: Routledge, 1997), p. 70.
3. Simmel, 'The Metropolis and Mental Life', p. 71.
4. Simmel, 'The Metropolis and Mental Life', p. 71.
5. Throughout this paper I shall be pursuing Baudrillard's tactic of 'the fatal strategy'. My argument will be deliberately exaggerated, so as to become less a representation of reality than a transcendence of it, while aiming to reveal, nonetheless, certain truths about the world.
6. On this see Andreas Huyssen, *Twilight Memories* (London: Routledge, 1996); Christopher Lasch, *Culture of Narcissism* (New York: Warner Books, 1979); and Neil Leach, *The Anaesthetics of Architecture* (Cambridge, MA: MIT Press, 1999).
7. Narcissus is the beautiful youth of Classical antiquity, with whom the nymph Echo had fallen in love. Echo is scorned by Narcissus, and she retreats into the woods, fading away to nothing as she nurses her broken heart. Nemesis punishes Narcissus for spurning the advances of Echo and other admirers. As Narcissus leans out over a pool for a drink following a hard day's hunting, he is captivated by his own image, mistaking the reflection for reality itself. He tries in vain to reach out and grasp the image, which also appears to reach out to him, but eventually, lying there without food or sleep, he wastes away in his own self love and dies. When they come to bury him, they discover

that his body is nowhere to be seen, but that a flower with white petals and a yellow centre has blossomed. To this day this flower still bears his name, Narcissus.

8   Lasch, *Culture of Narcissism*.
9   In that myth Narcissus gazes at his own reflection as though into a mirror, and through it seems to receive some form of aesthetic gratification. Yet the mirror is only a two-dimensional source of reflection. What I would like to suggest is that in terms of *Wallpaper\** person the 'reflective surface' needs to be perceived as an entire environment, a three-dimensional container, a cocoon.
10  The point here is that, as Herbert Marcuse has argued in *Eros and Civilisation* (London: Penguin, 1969), p. 194, the narcissist enjoys a certain existential oneness with the world. As such, we might recognise in this narcissistic individual someone content within a certain limited framework, oblivious to external concerns and fed by personal forms of gratification. The narcissist, then, attains a certain level of satisfaction. He or she fails to engage with the world as it actually is, but that does not prevent that person from achieving a certain balance and equilibrium. For the image of Narcissus is above all an image of harmony.
11  Leach, *Anaesthetics of Architecture*, p. 44.
12  'The aestheticization of the world induces a form of numbness. It reduces any notion of pain to the level of the seductive image. What is at risk in this process of aestheticization is that political and social content may be subsumed, absorbed and denied. The seduction of the image works against any underlying sense of social commitment ... The world becomes aestheticized and anaesthetized.' (Leach, *Anaesthetics of Architecture*, p. 45.)
13  Witness many of the recent trends, from Damien Hirst's sharks in formaldehyde in our art galleries to the mock military combat gear that is sold to kids even in 'respectable' stores such as Marks and Spencer. In a society where sliced cows, bisected sheep and rotting animal heads are proffered as art; in a society where films such as Cronenberg's *Crash* and other disaster movies receive top billing at our cinemas; in a society where former power stations are turned into art galleries, abattoirs into parks, and industrial warehouses into bijou apartments; and in a society where 'Dr Martens' industrial footwear and 'Diesel' clothing can become the height of fashion, there appears to be a fascination with the industrial and the brutal that underpins all aspects of cultural life. 'Dead hard' is dead cool.
14  Laura Mulvey, 'Visual Pleasure and Narrative Cinema', in Anthony Easthope (ed.), *Contemporary Film Theory* (London: Longman, 1993), pp. 111–24.
15  To some extent the very dumbness of much *Wallpaper\**-style advertising, the very hollowness of the images, invites viewers to fill that space with their own meaning, to appropriate that space, and see themselves within it. The argument can be derived from Roland Barthes's analysis of the Eiffel Tower. It is the very 'emptiness' and uselessness of the tower that allow it to be adopted as a universal symbol of Paris. See Roland Barthes, 'The Eiffel Tower', in Leach, *Rethinking Architecture*. The same principle applies on a broader scale to media personalities. Thus we find a preponderance of cultural icons today who are essentially hollow, emptied out of any real personality – as in the case of the Spice Girls, who have been recoded with virtual identities in the manner of Lara Croft – and ready to be filled with meaning. The narcissist colonises and 'inhabits' that cultural icon, as though it were a mannequin, reading it as the self.

16 Slavoj Zizek, *A Plague of Fantasies* (London: Verso, 1997); Marc Augé, *A War of Dreams,* trans. Liz Heron (London: Pluto, 1999).
17 Benjamin, *Arcades Project,* p. 391.
18 Graeme Gilloch, *Myth and Metropolis* (Cambridge: Polity, 1996), p. 104.
19 Gilloch, *Myth and Metropolis,* p. 105.
20 Rachel Bowlby, 'The Other Day: The Interpretation of Daydreams', *New Formations* 34 (Summer 1998), p. 16.
21 Supermarkets, as Daniel Miller reminds us, in *A Theory of Shopping* (Cambridge: Polity, 1998), are places where we make love.
22 Andrew Wernick, *Promotional Culture* (London: Sage, 1991).
23 Augé, *War of Dreams,* pp. 112–13.
24 Augé, *War of Dreams,* p. 113.
25 *Wallpaper\**, special edition (1998), p. 150.
26 Gilloch, *Myth and Metropolis,* p. 123.

Chapter 18
## Everything counts in large amounts
(The sound of geography collapsing)
**FAT**

A little after midday on 12 December 1901, three bursts of electromagnetic radiation travelled above the Atlantic ocean at 186,000 miles per second ... beep beep beep, from Poldhu, in the south-western corner of England to Marconi's cabin on top of a hill in St John's, Newfoundland, Canada. Three beeps that spelt 'S' in Morse code. These beeps were radio transmissions connecting two geographically distant people who, just before lunch and breakfast respectively, experienced something unique. They heard the sound of geography collapsing. Marconi had delivered with an induction coil and a spark discharger an experience previously promised and faked by mystics and shamans.

Proto-Modernists, meanwhile, had their eye on the tail end of the industrial revolution. They were enamoured with the formal characteristics of new machines, vehicles and industrial structures. These became the mainstays of the Modernist source book and part of the pseudo-functionalist quasi-logic of Modernist rhetoric. But it is possible that there was a subtext to Modernism which wasn't part of this rhetoric. A subtext born of wireless communication. Something that reaches out to us across a century of exponential development of radio communications and broadcasting.

With Marconi's radio in mind, those key Modernist concerns of the open plan and the glazed curtain wall may not just be accidents of evolution in construction technology. Perhaps they are the first signs of an architecture that seeks to respond to the new experiences of communications. Connecting places that once were separate, dissolving physical boundaries between rooms and the things that go on in them, blurring relationships between the inside and the outside. Maybe the hand basin at the Villa Savoye stands as a totem not of functionalism but of the electronic dissolution of space. Maybe Modernism is an architecture made by and for people who dream of being everywhere, all the time, simultaneously. Maybe this unacknowledged Modernist subtext is the one that is the most relevant to a world where ocean liners rust in breakers' yards while their sentimental image haunts us through digitally rendered, Oscar-winning romantic epics.

Almost a century after Marconi, Microsoft trademarked the advertising slogan 'Where do you want to go today?' They were unwittingly – but catchily – rephrasing David Greene and Mike Barnard's 1971 Archigram project 'The Electric Aborigine', which was, they suggested, a 'social chameleon'. Both of these ideas talk about the way electronic and communication technology affects our physical and social occupation of the world, the things that happen when we use our collection of high street electronics: TVs, laptops, modems, video cameras, phones (and whatever else our array of credit lines can stretch to). Our identities become fragmented and multiplied by them, whether it's the information transcribed magnetically on the back of credit cards, or cell phone SIM cards, multiple e-mail accounts, electronic avatars or customer profiles. While unidentified companies sweep our credit ratings, and web browser cookies collate our interests, we find our own identities and contexts shifting. Bill Gates says that by clicking and looking we are going somewhere; David Greene thinks we change ourselves. And they're both saying that when we're looking, reading and watching, we're being. Experience makes media part of us.

The medium is not the only message. It communicates particular and precise information. Marconi's Morse code 'S' and Rod Stewart's 'We are Sailing' heard on crackling AM are entirely different. Both the medium and the contents are important and let us engage with more intangible things. (You might say Rod is in the detail.) When Marshall McLuhan claimed that a light bulb is information, but that we can not recognise it as such because it is pure information, he was only half right. A trip to the local electrical store might have set him straight. A bulb is information all right, but there is content too. A plain-glass, 60 W bayonet bulb – or whatever the current local default type – might encourage the same mistake. But when we see a flickering element and a tapered bulb, we recognise an electric representation of a form of lighting associated with romantic evenings, religious ceremony and birthday cakes. SoftTone, EcoTone or ClassicTone bulbs have different meanings. A light bulb has a specific cultural content – any light bulb.

McLuhan's misreading is one commonly made by architects: the idea that objects and things can be 'pure', abstract and without meaning. The white walls of Modernism (as seen in international galleries, designer boutiques and luxury apartments) are conceptualised as things without cultural value – free from symbol, significance and origin. Abstraction (a.k.a. the banishment of representation and the diffusion of content) is what architects seem perversely interested in. Keeping content out of architecture is like trying to maintain a vacuum in a paper bag: stuff just keeps leaking in. To flip Le Corbusier's slogan, there are Modernist Eyes Which Do Not See.

The Modernist conceit of abstraction was welded to the idea that decoration could not be justified as a functional part of architecture. Decoration was derided as a trivial pursuit (the sober Modernist men compared it to the frivolity of ladies' fashions, as opposed to the serious nature of their own dress). The serious thing was function. Ornament was symbolic of historical forms of architecture, which were non-democratic, bourgeois and associated with the serfdom of the working class (interestingly, Pugin

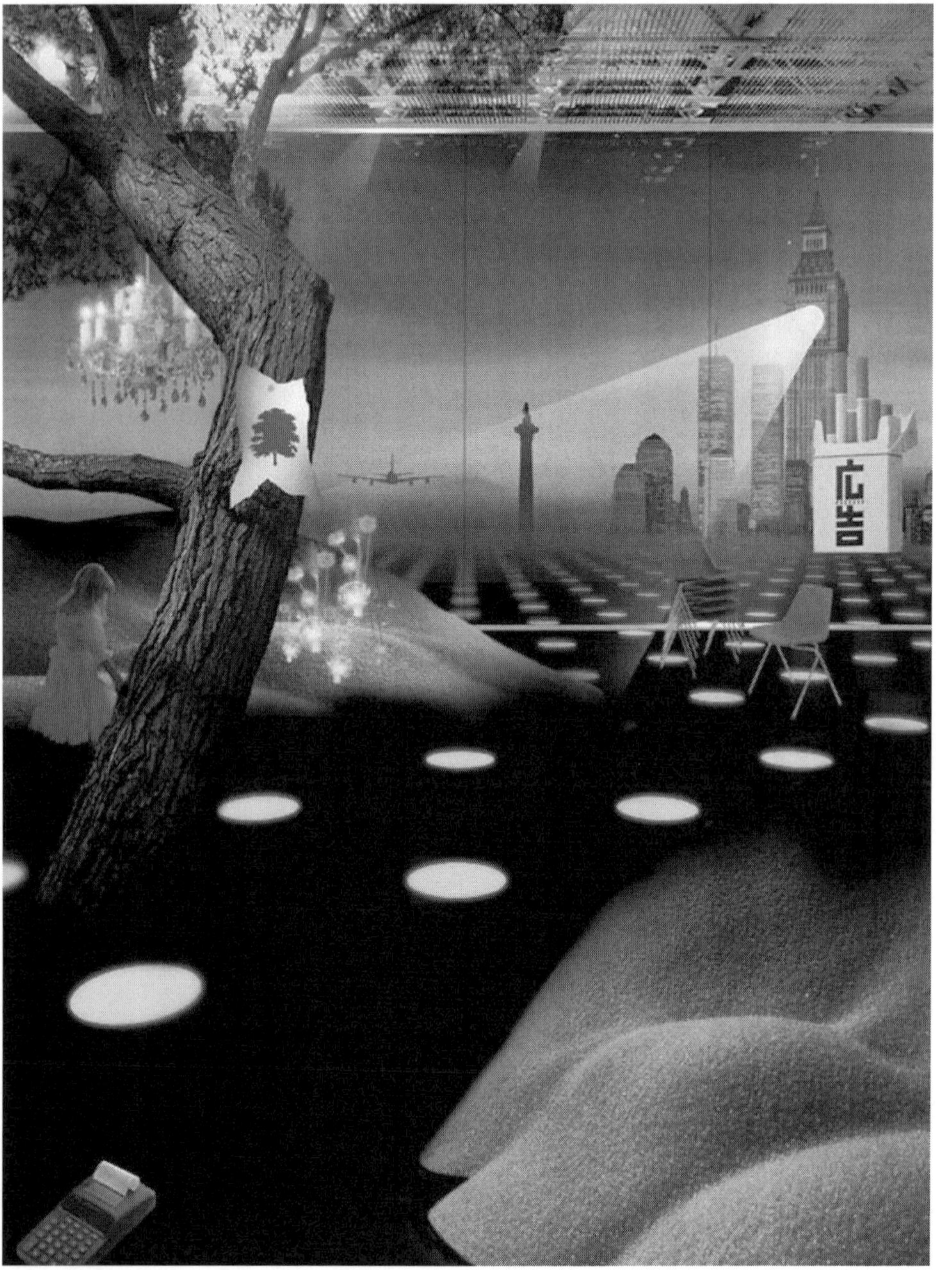
広告

had laid the blame for unsuitable decorative design on the appalling taste of the working man). Decorative and stylistic tropes were of the old order and, hence, anti-revolutionary. The banishment of ornament was a symbolic break with bourgeois tradition.

However misconceived this notion of abstraction was, it is now a central and unassailable tenet of the Modernist orthodoxy. Ornament, criminalised by Adolf Loos, remains taboo and stigmatised almost a century later. And this extreme position quickly moved from an articulate and progressive programme to an arcane and mystical belief. The importance of abstraction was tied up with changing politics, growing economic freedom and optimism in the promise of industrialisation. Strangely, the concern with appearance and surface was thought to be authentic and honest. A hundred years on, the Modernist cop who resides within us still attempts to police this moral and civil code.

Ironically, Modernism's enduring success has been as a status symbol, an aesthetic of First World luxury that looks just great in a double-page glossy spread. As Mies's clients might tell you, less costs more. Modernism's stylistic endurance is strangely associated with that which it sought to destroy. While this may ridicule the ethics of early Modernist architecture, it also demonstrates that our own conception of Modernist architecture needs revising. Authenticity and honesty are now attributes which are deliberately constructed as core brand values.

Maybe it's time to decriminalise decoration and arrange an amnesty on ornament. After all, a functionalist take on the information revolution would identify decoration as the functional apparatus of branding, the visible structure of communication. Decoration is precisely the way that the Pepsi can differentiates itself from a can of Coke in the newsagent's glass-fronted fridge. In a world where we have a surplus of everything – where all cars go, where all mobile phones work, where all computers will do the job, where all buildings can stand up, keep the rain out and comply with codes and regulations – the value is no longer in the hardware. It's in the communication of ideas. In other words, it is not the hardware, it is the experience that counts. It's the experience which changes the world.

In 1956 Dr Robert Adler led a team of engineers working on the first use of ultrasonic technology in the home as an approach for a practical wireless TV remote control. The transmitter used no batteries; it was built around aluminium rods that were light in weight and, when struck at one end, emitted distinctive high-frequency sounds. Zenith branded it 'Space Command', and it revolutionised TV tuning worldwide. The TV remote control caused households across America to rearrange their living room furniture. It also fundamentally altered our relationship with content, and so our experience of watching TV.

Life must have been restless before the invention of the remote control. Imagine having to walk up to the set and turn to a different channel. While the remote control was designed to ease navigation through proliferating channels, it had an indirect but profound consequence on the medium, causing us to casually fragment painstakingly constructed content and narrative as we flick through, hoping to find something that catches our eye. Countless virtual worlds flicker on cathode ray tubes while our thumb pumps the CH+ button, juxtaposing images which follow each other more quickly and strangely than all the buildings on the Las Vegas strip. Juxtapositions of narrative, scale, geography, real-time, recorded, genre, culture and subculture, point of view and atmosphere. Channel hopping changed the world.

If it changed our living rooms – and the way we see the world – it also changed our cities. It is often argued that Los Angeles is the first post-car city. This argument provides a Modernist/functionalist explanation for the centreless city and sprawling suburban metropolis (remember, next time you hear this, that the car is a potent Modernist symbol). Maybe a more instructive reading might be a city after wireless communication. The meaning of the city has been altered by the pressures that electronic communications have exerted on the public realm. Things which used to have a public physical presence are becoming invisible, transformed into activities conducted privately and individually. The contemporary city is riddled with intricate confusions of public and private, fragmented desires and needs – a strange cocktail of collective meanings and individual assertions that recalls Robert Venturi's remark, 'Americans don't need piazzas: they should be at home watching TV.'

Communication technology carries content that supersedes its urban incarnation. Not only functionally, but symbolically too. Cities are both physical and virtual. They exist as both images and bricks. We see banks that manifest themselves simultaneously as invisible electronics and as huge iconic towers. This mass of information bound up in and relating to urban places tells us that the contemporary city is about communication. It is a place that is very different from its various historical conceptions: the Classical model of the piazza, the Modernist idea of the plaza or the Situationist notion of the street. Which means that if contemporary design is about anything, it's about identity and communication. Or, to be more exact, about the contradictions and negotiations of the simultaneous identities that we slip in and out of.

Ralph Lauren's bank manager knows this well. A guy called Ralph Lifshitz from a New York Jewish ghetto works as a salesman at Brooks Brothers (home of conservative American tailoring) and unearths its more ethnic heritage. Mythologising the aesthetic of English public schools at the turn of the last century, lacing it with Ivy League memorabilia and creating a nostalgic version of wealth and privilege which he sells to young urban black America, whose streetwise patronage gives aspirational credibility to real life English public schoolboys and other white, middle-class markets. Lauren says (in language that has echoes of heroic utopian Modernism): 'My goal in design is to achieve the ultimate dream – the best reality imaginable.' And these are realities that exist as objects, images, aspirations and desires. They are as ephemeral as perfume and magazines, as real as James Cameron's *Titanic* or the Villa Savoye. We experience this reality through diverse media, including chairs, jumpers, household paint, as well as more conventional media. While the Modernists dismissed fashion as trivial, Ralph Lauren knows just how important it can be. Media become part of us.

This Laurenite conception perhaps allows us to understand Archigram's 'Cushicle' project as something other than the absurdist techno-fantasy that architects love. It is perhaps a cultural metaphor. You could say the Cushicle argues that the Anglo-Saxon home, redolent with symbolism and bound up with ideas of personal and social identity, has qualities that are (at least) equivalent to an architectural understanding of apparel. The place where one identifies oneself is no longer only the front lawn or the mantelpiece. From the labels on our jeans to the pediment of City Hall, we can't help but iterate identity.

What we see here is a kind of concentric family tree (albeit one that sometimes doubles back on itself in an incestuous way), a cultural lineage which spins out from the object. Meanings bounce and connect from one point to another with the complexity of traces of smashed atoms: the trails of quarks, electrons, positions and neutrinos, and unidentifiable other stuff. Objects are snagged and entwined with the world that surrounds them: cultural beacons as much as clothes. Truth and myth are entwined. The world constructed by Ralph Lauren could be said to resemble a (mostly pleasant) conspiracy theory where fact, suspicion and fiction multiply endlessly. The stories which spin out of Ralph's world are constructed, undermined, adjusted and rewritten in the pursuit of his (and our) dream. This is the Jencksian notion of double coding to the $n$th power. Which begins to erode the classic Post-Modern diametric position in relation to Modernism. In other words, it's more than just 'either/or' or 'both/and'. Everything counts.

Perhaps there is a future for architecture. Somewhere far from the ever-more-desperately extravagant Modernist manipulations which claim to present a constantly brand-new paradigm. Far from architects tied to their rendering packages and fascinated by the technology of production in exactly the same way as their Modernist forefathers. Far from architects performing a kind of unwitting karaoke homage to their heroes, whilst simultaneously claiming a break with that self-same tradition. A breath of fresh air that might involve retiring the long-in-the-tooth and frankly decrepit notional equation experimental/radical/avant-garde = formally original/heroically singular/

iconographically iconoclastic. A modern architecture that is immersed in its social and political contexts, saturated with information. An architecture that recognises that it is our experience of the world that is different and new. Not the hardware, and not the manipulation of abstract form. Architecture as media. Architecture as information for living in.

Modernist architecture is well served by its misleading moniker – which suggests that it was, is and will remain modern. We would say that it has never been. Will Hutton has argued that the decline in manufacturing and the rise in the service sector as sources of employment had begun some time before 1930.[1] Which were, of course, the halcyon days of unadulterated, capital-M Modernism. Architects, as ever, were a little behind the game. Modernism arose in the decaying tail end of the industrial revolution and, unsurprisingly, missed the yet-incomprehensible possibilities of the transmission from Cornwall to Canada, while Mackintosh, Perret and Wagner finished off the Scotland Street school, the rue de Ponthieu garage and the Post Office Savings Bank, respectively. The particular aesthetic, political and moral values of the Modernist social programme were built on a romanticised and ideologised historical period even at their emergence. They stumbled with the well-documented failure of social housing projects, while the communicative credo of Modernism's pure heroic aesthetics rode on into the age of turbo-capitalism. The new power of architecture and of architects is directly as part of the information revolution: communication, not programme.

## Postscript

Just outside Plano, Illinois, Peter Palumbo may well have been engaged in the production of an untitled artwork, whose meaning and ambitions may be as obscure as Stonehenge or the Freemasons. It is a mixed media piece about high Modernism, Cold War politics, international finance, the cream of twentieth-century fine art, society marriages, the British monarchy, patronage, heritage and air freight, regular flooding (the ominous symbol of global warming) and insurance claims. It is a piece of work about architecture, experience, narrative, about the real and virtual, about electronic communication, and about the best reality imaginable.

Glimpsed behind a Warhol Brillo box is a section of the Berlin Wall. The turret of the Mappin and Webb building is displayed by the gate like the head of a guilty medieval traitor. A letter from Margaret Thatcher hangs framed in the bathroom. Somewhere over the hill there is a K2 red phone box and a Royal Mail post box, reflected in the chrome body of an Airstream caravan.

As we all know, the Farnsworth House is a house that almost evaporates, a house that dematerialises. It's a house made with the sensation of being somewhere else whilst being here. The house is architecture for a wireless age, connected to, and being in, multiple places. Palumbo's additions write this subtext in large expensive script across the Miesian canvas. These are CNN trophies: objects used to the flash of the paparazzo's camera, whose importance is measured in their appearance in newscasts and coffee-table books. Maybe photographed more (though not in this context, where photography is strictly forbidden) than the house itself, whose importance as an image in the world of architectural representation secured its place in the Modernist canon (while its client expressed a desire to move to some country where women went around covered from head to toe). While a million images circulate, these objects are the unique relics. Twentieth-century Turin shrouds and holy grails sitting quietly in the snow: the calm, smug centre of an electronic data storm.

**Note**

1    Will Hutton and Anthony Giddens (eds), *On the Edge* (London: Vintage/Ebury, 2001).

# Index

Aalto, Alvar 22, 171, 198
ABK (National Gallery Extension) 136
Abramson, Daniel 67
abstraction 102–4, 175, 225, 245
Ackerman, James xii, 2, 26–36
Ackermann, Rudolph 166
Adam, James 162–3
Adam, Robert 61, 161–3
Adler, Robert 247
Adorno, Theodor 210
Advertisements for Architecture 218–19
advertising 237–8, 241; Le Corbusier and 65; engravings as 61; photography as 33, 135; comparison with architectural photography and pornography 122
aestheticisation 234; aesthetics of photography 30, 31; aesthetics as campaign tool 140, 151, 153
Aicher, Otl 171
Alberti, Leon Battista 7, 98
alienation 85, 113, 231–5
alternative tradition 198
American dream 46
American Institute of Architects 132
amnesia 174, 175, 232
Apollinaire, Guillaume 169
aquatint 33, 168
Aquinas, Thomas 7

Aragon, Louis 37–8
Archer, John 164
Archigram 94, 124, 244–5, 249; *Walking Cities* 62–3
Architectural Association (AA) 121, 172
architectural education xxi–xxii, 57–8, 110, 121, 124
architectural journalists 97, 141–5; relationships between 142–3
Architectural Photographic Association 28
ARCUK 140
Ariadne 207
*Arizona Republic* (newspaper) 133
Arnhem station project 101, 107
*Arts & Architecture* (magazine) 130, 131
'as found' 94–5
Ashbee, C.R. 169
AT&T Building 179
Augé, Marc 227–8, 235, 239
Aulenti, Gae: Musée d'Orsay (Paris) 185–6
authenticity 207–9
avant-garde 82, 169, 185, 211–12, 213, 249
avatars 116, 118, 120

Bacon, Francis 102, 103, 106
Badovici, Jean 169
Baillie-Scott, M.H. 170

Baldus, Edouard 28, 29
Banham, Peter Reyner 133
Bank of England 66–7
Barbaro, Daniele 10, 11, 13; edition of Vitruvius 12; *Prattica della Perspectiva* 11
Barcelona Pavilion 86–9, 215–6
Barnard, Mike 124, 244
Baroque period 13–17
Barthes, Roland 220, 242
Bath University 91
Batty, Michael 195–6
Baudrillard, Jean 241
Bauhaus 19, 63, 101, 174
Bauman, Zygmunt 189
Bayard, Hippolyte 28, 35; church of the Madeleine (Paris) 30
Beaux Arts 19, 33
Becher, Bernd and Hilla 38
Behrens, Peter 216
Bender, Barbara 228
Benjamin, Walter 39, 209, 210, 215, 217, 231, 235–6, 237
Bentham, Jeremy 103–4
Berlin Museum 113
Bernstein House 23
Betsky, Aaron 71
*Big Heat, The* 43
Bigness 194, 196
Bill, Max 171
Binney, Marcus 146–7, 148
*Blade Runner* 85, 90
Blake, Peter 133
Blake, William 163
Blanquart-Evrard, Louis-Desiré 29
blasé individual 231–2
*Blow-Up* 42
Boesiger, Willy 171
books 10, 17, 125, 126, 157–73, 175–96; children's 98; aimed at client 164; consumerism and 172; on cooking 98; guide 157, 199; history books 168; image-based 164; as luxury commodity 168; making money from 161; pattern books 159, 161; Smithsons and 96–7
Borromini, Francesco 159–60
Bosse, A.: *Les Perspecteurs* 16
Boullée, Étienne-Louis 164
Bowlby, Rachel 237
Boyarsky, Alvin 71, 172
Bozzolla, Angelo 213
Braham, Allan 164
brands 225; Repton and 166
Brown, Denise Scott 178, 182, 227
Buchli, Victor 226
*Building Design* (trade paper) 146
Bürger, Peter 211–12
Burgin, Victor 210, 211, 220
Burlington, Lord 161

Campbell, Colen 160, 161
Canary Wharf (London) 145, 184
capitalism 235–41
Cappucci, Pier Luigi 1
cartoons 181, 199
*Casabella* (magazine) 217
Case Study House #22 127–35
Case Study Program 130–1
Cendrars, Blaise 169
*Changing Rooms* (TV programme) 137, 198
Charles, Prince 136–8, 139, 144, 146–8; books and TV programmes 138; Mansion House scheme, role in 144–5, 147–8, 150, 186; Mansion House speech 136–8; Royal Opera House scheme, role in 144, 150, as source 144, 145, 146

Choisy, Auguste: *L'Art de Bâtir chez les Romains* 22
cinematography 37–43
Cirici, Christian 89
*Cities for a Small Planet* 195
Clérisseau, Charles-Louis 33, 161
Cohen, Jean-Louis 212
Coleridge, Samuel Taylor 61
Colomina, Beatriz xii–xiii, 65, 206, 207–21
colour 131, 132, 133, 168–9, 170, 172
comics 192
complexity theory 189–92
computer technologies 3, 5, 19–20, 22, 233; 3D Studio, AutoCAD 116; avatars 118, 120; computer-aided design 110; computer-generated worlds 110; computer graphics 19–20; Core Design 116; cyberspace 117; cyber-technology 229; designing gameplay 110–20; designing unease 113; Eidos 116; *Everquest* 45; game design techniques 111–13; game logic 112–13; narrative of 114; Tomb Raider 112–13, 116, 118; vulnerability of 49
Conran, Terence 94–5
conservation 29–30, 139, 140, 142, 146–9
conspiracy theories 153–4
Constable, John: *Salisbury Cathedral* 31
contextualism 225
Cook, Peter 98
copyright 198
Correa, Charles 137
Cottage Orné 167
Covent Garden Community Association 145–6, 150–3
credit cards 236, 237, 245
critical theory xxiv, 205–6, 207–30
criticism: nature of 214–20
Croft, Lara 116, 118, 242

Crosby, Theo 92
Croset, Pierre-Alain 217–18
Crow, Thomas 210, 212
Csordas, Thomas 226

Daedalus 207
Daguerre, Louis-Jacques-Mandé 26
Daly, César 216–17
Daumier, Honoré 168
décor 37–8, 41
decoration 247
de Quincey, Thomas 61
deconstruction 198–9
Deleuze, Gilles 102–4, 105, 106, 189
dematerialisation 222–30
Desargues, Gérard 16–17, 25
Descartes, René 14
descriptive geometry 19
desktop publishing 192
diagrams 99–109; Deleuze's abstract machine 102–4; instrumentalising 106–7; meaning of 101–2; operational dream 107–9, 181; selection and application 105, unplanned meanings of 109
Diderot, Denis 25
digital communications networks 45–53
discourse analysis 100–1
Disney xxiii, 187, 230, 239
dispersed systems 48–9
Dixon, Jeremy 150, 153
DNA 189
DoCoMo 47
documentary photography 26–30, 34, 121
Domenig, Günther 117
drawings: Archigram and xxi, 62–3; authorship of 67, 69; axonometry 19, 69; cone of vision 7–9; descriptive geometry 19; difference between

reality and 22, 77; 'greater than project' 71; illusionism 15; optical correction of 7–8; originality of 22; parallax and perception 7, 16; parody of 73; as performance 218; perspectival image 7, 13–15; perspective xxiii; perspective as 'idea' 15; perspective as 'invisible hinge' 19; as picture of 'building to come' 13; Piranesi and xxi; plan 'footprint' 9; project as picture 13; as construction of reality 15–16; during Renaissance 6–7; prior to Renaissance 5; relationship with objects 5; relationship with 'tyranny of graphics' 20; rules for 'real' projections 17; scaenographia 10–13; sections 9–10; vanishing point 7, 18; visual harmony of 7; worm's eye 69
Duchamp, Marcel 22
Duck and Decorated Shed 182, 183
Durand, Jean-Nicolas-Louis 3–4, 19, 24; 'mechanism of composition' 19; *Précis des Leçons d'Architecture* 3, 20
Dürer, Albrecht: *Underwysung der Messung* 6

Eames, Charles and Ray 96, 133
Eco, Umberto 175, 179, 181–2
École des Beaux Arts 19, 33
École Polytechnique 19
economics 50–1, 194, 231
Economist Building (London) 97
Edholm, Felicity 228
Eisenman, Peter 189, 227
Eisenstein, Sergey 61
Ellwood, Craig 133
*Engineer Prite's Project* 38
engravings 27, 28, 160–1, 162, 163, 164; as advertising 61; Piranesi and 61, 162–3
Entenza, John 130–1

Erenburg, Ilia 80
Euston Arch (London) 96–7, 142
Evans, Frederick H. 33
Evans, Robin 77
*Everquest* 45
exhibitions: German Pavilion (Barcelona) and 86–9, 215–16; *Exposition des Arts Decoratifs* 80; *Exhibitions of Artists of All Trends* 82; galleries and gallery system 214–15, 219; Mies van der Rohe and 96; *New Architecture: Foster Rogers Stirling* 141; Smithsons and: *House of the Future* 91–4; 'As Found' 94–6; Tatlin and 78–83; *This Is Tomorrow* 91–4, 96; Bernard Tschumi and 218–9
expenses 199

faciality 107–9
Farnsworth House 250–1
fashion 231
Fenton, Roger: Ely cathedral 31
Filarete, Antonio 6
film 37–44, 84–5; alienation and 40, 85; assemblage of fragments 38, 40, 85; colour versus black and white 41; dystopianism 85; editing 42; links between film and modernism 37–8, 85; *film noir* 40, 43; film space 38; film stock 40–2
Fine Arts Center (Tempe, Arizona) 187
Fischer von Erlach, Johann Bernhard 168; *Entwurf einer historischen Architektur* 158, 159
Florey Building (Queen's College, Oxford) 68–9
Fondation Corbusier 198
footnotes 163, 174
Ford, Henry 192

Ford Motor Company 121, 122
foreword 199
Foster, Norman 94, 171
Foucault, Michel 102, 103–4, 228
Frampton, Kenneth 199, 217
*Frankenstein* 40
Freud, Sigmund 233
Futurism 58, 81, 213

Galilei, Galileo 13–14
gallery system 214
Galli da Bibiena, Ferdinando: *scena per angolo* 17, 18
Gallop, Jane 214
gameplay 110–20
Gandy, Joseph Michael 67, 69
Gardiner, Stephen 122
Gates, Bill 245
Gaudi, Antoni 22
Gehry, Frank 191, 227; Guggenheim Museum (Bilbao) 191–2, 198, 225
George I, King 161
German Pavilion (Barcelona) *see* Barcelona Pavilion
Gibbs, James 161
Giedion, Sigfried 175
Ginzburg, Moisei 83
Girouard, Mark 69, 134
Gleye, Paul 133
global digital economy 45–6, 224–5, 248
global marketplace 185
globalisation 224–5
Goldberger, Paul 179
Gothic architecture 1, 5–6; Gothic revival 27, 31, 32
Gowan, James 69
GPS 48, 52
Graves, Michael 184, 187
Greenberg, Clement 210

Greene, David 244, 245
Greenspan, Alan 194
Gregotti, Vittorio 217
Gropius, Walter 101, 174, 175, 177
*Guardian* (newspaper) 151
Guggenheim Museum (Bilbao) 191–2, 198, 225
guides 157, 199

Hackney, Rod 140
Hadid, Zaha 203; The Peak (Hong Kong) 70–1
Hadrian's Villa, Tivoli 46–7, 60–1
Hara, Hiroshi 187
Harris, Eileen 160–1, 162, 163
Harris, Nigel 225
Haussmann, Baron 29
Hays, Michael 212, 215
Heidegger, Martin 25
Hejduk, John 22; Bernstein House 23
Hellman, Louis 199
*Hello!* (magazine) 240
Hencke, David 152
Henderson, Nigel 92, 93, 94; basement in Bethnal Green 95
Herron, Ron: *Walking Cities* 62–3
*Holiday* (magazine) 133
Holl, Steven 227
Hollein, Hans 184
Holston, James 228
home working 45–6
Hong Kong and Shanghai Bank 141
House of the Future 91–4
Hulsbergh, Henry 160
*Human Desire* 43
Humana Tower 184
Hutton, Will 250
Huxley, Aldous 61
Huxtable, Ada Louise 229–30

Huyssen, Andreas 210, 232

IBA (Berlin) 184
iconic pictures 57–90; 127–135; 200
*Image of the City, The* 48
industrialised construction 222–3
Institute of Electric Anthropology 121
Internet 45, 114, 222, 225
Izenour, Steven 182

Jack, Bill 150
Jacobs, Jane 176, 187, 189
Jameson, Fredric 210, 241
Jardine, Alice 211
Jeanneret, Pierre 169
Jencks, Charles xiv, 174–97, 200, 201
Jenkins, Simon 141
Jewish Museum (Berlin) 189, 190
Johnson, Philip 184, 202
Jones, Inigo 160, 161
journalism 126, 136–56, 216–17; autonomy of 138–9; Californian architectural 132–5; categorisation of 139–40; Entenza, John 130–1; influence of 137–8; Nairn, Iain 97; news values 138–9; partiality and bias 153–4; *Revue Générale de l'Architecture* 216–17; 'sources' 140, 144–6, 150–3; UK specialist journalists 141–5
journals and magazines 125, 126, 200–1, 215, 220, 236

Kahn, Louis 200
Kaplan, Sam Hall 134
Keiller, Patrick xiv, 38–44; Montalcino (Italy) 39
Kelly, Mary 210, 219
Kent, William 161
Kepler, Johannes 25

Kiasma (Helsinki) 225
Kipnis, Jeffrey 189, 197
Klein bottle 107, 108
Klein, Calvin 174
Koenig, Pierre 126; Case Study House #22 127–35
Koetter, Fred 180
Koolhaas, Rem 176, 182, 200; *S,M,L,XL* ii, 157, 172, 192–5, 200
Krier, Leon 69, 187
Krier, Robert 184
Kroll, Lucien 179
Kruft, Hanno-Walter 159
Kuleshov, Lev 38, 43
Kurokawa, Kisho 187; Museum of Contemporary Art (Hiroshima) 187–8

labyrinth 5
Lacan, Jacques 213–14
landscapes 30–1
Lang, Fritz 43; *Metropolis* 84–5
Langley, Batty 161
laptops 46, 51, 245
Las Vegas 182, 183, 194
Lasch, Christopher 232, 233
Lasdun, Denys 122
Laubin, Carl 151
Lauren, Ralph 248–9
Le Corbusier 22, 69, 97, 98, 118, 141, 174, 175, 176, 177, 192, 198, 213; books and 169–71, 176, 245; the Villa Savoye and the Villa at Garches 64–5
Le Gray, Gustave 28
Le Secq, Henri 28; church of the Madeleine (Paris) 29, 30
*Learning From Las Vegas* 72–3, 182, 200, 227
Ledoux, Claude-Nicolas 163–4, 165

Lefebvre, Henri 37
Leibniz, G.W. 25
Lenin, V.I. 80, 81
Leoni, Giacomo 160
Libeskind, Daniel 113, 172, 189; Jewish Museum (Berlin) 189, 190
Lipstadt, Hélène 216–17
Lipton, Stuart 145
Lissitzky, El 80, 82
lithography 33, 166–8, 209
Lloyd's Building 141
location 49–53, 239–40; SwarmCity 46–8, 49, 51–2; VatVille 45–6, 48, 49, 51
*London* 40–2
Longley, Paul 195–6
Loos, Adolf 65, 212–13, 217, 247
Lorrain, Claude 30
Los Angeles 133–4, 239
*Los Angeles Examiner* (newspaper) 132
Loutherberg, Philip de 166
Lunacharsky, Commissar 81
Lynch, Kevin 48
Lynn, Greg 189
Lyotard, Jean-François 179, 188–9

McCoy, Esther 133
McKendrick, Neil 162
McLuhan, Marshall 245
MacMasters, Dan 132
Macmillan, Harold 96
magazines 79–80, 83, 125, 126, 130, 181, 200–1, 215, 220, 229, 236
Magritte: *This is not a Pipe* xxi
Mailer, Norman 175
manifestos 193, 176, 218; *The Death and Life of the Great American Cities* 176; *Vers Une Architecture* 177; *Architectural Manifestoes* 218–9

Mansion House redevelopment (London) 136, 146–9
Manzini, Enzio 227
Maragall, Pasqual 184
Marconi 244–5
Marcuse, Herbert 242
Marker, Chris 39
Martin, Jean 8
Martin, Leslie 171
Marville, Charles 29
Marx, Karl 192, 237
*Matrix, The* 114
Matta-Clark, Gordon 4; *Office Baroque* 4
Mau, Bruce: *S,M,L,XL* ii,157, 172, 192–5
media theory 138–9
Melnikov, Konstantin 215
memory 115, 189; amnesia 174, 175, 232
*Men Only* (magazine) 122
Mestral, O. 28
*Metropolis* 84–5
Meyer, Hannes 215
Microsoft 244
Mies van der Rohe, Ludwig 96, 101, 136, 192; German Pavilion (Barcelona) 86–9, 215–16; Mansion House scheme 136, 146–9; Farnsworth House 250–1
minimalism 174, 175, 200
mirror stage of development 213–14
*Missions Héliographiques* 28
mobile phones 46–8, 52, 233–4
modernism 33, 85, 101, 146, 174, 175, 177, 179, 210, 222–3, 244–51; critical 186; definitions of 210, 211–12; links with film 85; links with emigration 37–8; mass culture and 212; problems besetting 184, 189; reinterpretation of 209–14; West Coast 125–7

Monge, Gaspard 17, 21
monographs 172, 192, 200
Montalcino (Italy) 39
*Monument to the Third International* (The Comintern) 78–83
Moore, Charles 182, 184; Piazza d'Italia (New Orleans) 180, 181
movement studies 107
Mulvey, Laura 235
Mumford, Lewis 175
Musée d'Orsay (Paris) 185–6
Museum of Contemporary Art (Hiroshima) 187–8
Museum of Contemporary Art (Los Angeles) 134
museums of architecture 214–15

Nairn, Iain 97
narcissism 232–5, 239
National Gallery (London) 136, 186
National Lottery 153
*National Photographer* (magazine) 132
nationalism 31
Nègre, Charles 30
neo-classicism 200
Neuestaatsgalerie (Stuttgart) 141, 148, 179, 180, 184
Neutra, Richard 131
newspapers 126, 136–54, 215; bias in 138–9; influence of 136–8; news values 138–40; sectional arrangement of 139–40; specialist journalists role in 141–4; underlying assumptions of 139–40
Newton, Isaac 192
*New York Times* (newspaper) 132
Nokia 47

O'Brien, Flann 114

*Oeuvre Complète* 171, 213
Oeuvres Complètes 201
Olivetti Building 180
Orientalism 32
Osborne, Trevor 145
Owings, Skidmore 97–8
Ozenfant, Amedée 169, 175

Palladio, Andrea 157; *I Quattro Libri* 157, 158, 159, 160; Study for San Petronio (Bologna) 76–7
Pallasmaa, Juhani 226, 227
Palumbo, Peter 145, 250–1; Mansion House scheme 146–9
panopticon 103–4
Paolozzi, Eduardo 92, 93
Papworth, J.B. 33, 166; Cottage Orné 167
parallax 30, 184
Parc de la Villette 74–5, 198
*Paris Match* (magazine) 240
Parsey, A.: *The Science of Vision* 21
Paternoster Square (London) 144, 151
Pawley, Martin 148
Pawson, John 174
*Paysan de Paris, Le* 37, 38
PDAs 52
Peak, The (Hong Kong) 70–1
Pelli, Cesar 184
Penn Station (New York) 103, 106
perspective 1, 7, 3–23; Baroque period 13–17; computer technologies and 3, 5, 19–20, 22; cone of vision 7–9; descriptive geometry and 19; devices 6, 8; as 'idea' 15; as 'invisible hinge' 19; medieval understanding 6–7; optical correction of 7–8; parallax 7, 16; as picture of 'building to come' 13; projection 4–5, 17; Renaissance and 6, 7; Rococo

**261** | Index

architecture 18; rules for 'real' projections 17; scaenographia 10–13; sections 9–11, 13; treatises on 9, 10, 17; vanishing point 7, 16; visual harmony of 7
Pevsner, Nikolaus 174, 179
photography 22, 26–36, 121–4, 126, 200, 201; as advertising 33, 135; aesthetics of 30, 31; as art history 87; 'authenticity' 209; 'authorship' 127–30; German Pavilion (Barcelona) and 86–9, 215–6; Benjamin and 208–9; Case Study House #22 127–35; cheapness and mass production 28; choice of subjects 31–2, 130–5; comparison of architectural with advertising and pornography 122; conventions of 27; as decontextualisation 129; as 'drawing its own picture' 26; 'documentary' 28, 34; enhancement of 123; as fake 123–4; as 'iconic' 57–9, 86–9, 127–35; as 'idea' 121; lenses 34; limitations of 27–8; mimicking perspective 30, 134; 'objectivity' of 28–9; as 'ordering' device 129; parallax and 30; parallels with painting at Bank of England 67; and the picturesque 33; as record of design 129; replacing buildings 86–9, 121–4; Shulman, Julius and 127–35; as representative of 'zeitgeist' 134; styling of photographs 130, 131, 134, 135; as survey 28–9; as unreliable documentary evidence 121–4
photogravure 170
Photoshop 121, 123–4
Piazza d'Italia (New Orleans) 180, 181
Picasso, Pablo 79

picturesque 30–1
Piranesi, Giovanni Battista 162–3; *Carceri* 23, 61; Ruins of Hadrian's Villa at Tivoli 60–1
Plaw, John 164
pluralism 179–83, 191, 201
pochoir technique 170
Poggiolo, Renato 212
Pollock, Jackson 124
portfolio publications 169, 170, 172
post-modernism 5, 176–97, 200, 201, 211, 226; beginnings 176–8; classicism and 184–6, 200; complexity and 189–92; propositions of 196–7; radical pluralism and radical eclecticism 179–83; small-block planning 186–9; time and 192–6
Pozzo, Andrea: drawing method 15; *quadratura* method 14; treatise on perspective 17
Predock, Antoine 187
pressure groups 145; Mansion House and 146–9; Royal Opera House and 149–53
Prigogine, Ilya 189
projection 4–5, 17
Proust, Marcel 102, 103, 106
public opinion, as defined in press 138, 154
publishing industry 126, 198–203, 209
Pugin, Augustus Charles 27; view of St Étienne (Caen) 27
Pugin, Augustus Welby Northmore 166, 245–7
Punin, Nikolai 80–3

*quadratura* method 14
Quetglas, Jose 216

Ramos, Fernando 89

rationality 100
real-time 115–16
*Recommendation for a Monument* 72–3
Reich, Lilly 216
remaindering 201
remote controls 247–8
Renaissance: architecture of 31; perspective and 6, 7
reproduction 202, 207–9, *see also* photography, photogravure
Repton, Humphry 166
restoration schemes 29–30
*Revue Générale de l'Architecture* (journal) 215–17
Richardson, Henry Hobson 33
Risselada, Max 91
Robertson, R.G.: *Descriptive Geometry* 21
Robertson, William 162
Robin Hood Gardens 91
*Robinson in Space* 42
Rococo architecture 18
Rogers, Richard 94, 195
Rossi, Aldo 184
Rouillard, Dominique 134
Rowe, Colin 180, 211
Royal Academy 141
Royal Institute of British Architects (RIBA) 136, 140
Royal Opera House (London) 144, 146, 149–53
Rushdie, Salman 179

Sabbagh, Karl 201
Sainsbury, Lord 150
Salines Royales, Arc et Senan 164
Salzmann, August 31
San Petronio (Bologna) 76–7
Sassens, Saskia 225
Savage, Nicholas 160–1, 162, 163

SAVE Britain's Heritage 142–3, 146–8
scaenographia 10, 11, 13
Scamozzi, Vincenzo: Villa Bardellini 9, 10
Scharoun, Hans 43
Schinkel, Karl Friedrich 166–8
Schumpeter, Joseph 67
sciagraphy 10–11, 13
scoop 151–2
Scott, George Gilbert 174–5
Scott, Ridley 85
Scott, Walter 26
Scully, Vincent 177
sections 9–11, 13
semiology/semiotics 121, 175
September 11th 48–9
Serraino, Pierluigi 126, 127–35
sex 182, 201
Shulman, Julius 126, 129–30; photography of Case Study House #22 127–35
Sim City 119
Simmel, Georg 231–2, 233, 235, 238
situationists 248
Slutzky, Robert 211
Smith, Elizabeth A.T. 134
Smithson, Alison and Peter 69, 91–8; 'As Found' exhibition 95–6; Bath University 91; Economist Building 97; Euston Arch book 96–7; House of the Future 91–4; Robin Hood Gardens 91
Soane, John 61, 69, 168; Cutaway of the Bank of England 66–7
Société Héliographique 28
Soja, Ed 195
Solà Morales, Ignasi de 89
Sony 45
Spada, Virgilio 160
spatial concentration 46–8
spatial flow 101

Spitalfields (London) 142
stage sets 10, 11
Stahl Residence (Case Study House #22) 127–35
Steichen, Edward 33
Steinberg, Saul 175
stereoscope 22
Sterne, Lawrence 172
Stieglitz, Alfred 33
Stirling, James 179–80, 187; Florey Building (Queen's College, Oxford) 68–9; Mansion House scheme (London) 148–9; Neuestaatsgalerie Stuttgart) 141, 148, 179, 180, 184
Stirling Prize 141
Stonehenge 228
structuralism 226
Stuttgart Museum/Gallery 141, 148, 179, 180, 184
Sudjic, Deyan 141, 171
*Sunset* (magazine) 132
supermarkets 236
Surrealism 37–8, 43, 232–4
SwarmCity 46–8, 49, 51–2

Tafuri, Manfredo 61, 210, 215
Talbot, William Henry Fox 26, 28
Tatlin, Vladimir: *Monument to the Third International* (The Comintern) 78–83
Taut, Bruno 216
taxonomic method 34
Team 10 97
technology 222–3, 229, *see also* computer technologies
telecommuting 46
television 139, 141, 198, 238; makeover shows 137; remote controls 247–8; 'You can't do architecture on TV' 139
terrorism 48–9

Terry, Quinlan 181, 201
text messaging 47
Thatcher, Margaret 147
Tilley, Christopher 225, 228
timing in publishing 202
Tisdall, Caroline 213
Tomb Raider 112–13, 116, 118
trade magazines 125–6
trompe l'oeil 111
Tschumi, Bernard 182, 227; 'Advertisements for Architecture' 218–19; Parc de la Villette 74–5, 198
Turner, J.M.W. 30
typesetting 169, 171

UCLA Medical Research Building (Los Angeles)178
Ungers, O.M. 184
UN Studio 99–109

van Ruisdael, Jacob 30
vanishing point 7, 16
vanity publishing 202
VatVille 45–6, 48, 49, 51
Venturi, Robert 182, 185, 189, 194–5, 200, 227, 248; *Complexity and Contradiction in Architecture* 177; Duck versus Decorated Shed 182, 183; *Learning From Las Vegas* 182, 200, 227; *Recommendation for a Monument* 72–3; UCLA Medical Research Building 178
Vidal, Gore 174
video 48
Vignola, Giacomo: *Due Regole della Prospectiva Prattica* 8, 9
Villalpando, Juan Bautista: *El Templo a Vista de Pajaro* 13
Villa Bardellini 9, 10

Villa Savoye and the Villa at Garches 64–5
Viollet-le-Duc, Eugène 29
Virilio, Paul 229
virtual reality 1–2
Vitruvius 7, 10, 11, 13, 24, 77
von Moos, Stanislaus 213
vulnerability 48–9

Walkman 46
*Wallpaper\** (magazine) 232–3, 238, 239–41
*Wallpaper\** person 231–43
Warhol, Andy: *Chelsea Girls* 41
Wasmuth, Ernst 168
Weldon, Huw 139
White, Stanford 201
Whitney Library of Design 133
Wilford, Michael 180
Wilton-Ely, John 61

Wolfe, Tom 182
woodcuts 160
Wordsworth, William 26
*Work of Art in the Age of Mechanical Reproduction, The* 207–8, 210
World Trade Center 48–9
Wren, Christopher 160
Wright, Frank Lloyd 168, 201, 202

Xerox 202

Yale 203
Yerbury, F.R. 67

Zentralsparkasse Bank (Vienna) 117
Zizek, Slavoj 235
Zumthor, Peter 203